Stuart Hall

Conversations, Projects and Legacies

Stuart Hall

Conversations, Projects and Legacies

Edited by
Julian Henriques & David Morley
with Vana Goblot

© 2017 Goldsmiths Press
Published in 2017 by Goldsmiths Press
Goldsmiths, University of London, New Cross
London SE14 6NW

Printed and bound in the United States of America.
Distribution by The MIT Press
Cambridge, Massachusetts, and London, England

A CIP record for this book is available from the British
Library

ISBN 978-1-906897-47-5 (hbk)
ISBN 978-1-906897-48-2 (ebk)

www.gold.ac.uk/goldsmiths-press

This book is dedicated to
Catherine, Jess and Becky Hall

Introduction

Stuart Hall has been described as an 'intellectual giant' whose influence now spans the work of several generations of intellectuals in the field of cultural studies—not simply in Britain, Europe and North America, but also in Latin America, Africa, Asia and the Caribbean. Importantly, he was also a public intellectual.

The field of cultural studies on which Hall has had such a formative influence has three key characteristics: First, it researches contemporary popular culture to show its influence and importance for understanding society as a whole. Second, especially in Hall's hands, cultural studies informs intellectual interventions in particular political moments—what Hall calls *conjunctures*. The collapse of the grand narratives, whether Marxism in the 1980s or the neoliberal consensus more recently, underlines the value of—and continuing need for—Hall's mode of political and intellectual engagement. Third, cultural studies often embodies a particular collaborative method of working and takes a specific instant as the spark to ignite the research. One example is the way that close scrutiny (reinvoking an almost Leavisite discourse) of a particular localised incident—the coverage of a single mugging in a Birmingham newspaper story—eventually led to the development of a theoretical analysis of authoritarian populism in the book *Policing the Crisis*, a work that resonates today perhaps more than ever, as Angela Davis's contribution makes clear.

Through his collaborators and colleagues—including, as just mentioned, Angela Davis, as well as Angela McRobbie, Dick Hebdige and John Akomfrah—*Conversations, Projects and Legacies* gives a uniquely valuable point of access to the increasing influence of Hall's work since his death in February 2014. However familiar or unfamiliar you might be with Hall's opus, this collection offers a rich array of personal, political, cultural and intellectual insights, entirely in keeping with the nature of Hall's distinctive contribution throughout his long career as a teacher and public intellectual.

Henry Louis Gates Jr. has said that he can think of 'no other theorist whose international standing is higher or whose work has had a greater influence in defining the studies of history, literature, art and the social sciences.' David Scott described Hall as 'one of the handful of intellectuals anywhere in the world who can claim to have literally transformed the character and practices of the social sciences and humanities in the 20th century.' Jacqueline Rose nominated Hall as 'one of the most prestigious, productive and creative intellectual figures of [his] time.' The influence of his work spans many different regions—as witnessed when Kuan-Hsing Chen said, 'There is no one else who has the same degree of intellectual influence in East Asian humanities and social science', or in Liv Sovik's essay (chapter 20), which demonstrates the wide resonance of Hall's work in the cultural and racial politics of Latin America.[1]

Hall was among the founding figures of what has now internationally become known as *cultural studies* and is internationally recognised as such. His work has become canonical in the study of media representations, audiences, cultural theory, postcolonialism, subcultures and studies of ethnicity, identity, 'race' and diaspora. It has been translated into Italian, Korean, French, Arabic, Finnish, German, Turkish, Spanish, Hebrew, Chinese, Portuguese, Japanese and Dutch, among other languages.

The speed of political change appears to be accelerating, but this does nothing to diminish the relevance of Hall's work to the issues facing contemporary societies worldwide. Central to the politics of today are urgent questions of nationhood, identity, race, multiculturalism and fundamentalism, along with the rise of a variety of forms of authoritarian populism—represented not only by figures like Donald Trump in the United States and Marie Le Pen in France, but also by right-wing parties in many other parts of the world. These are all issues to which Hall made significant contributions—and they remain atop our political agenda today, in the wake of the financial crash of the first part of the twenty-first century, as the worldwide hegemony of neoliberalism now creaks under the pressure of stagflation, rising structural unemployment and the growth of resistance to globalisation from both ends of the political spectrum. One of the reasons that Hall's work remains resonant in this way is because of his working *method*, as many of our contributors note.

Hall's relevance, above all, stems from the methodology of his work and from his contribution to the development of a certain way of being a public intellectual and using academic theoretical terminology to contribute to the analysis of contemporary culture and politics. That way of proceeding is what he taught—and still teaches us now—and is what he exemplified in his own work. This was dialogical and collective in its mode of conduct and conjunctural in the application of its intellectual product. Hall's articles, essays and chapters were invariably conceived strategically, as an *intervention* in the *contingencies*—to use two of his key terms—of a specific political moment. His coining of the term *Thatcherism* in 'The Great Moving Right Show' (1979)[2] is just one example—and one in which he presciently conceptualised what turned out to be the dominant mode of governmentality in the United Kingdom over the subsequent thirty years. Nor was he satisfied with merely identifying the early beginnings of that politics; he then pursued its development in a series of subsequent articles from 'The Great Moving Centre Show' and 'Tony Blair: The Greatest Tory since Thatcher?' in 1997 through to 'New Labour's Double Shuffle' in 2003 and 'The Neo-liberal Revolution' in 2011.[3] Contrary to what might be expected in some quarters of the left, this eschewing of grand theory for ideas born from trying to understand the specifics of the moment, offers the best guarantee of their continuing relevance—even if Hall always pointedly insisted that in the end, there were no absolute guarantees to be had.

Stuart Hall arrived in England from Jamaica to study at Oxford University in the early 1950s, in the wake of the first wave of postwar Afro-Caribbean immigration now known, retrospectively, as the *Windrush generation* (after the *Empire Windrush*, the ship that brought the first of these immigrants to the United Kingdom). At Oxford, Hall rapidly became part of a network of international students involved in the heady beginnings of postcolonial politics, as the world's major empires moved into the era of crises in Suez and in Hungary in 1956 and as, during the Cold War, the Non-Aligned Movement was born in the Third World. These were also the beginnings of what came to be known as the New Left in the United

Kingdom, in which Hall played a central part; indeed, on finishing his studies, Hall became the editor of *New Left Review*.

This was also the beginning of Hall's long involvement in the politics of popular culture. After Oxford, he taught what would now be known as *media studies* in South London schools and produced his first book, *The Popular Arts*, co-written with the film scholar Paddy Whannel. When Richard Hoggart then set up the path-breaking Centre for Contemporary Cultural Studies (CCCS) at the University of Birmingham in the mid-1960s, Hall was the person Hoggart invited to join him as his assistant based on his work. In the early 1970s, Hall took over as director of the Centre and rapidly became the single most important figure in what became known as *British cultural studies*. In that project, Hall and his graduate students worked to develop—and later, internationalise—the insights into popular culture initiated by Hoggart and Raymond Williams to the point at which it became the global phenomenon that it is today.

In the early 1980s, in search of a broader constituency than could be provided in a graduate research institution, Hall moved to the Open University, where he worked until his retirement; over a decade and a half, he produced many innovative courses on questions of media politics, society, race, ethnicity and identity. In that work, the question of culture and its relation to power was always central, and over his working lifetime he contributed massively to what retrospectively became known as the *cultural turn* across the social sciences and humanities. However, although Hall was both an intellectually innovative academic and a uniquely gifted teacher, he was also a public intellectual. Through his writing for non-academic outlets and his many media appearances, he also played a large part in defining the major shifts in British political culture during his lifetime. In the Thatcher-Reagan era this was particularly evident in his enormously prescient analysis of the phenomenon of Thatcherism, developed in the late 1970s in the context of the transformations undergone by post-war Britain as it entered the age of globalisation. Throughout his life, he played a major part in political debates about race, ethnicity and multiculturalism in the United Kingdom—and was active in spreading those ideas internationally. From his viewpoint as a 'familiar stranger' (to use his own phrase) who no longer felt completely at home in either Jamaica or Britain, he was perhaps better able to perceive important aspects of both societies more clearly than their own 'natives.' He was, above all, a much-loved and globally admired 'diasporic intellectual' of enormous stature and influence.

Within the British context, Hall was not simply an outstanding academic but also a public intellectual with a strong commitment to the exploration of issues surrounding questions of race, ethnicity, migrancy, identity and culture. Through this connection, he served in many public bodies and committees, including the Runnymede Commission on the Future of Multi-Ethnic Britain. In his later years, through his involvement with Autograph ABP (Association of Black Photographers) and the Institute for the International Visual Arts (INIVA), he also helped to inspire a whole generation of Britain's leading black and postcolonial photographers, filmmakers and artists—such as David Bailey, Sonia Boyce, Isaac Julien and John Akomfrah, whose acclaimed installation (*The Unfinished Conversation*, 2012) and film (*The Stuart Hall Project*, 2013) brought Hall's work to the attention of a new generation.

By the time of his death in February 2014, Hall had already received many honours, including the European Cultural Foundation's Diversity Prize, the British Sociological Association's Lifetime Achievement Award and a nomination for the American International Communications Association's Career Achievement Award. He was a fellow or honorary degree holder at thirty-two universities in eight countries.

The pieces in this collection have their origin in a conference that took place at Goldsmiths, University of London. In many respects, some of which are mentioned in the introduction to part VII of the book, Hall is a central figure for the ethos of the college. Goldsmiths' character is shaped by its position as a comparatively small, single-campus research-intensive institution located in an inner-city area, far from central London. Hall's intellectual legacy of cultural studies is entirely at home in—and indeed a strength for—Goldsmiths' arts and humanities and social sciences traditions. Not being government-approved STEM[4] subjects, these traditions face an increasingly hostile funding environment. There is no one better than Hall to evince the lasting value and importance of the kind of cultural work we do—inspired in no small part by his example.

The collection is organised into seven sections, each with its own introduction. There is no need to anticipate their words here, but the titles of the sections alone give some idea of the scope of this volume. We hope that this collection can contribute to the continuing of such conversations and, thereby, our projects and Hall's legacies.

Notes

1. The comments by Henry Louis Gates Jr., David Scott, Jacqueline Rose and Kuan-Hsing Chen were all made in the context of Hall's nomination for a career achievement award from the International Communication Association in 2014.
2. 'Stuart Hall, 'The Great Moving Right Show', *Marxism Today* 23, no. 1 (1979): 14–20.
3. 'Martin Jacques and Stuart Hall, 'The Great Moving Centre Show', *New Statesman*, November 21, 1997; Martin Jacques and Stuart Hall, 'Tony Blair: The Greatest Tory Since Thatcher?', *The Guardian*, April 13, 1997; Stuart Hall, 'New Labour's Double-Shuffle', *Soundings: A Journal of Politics and Culture*, no. 24 (Summer 2003): 10–24; Stuart Hall, 'The Neoliberal Revolution', *Soundings: A Journal of Politics and Culture*, no. 48 (Summer 2011): 9–27.
4. STEM subjects are science, technology and mathematics.

Stuart Hall International Conference:
Conversations, Projects + Legacies

Friday, 28th November 2014
9am - 6pm Professor Stuart
Hall Building [PSH], LG02

**Keynote: Angela Davis -
Policing the Crisis Today**

+ Screening of live web-stream,
PSH LG01, MRB Screen 1

+ 2pm Naming of the Professor
Stuart Hall Building Ceremony

+ 6pm Drinks Reception

With:

Sara Ahmed
John Akomfrah
Lucy Bland
Avtar Brah
Charlotte Brunsdon
Iain Chambers
Kuan-Hsing Chen
John Clarke
James Curran
Lawrence Grossberg
Dick Hebdige
Julian Henriques
Tony Jefferson
Angela McRobbie
Caspar Melville
Doreen Massey
David Morley
Frank Mort
Irit Rogoff
Mike Rustin
Bill Schwarz
David Scott
Mark Sealy
Liv Sovik
Lola Young

Live web-streaming and more information from:
www.gold.ac.uk/media-communications/stuart-hall-conference/
email - z.arabadji@gold.ac.uk

Department of Media
and Communications

Goldsmiths
UNIVERSITY OF LONDON

Angela Y. Davis

Julian Henriques

Bill Schwarz

John Akomfrah

David Morley

Mark Sealy

Student audience.
Deborah Findlater, Laurel Hadleigh,
Mahamed Abdullahi and Yusuf Musse

Dick Hebdige

Irit Rogoff, James Curran,
Angela McRobbie,
David Morley and Bill Schwarz

David Scott

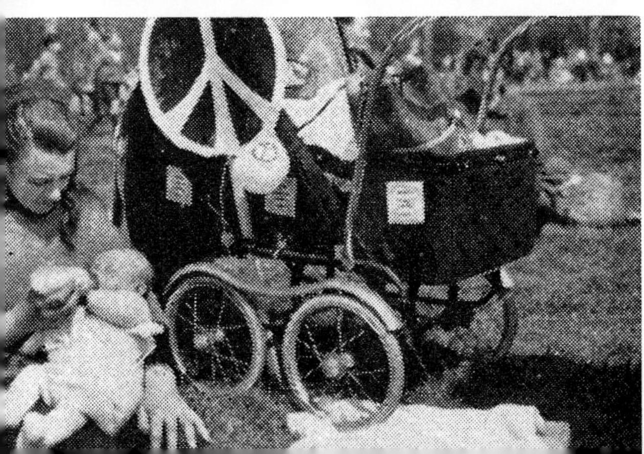

new left review

Revolution — E. P. Thompson

Men and Motors — Denis Butt

Transport Muddle — John Hughes

Health Service Revisited — Sheila Lynd

Discussion on "Dinlock"

Lady Albemarle's Modesty — Peter Massie

Republicanism After The Restoration — Christopher Hill

Dream Boy — Ray Gosling

Sharpeville — Drawings by Paul Hogarth

3 **MAY JUNE 1960** **3/6**

NEW LEFT REVIEW

Previous: Stuart Hall with fellow members of the *New Left Review*/New Left Clubs initiative

Part I
Cultural Studies:
Multiple Legacies

Cultural Studies: Multiple Legacies

The chapters in part I all explore Hall's legacy—not just at Goldsmiths, but in cultural studies more generally. Bill Schwarz's contribution in chapter 1 begins with a revealing anecdote about the extent to which Hall's work simultaneously influenced so many of Goldsmiths' different departments. However, as he turns to his evocative imaginary scenario—in which he pictures Hall in nightly conversation among the dead intellectual giants of Highgate Cemetery, where Hall was buried—he also recalls the strength of Hall's own continuing investments in earlier intellectual traditions. Not least of these was the Marxism into which, as Hall once put it, he felt 'dragged backwards' in 1956, against both the Soviet tanks in Budapest and the British paratroopers in Egypt. As Schwarz rightly indicates, Marxism—or rather, one very particular strand of non-reductionist Marxism—was the single most important intellectual tradition for Hall, the overarching problematic with which he remained (always argumentatively) engaged, right up to the end of his life. This engagement is, indeed, registered vividly in the section of Isaac Julien's installation *Kapital* (2013), in which, only a couple of months before his death, Hall (in his ever-pleasant manner) relentlessly pursues his disagreement with the more determinist form of Marxist analysis made popular among some quarters, in recent years, by scholars such as David Harvey. Indeed, as those who continued discussions with him up to the end will testify, in the last years of his life, the questions initially raised for Hall by the *Grundrisse* and those associated with the thorny problems of the circuit of capital, along with questions of political and economic periodisation, were never far from his mind.

James Curran's contribution in chapter 2 also addresses Stuart Hall's early work; like Schwarz, he is concerned with emphasising the continuing importance for Hall of Marxism as a point of reference, most notably in his development of Gramscian theories of the continuous and always provisional struggle over forms of cultural hegemony. In that work, as Curran points out—and particularly with the massive impact of the now-canonical *Policing the Crisis*—he and his colleagues at the CCCS succeeded in transforming not just the discipline of sociology but also that of political communications. However, Curran also reminds us of the importance of the skills and concerns that Hall brought to the field from his earlier background in literary studies. In this respect, we are reminded of the influential work Hall performed with Paddy Whannel in their attempt to not only take seriously the aesthetics of popular arts and popular culture, but also, in so doing, to move beyond the dismissal of mass culture that had previously been the standard leftist response. Evidently, this was a concern Hall shared, at an early stage, with Richard Hoggart in their argument that their research centre in Birmingham would give serious critical attention to cultural products that had previously been merely scorned.

However, although Curran takes the view that this thread of Hall's work was perhaps somewhat obscured by his later concerns with questions of ethnicity, race and identity, we can readily find moments in which these concerns with matters of aesthetics are still very much alive in Hall's thinking. Thus, in the interview with Colin McCabe—from 2007, later in his life—Hall expounds a detailed analysis of exactly why, on aesthetic grounds, Billie Holliday must be judged a better singer than others with whom she is often compared, very much in the manner of the 'discriminating' arguments in *The Popular Arts*. Similarly, even if the visible themes and contents of much of his work were articulated in different terms, Hall's continuing engagement with the visual arts in the last twenty years of his life cannot be understood outside the continuity of his concerns with the relation between the aesthetic and the political.

In chapter 3, David Morley's concerns are focused centrally on the theoretical and methodological legacy of Stuart's modality of cultural analysis. Like Curran and Schwarz, Morley recognises the continuing relevance of Marxism to Hall's work, but his starting point here is found in the protocols for the uses of theory, which Stuart derives from his analysis of Marx's '1857 Introduction' to the *Grundrisse*. Evidently, this is a point of considerable contention in terms of the subsequent development of cultural studies over the last twenty years or so, as it has moved towards a stronger investment in '(High) Theory' than Hall was ever comfortable with. As outlined in Morley's account, Hall was strongly averse to abstract forms of theorisation which lack empirical grounding—and which themselves often scorn the kinds of grounded theory produced at Birmingham as no more than 'middlebrow'. By way of explicating this issue, Morley offers an analogy between Hall's work and that of the French philosopher Michel Serres, who, like Hall, always dismissed what he regarded as the 'lazy' forms of universal metatheory and insisted on the development of customised methods of analysis for particular purposes—an injunction that fits well with Hall's own strong commitment to conjunctural forms of analysis. To this extent, it can be argued that Hall's strongest legacy is this methodological one—concerning *how* we should engage in cultural studies.

In this respect, Angela McRobbie's contribution in chapter 4 offers a tightly focused account of how Hall's commitment to interdisciplinary forms of conjunctural analysis can be mobilised to produce a case study of the cultural politics of meaning. Her case study concerns the struggle over the meaning of the word *welfare*, which, as McRobbie points out, has endured over the last twenty years. In this process, the cultural precondition for the economic and political dismantling of large parts of the welfare state has been the redefinition of *welfare discourse* to no longer refer to honourable or valuable forms of public goods, but rather its insistent devaluation in relation to a damaging process of negative stereotyping. As she points out, alongside the changing welfare policies dictated by neoliberalism, we have seen the creation of a new moral climate in which the very word *welfare* has been associated consistently with negative qualities. As she notes, all this has been articulated in phrases concerning the supposed *dependency culture* of the *undeserving poor*. Thus, the responsibility for poverty has been individualised and is now presumed to be, in large part, the consequence of some type of personality/character deficiency or of an individual's own failure to make the appropriate effort to escape their unhappy circumstances. Thus, poverty—rather than requiring a sociological explanation or better forms of institutional and material support for those in difficulty—comes to be associated with the 'mismanaged lives' of the 'slovenly bodies' of those represented in various mediated forms of what she calls 'poverty porn'.

McRobbie's incisive case study shows how, as Hall gradually adapted his early investments in Marxism, he was able to take on board the important insights generated by poststructuralism and critical discourse theory. The great strength of such an approach, as McRobbie demonstrates, is to produce a perspective that allows us to recognise the very real importance of the economic transformations wrought by neoliberalism, without returning to the crude determinism of fundamentalist Marxism—precisely because his perspective can recognise the crucial cultural, ideological and discursive dimensions of economics itself. From this perspective, rather than neglecting the sphere of the economic, as is sometimes alleged, we can see that Hall was in fact concerned with the production of a better mode of economic analysis, which was the more powerful for being conceived on an interdisciplinary basis, and thus was able to take into account the articulation of economic policy with public forms of cultural and political discourse, in the media and elsewhere.

1 *The Red Plot*

Bill Schwarz

Since Stuart Hall died, I've gone back and read widely across his body of work, returning to pieces that were familiar and discovering new writings I never knew existed. Yet even the work I thought I knew well has presented surprises, creating unexpected turns and catching me off guard. Month by month, these experiences vary. It's not that they are cumulative, leading to a coherent or integrated summation that allows me to conclude that Hall's work is about *this* or *that*; instead, I twist and turn, carried hither and thither, and arrive at unscheduled destinations.

When it comes to putting pen to paper—or rather, when I am confronted by the abstract illumination of the blank screen—I discover that there is no obvious place for me to go. I've completed a couple of written papers, but they remain on my machine, and I reckon that's where they'll stay. The more I read, the less I seem to know, and the more the animated person of Stuart Hall recedes. What I write this week is not what I'd have written last week, nor what I imagine I'll write next week. This is, I know, to take contingency and the determination to avoid the consolidation of an orthodoxy too far. Recognition of the virtues of unknowability has value—but there are limits.

Even so, here I am back at Goldsmiths. It's a properly Goldsmiths occasion, and it's right that it should be so. I loved my years at Goldsmiths. I remember them (mainly) as a ferment of creative thinking, at its best existing at some remove from even the radical conventions of more centred academic, more familiar thought. Here we are in a brand-new auditorium in which everything works; that's a delight, of course, and I'm pleased to see it—but it doesn't conform to my memories of rough-and-ready, improvised, rocky Goldsmiths. Maybe the pull of nostalgia possesses me. We know enough, though, about the relations between institutions and the ideas produced inside them to appreciate that, at its most engaging, there was always something attractively unruly about the ideas that emanated from Goldsmiths.

Shortly after I first arrived, I was invigilating an exam for master's students from anthropology, sociology, media studies and literature. With time on my hands, I read through the exam papers and was instantly struck by the fact that all the students, whatever they were studying, were reading Hall. This wasn't a matter of academic disciplines, an anticipation of what has come to be institutionalized as the vaunted injunction for interdisciplinarity. It was more than that. It was that students and their tutors were, with markedly different theoretical commitments and with distinct intellectual and political temperaments, all engaging with Hall. There were the Deleuzians, those who worked in the slipstream of Judith Butler, the Marxists with no liking for any of the epistemic 'posts', Foucauldians of different stripes, champions of critical race approaches, queer theorists, those who were militant in their rejection of theory in the name of theory and many more I couldn't fathom. There was something protean about Stuart Hall, in the sense that bits of him could be allied to multiple, contrary positions. I'm sure there were occasions when he wasn't thrilled by many of these appropriations and would look forward to the day when the arguments could be had. Yet at the same time, there was something invigorating—very Goldsmiths—about these investments and about the passions that drove them. There was no question of a singular, consensual Stuart Hall taking command. This was to the good. As he was fond of reporting when he returned from a conference: 'I had a good time. I didn't agree with anyone.'

With these thoughts in mind I've recently returned to Hall's essay 'Epilogue: Through the Prism of an Intellectual Life'.[1] The essay moved me greatly; it took me by surprise when I re-encountered it; and it touches on questions of what we can expect thought to do. It's the transcript of his closing remarks to the conference devoted to his work that was held at the Mona campus of the University of the West Indies in Kingston in 2004, marking a celebrated, if inevitably difficult, return to his native land. He sat quietly for a couple of days, listening and observing; when the time came for him to talk, he was on a roll. He was airborne, playfully defying gravity, at one moment swooping down to press home a point of detail, the next doing daredevil acrobatics in the sky. He was flying high. He talked long past his allotted time. The only factor that brought him down to earth was the necessity of his speedily getting to the hospital—the imperatives of his ailing, material body intervening—for an appointment that required him to miss the exuberant African drumming that started the moment he'd finished talking, extending the excited buzz of the finale.

After acknowledging the manifold misrecognitions at large ('I kept looking around trying to discover this person "Stuart Hall" that everybody is talking about'), he chose to ruminate on the properties of theory—of 'thinking about thinking'.

When one *thinks*, he said, 'one confronts the absolute unknowingness, the opacity, the density of reality, of the subject one is trying to understand'. To work through the morass of *unknowingness*, it's necessary, Hall contended, to separate *oneself* from *one's self*. Such an act of mental and psychic separation works as a foundational property of thought, as opposed to the immediacy of living in 'the density of reality'. To think, he went on, 'one needs the act of distancing oneself', such that critical thought *itself* derives 'from the place of the other':

> Marx once suggested that one should use concepts like a scientist uses a microscope, to change the magnification, in order to 'see differently'—to penetrate the disorderly surface of things to another level of understanding. There is a sense in which one has to stand back, outside of oneself, in order to make *the detour through thought*, to approach what it is one is trying to think about indirectly, obliquely, in another way, in another mode. I think the world is fundamentally resistant to thought. I think it is resistant to 'theory'. I do not think that it likes to be thought. I do not think it wants to be understood . . . It is not something that simply flows naturally from inside oneself. (269–270)

He then continued: 'One is always unconsciously escaping the attempt to self-knowledge, the attempt to become identical with myself. That is not possible. I cannot become identical with myself. That is the paradox of identity . . . one can only think of identity through difference. To think is to construct that inevitable distance between the subject that is thinking and the subject that is being thought about. That is just a condition of intellectual work.'

This affirms the strangeness of an intellectual vocation in the face of a world which, in Hall's winning formulation, 'does not like to be thought.' It affirms too the consequent splitting of the self required to live one's life in this way. In the strangeness of this mode of being—in the necessity of locating oneself 'elsewhere', as the other—lies much of the impetus for Hall's practice of thinking diasporically. For Hall, this is exactly to think from somewhere other than the 'densities' of given, socially sanctioned realities. It's here too that his allegiance to thinking deconstructively occurs.

However, as readers will know, it was common for Hall to embark upon a deconstructive journey, only to pull back en route. He couldn't countenance, personally or politically, the prospect of a vertiginous, ever-continuing spiral of deconstruction. For him, theory was exactly the detour that comprised the necessary moment of abstraction but that would, just as necessarily, bring us back to the historical real. Although he was insistent on the impossibility of our ever becoming 'identical with ourselves', the psychic drive underwriting intellectual endeavour was in his view, nonetheless, to reach for what could never be—to bridge, that is, and to live as best we can with the chasm between the self and the other inside us: to bridge the chasm between the self and the world.

In his writings, his preoccupation with his own selfhood came to be more visible as he aged. Simultaneously, he found himself having to confront once more, as he did throughout much of his life, the gravitational pull of Marxism, close up and drawn into the vortex of the paradigm. Not for a moment was he surprised or disturbed by the conjunction of these contending intellectual forces. Such were the consequences of his privileging not the formalized geometries of abstraction, but the political imperatives of his determination to bring the theoretical detour back to the self, back to the world.

Such thoughts have been preoccupying me of late: both formally as part of my day job and in the interstices of my daily, unprofessional routine, when—for significant portions of the day—intellectual concerns of this intensity gently pass me by, submerged as I am in the 'density of the real'. I've been spending the year at a research centre in North America preparing Hall's work for publication, or for republication. This has been, amongst much else, a time of unparalleled privilege, radically different from my everyday life in London. It's like an unhomely, monastic retreat resonant of a different age. I sit in my office on the edge of the forest and have no other duties than to work with Stuart. While my colleagues immerse themselves in ancient Assyrian or Judaic manuscripts or in arcane fragments of Latin poetry or in the question of the first-person singular in Cartesian philosophy, I have a different experience. My office door closes, and it's Stuart and me. Every day, his voice enters my soul, and it's there when I go to bed. This routine has its pleasures. It's also unnerving, as conversing intimately with the dead always is. Although of course—despite what I desperately tell myself—my conversations aren't conversations at all. It falls to me to supply the answers to my own questions. I'm never surprised by the answers I receive.

Only in the larger, less intimate sense is this a conversation. Much of intellectual life, and all of what we call *history*, turn on our questioning of those who have departed the world. In this respect, my intellectual experience isn't so different, after all, from those who contend with the fragments of Assyrian or Latin civilization. Yet I'm living more immediately than is customary that which George Lamming recounts, in his *The Pleasures of Exile*[2] as the Haitian experience of the Ceremony of Souls, when the dead and the living converse. In the ceremony, those condemned to Purgatory depend on the living to affect their onward journey to a better place. In my—in our—case, the axis shifts. It is the living who need to negotiate a means to accommodate ourselves to the past.

In these circumstances, in my office day by day with no students or colleagues insistently banging on the door or manically occupying my inbox, my mind has the space to wander. As the hours pass, my reveries incrementally take command. While the fantasies accumulate, one leading to the other, it's still just Stuart and me. In such moments, I find myself drawn to Stuart interred, to the final freeze-frame of his being lowered slowly into his grave. It's a heart-breaking memory, held in my being.

He's buried in Highgate Cemetery in North London. The cemetery is well-known for the fact that Karl Marx's grave is there, just up the road from where Marx and his long-suffering family used to live. Right next to him, although without the same magnitude of monumentality, is the resting place of the great Trinidadian feminist-Marxist Claudia Jones; thanks to the diktats of the US State Department, Jones spent her final years in London, where with her incandescent bravura she launched the idea of Caribbean carnival in the colonial metropole. Stuart lies close by the Victorian luminaries George Eliot, Herbert Spencer and Leslie Stephen. Readers of more contemporary sensibilities might, or might not, relish the fact that he's also proximate to Patrick Caulfield, Bert Jansch and Malcolm McLaren.

This, though, is the Baedeker reading. There are more personal attachments to relate. Grouped around Marx, or in his vicinity, are a cluster of British Marxists of Hall's generation. There's Raphael Samuel, a political comrade from the days of the early New Left at the end of the fifties. There are Eric Hobsbawm and Ralph Miliband, as well as a sprinkling of prominent Trotskyists with whom, over the years, Hall engaged in political disputation. They crowd together in Marx's shadow, turning that little corner of Highgate into what, in my fancies, I've come to think of as the Red Plot.

Stuart isn't actually a signatory to the Red Plot. He's at a tangent to Marx and to the Marxists: down the hill a bit, around the corner and within sight of the borders of the cemetery, beyond which ordinary folk can be seen attending to their daily business—not quite in Marx's shadow, but within hailing distance.

As I entertain my reverie, when darkness falls and the living depart the cemetery, and when the gates swing shut and the key in the lock is turned, gradually the Red Plot comes alive with the murmur of collective subversion, enacting something like a mighty Marxist sleepover. There continues to be much marvelling at the perspicacity of the master. Those endorsing the theory of the falling rate of profit have, if anything, increased in the past years. Even so, there remains much to detain them. So much remains unresolved: The revolutionary potential of the global dispossessed; war, famine and disease, and new barbarisms of unanticipated brutality; China. They're kept busy, these unquiet souls, as they had been when they lived as mortals.

Stuart was always attracted to subversion, and political disputation lay close to his heart. He couldn't help but be drawn into such nocturnal dramas, if ever they were to occur. From his outpost, he'd have much to contribute on the ideas of the master and on the fate of social transformation in the current epoch. This is his political generation. He'd know exactly where everyone was coming from and how they'd assemble their arguments. He'd know their script, just as they'd be accustomed to his own insistent revisionism. As darkness falls, still somehow a degree out of place, he'd join the spirited exchange of ideas. But after a while, I imagine him yearning to hear something new and turning over, wondering what secrets are carried in the night sky above him.

Just like the answers I receive from him each day, these are my reveries. How could it be otherwise? Sometimes, I imagine sharing this story with him. He smiles politely while looking over his shoulder, in a backward glance, endeavouring to spot this 'Stuart Hall' that I've been talking about.

Notes

1. Stuart Hall, 'Epilogue: Through the Prism of an Intellectual Life', in *Culture, Politics, Race and Diaspora: The Thought of Stuart Hall*, ed. Brian Meeks (Kingston & London: Ian Randle and Lawrence and Wishart, 2007), 269–270.
2. George Lamming, *The Pleasures of Exile* (London: Pluto Press, 2005).

Stuart Hall Redux: His Early Work, 1964–1984

2

James Curran

Stuart Hall's stardom as a theorist of ethnicity and cultural identity has caused the value of his earlier work to be underestimated, except for his canonical 1973 encoding/decoding essay.[1] Take, for example, his first co-authored book, *The Popular Arts*, published in 1964: It goes undiscussed in a Festschrift dedicated to him.[2] It is ignored in an anthology examining the issues raised by his cultural studies work, mostly written by his former admiring students.[3] It is disparaged in the two book-length studies of Stuart Hall's work, by James Procter and Helen Davis, respectively.[4] There is not even a copy of the book in the Goldsmiths College library—the library of an institution that has a building dedicated to the memory of Stuart Hall.

Yet it is an important work, the significance of which can only be appreciated properly if it is set in the context of its time. In the early 1960s, it was still conventional to dismiss commercial popular culture as ephemeral, emotionally impoverished and formulaic and to contrast it with high culture of intrinsic merit that endured through time. Not to recognise this was to invite ridicule and be consigned, in the words of influential critic José Ortega Y Gasset, to those with a 'commonplace mind'.[5] It also meant failing to recognise that the mass market leads, as Q. D. Leavis argued in a celebrated study of popular culture, to the 'levelling down' of popular taste[6] and to standardisation 'approved by the herd'.[7]

Others more explicitly on the left, like the American critic Gilbert Seldes, blamed 'the failure of the popular arts' on 'the low value placed on them by the exploiters' who controlled popular culture.[8] In this view, it was not the masses who were at fault, but the capitalists who short-changed them. Others argued that the limitations of mass culture were the consequence of the development of a 'mass society' in which people had become detached from their stable roots and social ties and were becoming atomised, homogenous and vulnerable to manipulation.[9]

There was thus an intimidating legacy of established thought in the early 1960s that dismissed commercial popular culture as impoverished, whether due to the defects of the public, the deficiencies of the market or profound sociological change. This position had adherents on both left and right and on both sides of the Atlantic, but a shift of orientation was nonetheless discernible in the early 1960s.[10] It found its most coherent expression in *The Popular Arts*, a book Stuart Hall co-authored with Paddy Whannel.[11] Instead of dismissing popular culture, the two authors distinguished between what was good and bad within popular culture. Thus, they specified what were, in their view, the shortcomings of some contemporary popular newspapers.[12] By contrast, they hailed a new TV series called *Z-Cars* as a major advance in TV drama because of its ground-breaking, warts-and-all portrayal of the police, its powerful evocation of place and community, its depiction of closely observed and well-delineated characters, its technical virtuosity and its progressive depiction of both the social causes of violence and the devastating consequences of this violence.

Back in 1964, to examine a cop show as if it was a Henry James novel and to argue that popular culture could excel (at a time when some leading intellectuals were still refusing on principle to own a TV set)[13] was to be profoundly innovative. Yet this book soon came to be viewed as outdated, because the rise of cultural studies transformed the analysis of popular culture. Celebrated research documented the active role of the audience in the creation of meaning,[14] examined the place of popular culture in symbolic struggle,[15] championed the aesthetic of pleasure,[16] depicted taste as an extension of class and education[17] and relativized cultural value in response to postmodernism,[18] some versions of which chimed with the market liberal view that the only valid way to judge a programme is by how many people watch it.[19] All this seemed at odds with the approach of *The Popular Arts*, perhaps explaining why the book was so quickly forgotten.

However, *The Popular Arts* remains an important book not merely for the historical reason that it was a landmark study opposing the then-dominant elitism of cultural analysis. It offers, in my view, a still valid—if unfashionable—way of evaluating popular culture. It is a product of a period before neoliberalism was hegemonic. It implicitly mobilises a variety of criteria in assessing cultural value: moral (empathy and understanding), democratic (extending social representation), political (is it progressive?), literary (originality, insight, evocation, etc.) and aesthetic (is it well made?). This composite regime of value can be debated and revised, but the key point is that it offers a roadmap based on a different compass setting from that of the market for evaluating the worth of media content. If we are to make a persuasive case for defending public service broadcasting, for sustaining its funding and for reforming its functioning, we must explain what programme 'quality' means and why it should be supported. That is why it is worth returning to the rocky path that Hall and Whannel scouted years ago.

The second way in which Stuart Hall's early work broke new ground in Britain was that it revealed how literary studies could be deployed in concrete, revelatory ways. In its initial pioneer phase, media research in Britain was shaped by communications research in the United States and grounded in the social sciences.[20] Its weapons of choice were social surveys and semi-structured interviews. Hall did something utterly different: He interpreted the world of the gossip column,[21] anatomised the premises of current affair programmes,[22] analysed the demonization of radical students[23] and decoded photographs.[24] He offered a different way of engaging in media research that would now be called *critical discourse analysis.*

The third way in which Hall shaped the field was to reconceive political communications research through a seminal, co-authored book published in 1978. Entitled *Policing the Crisis*, it begins in a discouraging way with a neurotic self-denunciation. 'The book', its authors warn in the introduction, 'has been longer in preparation than its ultimate quality deserves'.[25] In fact, the book proved to be one of the foundation texts of critical political communications research in Britain.[26] Instead of relying on a single data set to examine a narrowly circumscribed topic, the book roams across two decades to offer a Marxist interpretation of the role of the media in the renewal of a regime of power—and instead of relying on longitudinal panel studies, the book situates its investigation of media influence within a panoramic historical setting that contextualised audience responses. Large numbers of people were predisposed to respond in the 1970s, the book argues, to a popular press campaign against black criminals and to the way it was spun as being symptomatic of a deep social malaise, because public indignation had already been aroused against a succession of outsider groups, because the campaign tapped into deeply rooted social values and because it provided a focus for feelings of loss arising from national decline, social dislocation and generational change.

The book's originality even extended to taking a well-aimed swipe at radical media political economists, allies on the left. News sources, Stuart Hall and his colleagues argued, were more important than media ownership in shaping the reporting of news. Powerful institutions and groups were, they maintained, the primary definers of news; journalists were merely secondary, translating the definitions supplied to them into a popular idiom. This generalisation arose from their case study, which showed that the police, judiciary and politicians, with popular amplification, provided a closed loop in defining law and order news.

This analysis fitted with a specific historical period—the dying days of liberal corporatism in the 1970s. It accorded less well with the evidence of the next decade, when press owners became more assertive and news source conflict became more marked as a consequence of political polarisation.[27] However, it was a tribute to the fertile creativity of Stuart Hall and his colleagues that just one chapter in their book generated a debate that persisted for decades.

The overarching theme of their book was that the capitalist state had moved towards a more authoritarian mode in the 1970s due to the exhaustion of consent. This theme drew upon a standard Marxist analysis in which authority is portrayed as being both coercive and reliant on persuasion. What made this book different was that it emphasised the extent to which persuasion— 'cultural hegemony'—was being resisted and had to be renewed.[28]

This last theme was developed by Stuart Hall in several theoretical essays, marking his third distinctive, early contribution to the field: as a Marxist theorist and expositor. Hegemony, in his account, is not to be conceived as a single ideology imposed by the ruling class to prevent the working class from fulfilling its historic destiny. Rather, it is better understood as a network of discourses, which are sometimes inconsistent. To be persuasive, these discourses need to have a seeming rationality that connects to the social experiences and 'lived reality' of people and need to be articulated together. Even then, they need to overcome mistrust and disbelief arising from multiple sources of resistance that cannot be adequately understood, in conventional Marxist terms, as arising from the social relations of production. Dominant discourses also have to be updated and revised in response to new challenges and developments if they are to remain persuasive.

This analysis was clearly influenced by the social and cultural conflicts, as well as those political and economic, that became prominent in the late 1960s and 1970s. Its effect was to weaken the pessimistic radical functionalism that had dominated the critical tradition of the earlier era, represented in different ways by Herbert Marcuse[29] and Ralph Miliband,[30] and it helped to unleash a wave of creativity at the CCCS. Imaginative empirical research portrayed dress codes, hair styles, music and other forms of cultural expression as being an arena in which class, ethnic, gender and generational protests were being expressed in a symbolic form.[31] This led to the reconception of the media as a contested space rather than as an agency automatically manufacturing consent and conformity.

The appropriation of Gramsci was enormously productive, but also selective. Gramsci had conceived of cultural contest as being part of a political struggle to *gain state power*, a precondition of transforming society.[32] However, winning state power was never a theme that was given much attention in cultural studies' appropriation of his work. Indeed, cultural struggle came to be seen in some studies as the pursuits of self-actualisation and of social transformation through changes of sensibility.[33] Increasingly, mainstream British cultural studies became disconnected from the practice of politics, at least in a form that related to government and public policy. However, this was not true of Stuart Hall, who sought to intervene directly in the political life of Britain as a public intellectual. This is the fourth dimension of his early work: his emergence as a political sage.[34]

In a seminal essay published in 1979, Stuart Hall argued that the right had successfully changed the terrain of public debate in a way that connected to shifting currents of public feeling.[35] The Thatcherite right had articulated organic conservatism (nation, family, duty, standards, authority and tradition) to a revived neoliberalism (self-interest, competitive individualism and anti-statism) in a way that rendered it a potent force. Labourism, by contrast, was becoming increasingly disconnected from the public and was seemingly unable to resolve the contradictions that beset it. At approximately the same time, the historian Eric Hobsbawm published an important essay documenting long-term structural changes in British society that favoured the right.[36] These were remarkably prescient commentaries, published before Margaret Thatcher's victory in 1979. They were like red flares fired into the sky, alerting the labour movement that it faced a deep-seated crisis requiring a fundamental reorientation.

Stuart Hall returned to 'the crisis of labourism' in a lengthy essay four years later. The 1975–1979 period, he argued, was 'when the basis of post-war reformism was destroyed'.[37] Labour's problems were further compounded by the hegemonic force of Thatcherism, an internal split, de-industrialisation and a fragmenting class culture, Labour's narrow parliamentary focus and its seeming inability to grasp the extent of its crisis. Only the building of a new social alliance, the formation of a programme needed to sustain this alliance and engagement on multiple fronts making Labour the focal point of popular aspiration could reverse Labour's continued decline, he argued.

This was part of a wide-ranging analysis that proved to be enormously influential.[38] In retrospect, Stuart Hall probably overstated the popular appeal of Thatcherism; surveys in the 1980s documented the underlying resilience of welfarist values, continued support for state economic intervention and an anti-authoritarian reaction.[39] Thatcher won elections partly because the opposition was split in a majoritarian electoral system. Indeed, there developed an anti-Tory, not just an anti-Labour, sentiment, which found expression in the rise of third-party support from the 1970s onwards.[40]

Stuart Hall was fundamentally right in arguing that Thatcher changed the terms of public debate and redefined the political terrain, however. He was right also in fearing that Labour lacked the inner resources and vision to renew itself as a radical force in the 1980s. When Labour adapted and achieved electoral success under Tony Blair in 1997, it was partly by incorporating neoliberal and some authoritarian populist elements from the Thatcherite legacy. This was not the project that Stuart Hall advocated when he made the case that Labour needed to change.[41]

Thus, my simple point is that Stuart Hall's acclaimed work as a theorist of ethnicity and multiculturalism—the centrepiece of what an influential documentary calls the *Stuart Hall Project*[42]— fails to do full justice to the extent of his achievement. His later work was the culmination, not the beginning, of a remarkable career. From 1964 to 1984, he examined popular culture in a new way; redefined the nature of political communication research; developed new insights into the relationship between discourse, culture and change; and became an influential public intellectual (to say nothing of his inspirational roles as a teacher and as director of the CCCS).

Public intellectuals often find themselves opining about things they have no expertise in.[43] What gave Stuart Hall an edge as a political seer was that he drew directly upon his academic research. His co-authored text *Policing the Crisis* laid the foundation for his argument that Thatcherism had renewed the right in a novel way, while Labourism had become an exhausted tradition. His Gramscian theorising highlighted the importance of how public discourse is framed and integrated, how it can cohere different groups within its horizon of thought and how it can gain traction by connecting to popular feelings and social experiences. This theoretical analysis was then applied by Hall to highlight the discursive power of Thatcherism and the weakness of Labourism. To an unusual degree, the work of Stuart Hall as a scholar meshed with his role as a public intellectual.

This is partly why as early as December 1983, when *New Statesman* rounded up left thinkers and activists to ask them which writer had influenced them the most, I chose Stuart Hall. The passage of time has consolidated this judgement.

Notes

1. Stuart Hall, 'Encoding and Decoding in the Television Discourse', CCCS Stencilled Paper 7, University of Birmingham, 1973.
2. Paul Gilroy, Lawrence Grossberg and Angela McRobbie, eds., *Without Guarantees: In Honour of Stuart Hall* (London: Verso, 2000).
3. David Morley and Kuan-Hsing Chen, eds., *Stuart Hall: Critical Dialogues in Cultural Studies* (London: Routledge, 1996).
4. James Procter, *Stuart Hall* (London: Routledge, 2004); Helen Davis, *Understanding Stuart Hall* (London: Sage, 2004).
5. José Ortega Y Gasset, 'The Coming of the Masses', in *Mass Culture*, ed. Bernard Rosenberg and David M. White (New York: Free Press, 1957), 41–45, 45.
6. Queenie Dorothy Leavis, *Fiction and the Reading Public* (Harmondsworth: Peregrine Books, [1932] 1979), 151.
7. Ibid., 157.
8. Gilbert Seldes, 'The People and the Arts', in *Mass Culture*, ed. Bernard Rosenberg and David M. White (New York: Free Press, 1957), 74–97, 82.
9. Barnard Rosenberg, 'Mass Culture in America', in *Mass Culture*, ed. Bernard Rosenberg and David M. White (New York: Free Press, 1957), 3–12.
10. Denys Thompson, ed., *Discrimination and Popular Culture* (Harmondsworth: Pelican Books, 1964).
11. Stuart Hall and Paddy Whannel, *The Popular Arts* (London: Hutchinson Educational, 1964).
12. Its argument was developed in a good, oft-overlooked book: Anthony Charles Hockley Smith, *Paper Voices* (London: Chatto and Windus, 1975).
13. John Carey, *Intellectuals and the Masses* (London: Faber and Faber, 1992).
14. John Fiske, *Television Culture* (London: Methuen, 1987).
15. Dick Hebdige, *Subculture* (London: Routledge, 1979).
16. Icn Ang, *Watching Dallas* (London: Methuen, 1985).
17. Pierre Bourdieu, 'The Aristocracy of Culture', in *Media, Culture and Society: A Critical Reader*, ed. Richard Collins et al. (London: Sage, 1986), 164–193.
18. Angela McRobbie, *Postmodernism and Popular Culture* (London: Routledge, 1994).
19. Adam Smith Institute (ASI), *Omega Report: Communications Policy* (London: ASI, 1985).
20. For a glimpse into this early, social science–dominated phase, see James Curran, 'Jay Blumler: A Founding Father of British Media Studies', in *Can the Media Save Democracy?*, ed. Stephen Coleman, Giles Moss and Katy Parry (Basingstoke: Palgrave Macmillan, 2015), 197–209.
21. Stuart Hall, 'The World of the Gossip Column', in *Your Sunday Newspaper*, ed. Richard Hoggart (London: University of London Press, 1967), 68–80
22. Stuart Hall, Ian Connell and Lidia Curti, 'The "Unity" of Current Affairs Television', *Working Papers in Cultural Studies*, no. 9 (1976): 51–94.
23. Stuart Hall, 'Deviancy, Politics and the Media', in *Deviance and Social Control*, ed. Paul Rock and Mary McIntosh (London: Tavistock, 1973), 261–305.
24. Stuart Hall, 'The Determination of News Photographs', in *The Manufacture of News*, ed. Stanley Cohen and Jock Young (London: Constable, 1973), 176–190.
25. Stuart Hall et al., *Policing the Crisis* (Basingstoke: Macmillan, 1978), ix.
26. Along with another fine book: Peter Golding and Sue Middleton, *Images of Welfare* (Oxford: Martin Robertson, 1982).

27. This contrast was projected at the time as a principled theoretical difference; see Philip Schlesinger and Howard Tumber, *Reporting Crime* (Oxford: Oxford University Press, 1994). It may have been this in part, but it also reflected a contextual shift.

28. Hall's critical exposition of Gramsci is first presented in Stuart Hall, Robert Lumley and Gregor McLennan, 'Politics and Ideology: Gramsci', *Working Papers in Cultural Studies*, no. 10 (1977): 45–76; and in his influential essay, Stuart Hall, 'Culture, the Media and the 'Ideological Effect', in *Mass Communication and Society*, ed. James Curran, Michael Gurevitch and Janet Woollacott (London: Edward Arnold, 1977), 315–348. His exposition and interpretation of Grasmci was developed in subsequent essays, notably in Stuart Hall, 'The Rediscovery of "Ideology": The Return of the Repressed in Media Studies', in *Culture, Society and the Media*, ed. Michael Gurevitch et al. (London: Methuen, 1982), 56–90.

29. Herbert Marcuse, *One-Dimensional Man* (London: Routledge and Kegan Paul, 1964).

30. Ralph Miliband, *The State in Capitalist Society* (London: Quartet Books, 1973).

31. Hebdige, *Subculture*; Stuart Hall and Tony Jefferson, eds., *Resistance through Rituals* (London: Hutchinson, 1976).

32. Antonio Gramsci, *Selections from the Prison Notebooks of Antonio Gramsci* (London: Lawrence and Wishart, 1971).

33. Paul Willis, *Common Culture* (Milton Keynes: Open University Press, 1990).

34. His political commentary during this period is collected in Stuart Hall, *The Hard Road to Renewal* (London: Verso, 1988).

35. Stuart Hall, 'The Great Moving Right Show', *Marxism Today* (January 1979), 14–20; reprinted in Stuart Hall, *The Hard Road to Renewal* (London: Verso, 1988), 39–56.

36. Eric Hobsbawm, 'The Forward March of Labour Halted?', *Marxism Today* (September 1978); reprinted with critiques and responses in Martin Jacques and Francis Mulhern, *The Forward March of Labour Halted?* (London: Verso, 1981), 1–19.

37. Stuart Hall, 'The Crisis of Labourism', in *The Future of the Left*, ed. James Curran (Cambridge: Polity, 1984), 23–36.

38. See, in particular, Stuart Hall, 'Introduction: Thatcherism and the Crisis of the Left' in Stuart Hall, *The Hard Road to Renewal* (London: Verso, 1988), 1–15.

39. James Curran, 'The Crisis of Opposition: A Reappraisal', in *The Alternative*, ed. Ben Pimlott, Anthony Wright and Tony Flower (London: W. H. Allen, 1990) 231–242; Ivor Crewe, 'Has the Electorate Become Thatcherite?', in *Thatcherism*, ed. Robert Skidelsky (London: Chatto and Windus, 1988), 25–49.

40. Anthony King, *Who Governs Britain*? (London: Pelican Books, 2015).

41. Stuart Hall, *The Hard Road to Renewal* (London: Verso, 1988).

42. *The Stuart Hall Project*, documentary directed by John Akomfrah, 2013, available at BFI Film Forever, http://www.bfi.org.uk/blu-rays-dvds/stuart-hall-project.

43. 'Leading Lights', *New Statesman* (December 16–23, 1983): 32.

3 The Politics of Theory and Method in Cultural Studies

David Morley

In this chapter, I want to address some very old problems concerning the politics of theory and method and the politics of what it means now to engage in cultural studies in a way that honours Stuart Hall's legacy.

A couple of years before he died, the North American–based International Communication Association (ICA) approached Stuart to nominate him for a career achievement award. Naturally, he was flattered, but when he saw the terms of reference he demurred—because they insisted that the person nominated for the prize should have 'conclusively solved an identifiable problem' in the field of communications. Stuart simply observed that the definitive solving of problems had never been his business; that business, of course, was the production of better questions and the reformulation of problems into more productive modalities. Happily, the ICA members were so keen to have Stuart nominated for their prize that they promptly changed their terms of reference to accommodate him. My remarks here are intended in the same spirit of provisionality: I have no definitive resolution to offer for the tensions to which I will refer between theoretical and empirical work, nor for those between the methodological dangers I discuss later in relation to 'closed' forms of determinist essentialism and their poststructuralist critics. All I can offer is to explore how we might perhaps better understand the significance of these questions and make such decisions as we need to make—and live with their consequent contradictions.

In recent years, there seems to have been a feeling in some places that cultural studies needs a kind of 'theoretical facelift'.[1] This usually involves the idea that it's time to abandon all that 'old-fashioned', messy, interdisciplinary stuff that came out of Birmingham and get things reorganised around a more systematically theorised and clearly codified philosophy or sociology of culture. Circumstantially, in the United Kingdom, this feeling has probably been exacerbated by the pressures to achieve 'respectability' introduced by the Higher Education Funding Council's various schemes for the construction of league tables based on 'research assessment/excellence' procedures, in which all work is accorded a number of stars (on the principle of the Michelin restaurant guides) and funding follows the stars. One tactic here has been for people to attempt to achieve higher scores by emphasising the status of their work as High Theory. In that respect, Theory has thus sometimes functioned as a kind of trump card in relation to any position based on 'merely empirical' observation; from that point of view, the kind of grounded cultural studies produced in Birmingham could only ever have been seen as, at best, middlebrow.

Thus, claims are sometimes now made in favour of what has been called a *new cultural studies*, which regards itself as more theoretical than what went before.[2] However, I confess that is a claim that quite confounds me; I can see that the authors commonly quoted in this more recent cultural studies work, such as Deleuze or Derrida or Agamben or Badiou—offer *different* theories than those provided by Ferdinand de Saussure, Barthes, Volosinov and Gramsci, but I cannot see that they are *more* theoretical. Indeed, for anyone who ever visited the CCCS in that earlier period, the implicit claim that it existed in a (naïve? innocent?) pre-theoretical period is quite bizarre.

In any case, I think that to head in the direction of High Theory would be the death of, rather than—as has been proposed—any kind of 'renewal' of, cultural studies. That kind of work tends towards the production of a worryingly generalised form of abstracted Cultural Theory. In my own field, its worst (and worryingly prevalent) versions often feature an uninterrogated 'we' who 'nowadays' live in an undifferentiated globalised technoverse, in which everything is quite transformed by the 'new media.' This world is often presumed to be unproblematically integrated into a virtual cyberspace, which has apparently overcome all material and cultural divisions. Further, the analytical task is then understood as identifying, by a process of philosophical reflection, the essence of a given medium (or technology) and then deducing its inevitable effects.

That kind of work has little to do with Stuart's idea of cultural studies, which was always founded on a particular view of the appropriate uses—and misuses—of theory. From that perspective, theory and abstraction are recognised as powerful analytical tools, without which we would be unable to sort the myriad facts of the world into their significant patterns, but they are also seen (rather like a power saw) as potentially dangerous; if not handled carefully, they can easily do more harm than good. In Stuart's most well-known version of this argument, though we begin from the concrete, we must then proceed to make abstractions from its detail to produce concepts that will better allow us to analyse what is going on.[3] However, he insists, having done so, then rather than remaining in the realm of theory we must return to the concrete, to see how useful these theoretical abstractions are in analysing a particular conjuncture. In another formulation, Stuart goes on to argue that you cannot do without theory, 'because the world presents itself in a chaos of appearances, and the only way one can . . . analyse them . . . is to break into that series of congealed and opaque appearances (using) the tools of concepts'[4]—that is the 'necessary detour' through theory, the necessary moment of abstraction. However, as he says, 'you cannot stop there . . . and simply *refine* your abstractions [like] a great deal of theory does . . . instead, you have to return to the [concrete] world of many determinations, where attempts to explain and understand are [always] open and never ending.'[5]

Here, I want to offer an analogy between Stuart's work and that of the French philosopher Michel Serres. Like Stuart, Serres is trenchantly critical of modes of analysis that try to use a single passkey to open all doors (whether that key be psychoanalytic, Marxist, semiotic or deconstructionist). He is fiercely opposed to the reductionism of this kind of universal metalanguage, which, he avers, is too 'comfortable and lazy.' For him, as for Stuart, analytical method does not consist of 'marshalling ready-made solutions proffered by a particular method.' Because of the importance he attaches to singularities and local detail, he argues that we always need a 'customised' method, adapted to the problem at hand—so that 'each time you try to open a different lock, you have to forge a specific key adapted to that purpose.'[6]

In this context, Sean Cubitt has made a comparable argument in favour of particularity—and specifically in favour of the anecdote as a vital form of evidence. He argues that the 'high resolution' of the anecdotal method provides the correctives of depth and colour to the generalist findings of methods that deal only with multiple instances and large-scale tendencies—and statements (and explanatory claims) about larger, more abstract formations can then be grounded in specific instances.[7] To that extent, as he claims, though anecdotal analysis sacrifices generalisation and typicality, it is able to address how the multiple factors in play in a given situation operate simultaneously in a specific instance; it is thus, in Stuart's sense, an inherently conjunctural form of analysis.

As Serres explains, because he uses diverse methods, the overall coherence of his project is sometimes treated as suspect—or guilty of some kind of theoretical incoherence (a charge those with long memories will perhaps recall Barry Hindess and Paul Hirst raising against Stuart many years ago). As Serres puts it, it may perhaps seem, when judging by his apparently eclectic working methods, that he is 'like a man who takes a plane from Toulouse to Madrid, travels by car from Geneva to Lausanne, goes on foot from Paris towards the Chevreux's Valley . . . to the top of the Matterhorn (with spikes on his shoes . . .) . . . who goes by boat . . . to New York . . . swims from Calais to Dover . . . travels by rocket towards the moon . . . (and) by semaphore, telephone or fax, by diaries from childhood to old age, by monuments from antiquity to the present'. Faced with this seemingly incoherent set of choices, Serres notes, 'one may well ask—what in the world is that man doing?' However, after making an analogy between methodological choices and planning a trip, he explains that these particular modes of travel, while disparate, are nonetheless carefully chosen—far from being fanciful—in relation to 'the specific reasons for that trip, the point of departure and destination, the nature of the places through which one will pass and the particular nature of the obstacles to be overcome.'[8]

Despite his commitment to the localised understanding of phenomena and to the 'systematic destruction of the metalanguages of essence', Serres, like Stuart, does not romanticise the fragmentary; rather, he aims for a form of synthetic analysis founded on the fullest grasp of the particulars in play in a given situation: 'The best synthesis only takes place on a field of maximal differences'; otherwise, it is 'merely the repetition of a slogan.'[9] This is no anti-theoretical position: on the contrary, Serres is in search of theoretical elegance. Just as the philosophical principle of Occam's razor enjoins us always to accept the simplest possible explanation of any phenomenon until reason is shown to the contrary, Serres defines theoretical elegance as the art of 'drawing the maximum number of results from a minimum number of suppositions.'[10]

By contrast, in this respect, abstract cultural theory fares little better than classical economics, insofar as both approaches rest on an implausible number of *ceteris paribus* assumptions. The problem is that there is always a high price to pay for stripping out cultural context, or 'assuming it away'—because things rarely turn out to be equal in the manner that such theories assume. To put it more concretely, in relation to my own field of research, abstract models of the new media or of digitalisation or of cyberspace in general seem to me far less helpful than conjunctural analyses of the ways in which material and virtual worlds are now being articulated together in different ways, in specific cultural, historical and geographical conjunctures. That is the kind of work that best characterises Stuart's legacy, the siren call of High Theory notwithstanding.

Poststructuralism and Essentialism

Let me turn now briefly to the question of poststructuralism, and to the dangers of essentialism, on which it often focuses. In this context, it is worth remembering that rather than dismissing all forms of social science, Stuart's declared ambition was to do sociology better than sociologists.[11] To that extent, although he was always sensitive to the need to avoid any heavy-handed form of determinist essentialism, he also, to say the least, had an ambivalent relation to the moment in which Raymond Williams declared that there are no masses, only ways of seeing other people as masses.[12] The difficulty with that classically humanist assertion—which perhaps becomes clearer if we substitute the analytical term *classes* for the pejorative *masses*—is that there are many situations in which it is, in fact, useful to think of people as members of classes—or, indeed, of other kinds of groups (genders, ethnicities, etc.).

To simply reduce anyone to his or her status as a member of a category and to assume that said person's thoughts and actions are automatically determined by his or her social position would clearly be a ludicrous form of essentialism. However, conversely, to reject the notion that such factors set parameters for the different possibilities that are more (or less) open (or closed) to people in particular social positions would simply be to return, via poststructuralism, to an updated form of methodological individualism. An anti-essentialism that simply refuses, on principle, to use any system of categorisation, due to its being *ipso facto* reductive, simply consigns us to a situation in which we see the world as a chaotic realm of individual and particular occurrences without patterns—the very problem that, as Stuart says, certain forms of judiciously handled abstraction can help us avoid.

In this vein, the anthropologist John Postill, tracing the shifting metaphors of media and cultural studies work since the late 1970s, has identified a clear shift across the field, away from metaphors of structure, system and boundedness and towards a strong preference for metaphors of flows, blurs and contingencies.[13] However, his point is that in general terms, to claim that identity is always fluid is no more helpful than it would be to claim that it is 'always fixed'. The question is rather which identities are limited, to what extent, by which structures and in which contexts. Identity is not well understood only as a voluntarist issue—a simple question of what you decide to make yourself into—but also of what (specific and limited) forms of cultural and economic capital your social position provides you with, out of which you can construct your identity. To put it another way, by returning to where I started in relation to the uses of grounded theory, that is the specific potential of the kind of theoretically informed conjunctural analysis that Stuart always advocated.

Notes

1. See, for example, Paul Smith, ed., *The Renewal of Cultural Studies* (Philadelphia: Temple University Press, 2011).
2. Gary Hall and Claire Burchell, 'Cultural Studies and Theory: Once More from the Top with Feeling', in *The Renewal of Cultural Studies*, ed. Paul Smith (Philadelphia: Temple University Press, 2011).
3. Stuart Hall, 'A Reading of Marx's 1857 Notes to the Grundrisse', CCCS Stencilled Paper 1, University of Birmingham, 1973.
4. Stuart Hall, 'Epilogue: Through the Prism of an Intellectual Life', in *Culture, Politics, Race and Diaspora*, ed. B. Meeks (London: Lawrence & Wishart, 2007), 269–291, 277.
5. Ibid, 278.
6. Michel Serres, in Bruno Latour and Michel Serres, *Conversations on Science Culture and Time* (Ann Arbor: University of Michigan Press, 1995), 91–92.
7. Sean Cubitt, 'Anecdotal Evidence', *NECSUS European Journal of Media Studies* 2, no. 1 (Spring 2013): 5–18, http://www.necsus-ejms.org/portfolio/spring-2013-the-green-issue/.
8. Latour and Serres, *Conversations*, 110–111.
9. Ibid., 91.
10. Ibid., 96.
11. See Stuart Hall, 'The Hinterland of Science: Ideology and the "Sociology of Knowledge"', in *Working Papers in Cultural Studies*, no. 10 (1977): 9–32.
12. See Raymond Williams, 'Culture Is Ordinary', in *Culture and Society* (Harmondsworth: Penguin, 1958), 289.
13. See John Postill, *Media and Nation-Building* (Oxford; New York: Berghahn, 2006); and also John Postill, *The Cultural Effects of Media* (forthcoming).

Stuart Hall and the Fate of Welfare in Neoliberal Times

4

Angela McRobbie

Images and Texts and Genres

In the final years of Stuart Hall's life, he made various comments on the remarkable treatment he had received during years of illness from the UK's National Health Service (NHS). He said, in a number of interviews, that the NHS was one of the most humane institutions ever invented, and he was continually thankful for the care he received during his three times per week dialysis. He emphasized that this was a universal provision 'free at the point of delivery', as the saying goes, and one of the products of the post-war years of social democracy. The NHS is and has been an employer of thousands of people from the Caribbean, especially nursing staff, many of whom arrived in Britain in the early 1950s as part of the *Windrush* generation. Hall would often talk about how he enjoyed the familiar atmosphere in the ward, even finding himself advising nurses on the A-level choices and university entrance applications of their children or grandchildren.

In this chapter, I will pursue the question of welfare and social provision and how its dismantling has provided the key axis for the transition to a fully fledged neoliberal order in the United Kingdom. My claim is that *multimediated anti-welfarism* is the instrument for producing conditions propitious to establishing neoliberalism and the widening of social inequalities which ensue. Hence I draw attention to the popular media and its role in building up a groundswell of approval for the dismantling of welfare. This account also brings me into proximity with Hall's writing over three decades—from *Policing the Crisis* to his co-authorship with Martin Jacques on Thatcherism, to his analysis of the Blair years and, shortly before he died, the times of the Cameron government.[1] A defining element of these governments, across party lines, is a determination to 'reform the welfare state'—words which are in effect euphemisms for transforming its fundamental features, almost to the point of extinction. This determination can be traced from the point at which Margaret Thatcher listened closely to Sir Keith Joseph, a strong exponent of the ideas coming out of the Chicago school of economists, right through into the era of Cameron and his Chancellor George Osborne and beyond to the present-day government of Theresa May. I argue here that Hall's analysis of the distinctive anti-welfare characteristics of the neoliberal regime has been deeply inflected by his distinctively 'cultural studies' style of poststructuralism, and more recently, by what is often referred to as biopolitics, that is, the micro-management of populations by means of specific modes of address to the body and to conduct.[2] This focus permits an analysis of social power across the terrain of *multimediatised* everyday life. Where Foucault put the body at the centre of attention and the range of addresses to the body, Hall instead considered the wider milieu of media and popular culture. Foucault had little or no sense of the integral role of either media or culture in the field of power. For Hall, in contrast, these were the key institutions and agencies which talked directly to the bodies of the populace. Hall also had a historical definition of culture carved out of his long-standing engagement with Marxism, where Foucault's work, especially the lectures on biopolitics (incidentally delivered at more or less the same point in time when Hall was publishing *Policing the Crisis)* marked out a decisive departure from Marxism. However, as I have pointed out elsewhere, there was indeed some similarity of interests in these parallel undertakings.[3]

Hall was perhaps less overtly influenced by Foucault than others working in the cultural studies tradition. In Birmingham times (1976–1981) the key advocates of Foucault's thought were the cultural historian Frank Mort and the art historian Andy Lowe. Despite this, there is, arguably, a compatibility between Hall's writing and the Foucault tradition focusing on the microphysics of power and the politics of the body. Such a convergence warrants further consideration. (Later in his life, Hall listened closely to the debates often led by Jeremy Gilbert, which developed the kind of politics that emerged from Deleuze's reading of Foucault.)[4]

But in the early days of cultural studies Hall looked to Althusser and Gramsci, and from his early essay 'Two Paradigms in Cultural Studies', the stage is set for a preference to pursue the politics of meaning and to dissect the array of ideological practices that are such key instruments for gaining consent to social transformation.[5] In that essay Hall was indicating that those critical approaches concerned with revealing the mechanisms that helped create political consensus or acquiescence with the existing social order was more pressing for academic work than the kinds of 'culturalist' approaches associated with early Marx, and with the many Birmingham studies of agency and resistance, including perhaps, the earlier work on youth cultures. We can call this a focus on the microphysics of power, or we can see it as Hall's own distinctive approach, one in which the concepts of culture and ideology come to be almost interwoven, suffused one into the other, to demarcate a site of tension and struggle as ideological forces seek to reshape the terrain of everyday life and to draw on popular cultures to create new kinds of moral climates. From quite early on Hall was looking for a theoretical escape route from the rigidity or even the straitjacket of the base/superstructure model, even as Althusser insisted on the materiality of ideology and on the autonomy of the ISAs. Hall was edging towards the politics of meaning encapsulated through the idea of *différance*.[6]

Nor should we forget Hall's debt to Ernesto Laclau and Chantal Mouffe, not least for the concept of articulation and for the decisive post-Marxist move those theorists made as they drew on poststructuralist theories of language to challenge some of the foundational vocabularies of Marx and Marxism—for example, the 'transcendental signifier' of *revolution*.[7] These shifts in theory (including the use of psychoanalysis) also gave Hall the impulse to make a decisive break with the primacy given to class in orthodox Marxist accounts, a focus that inevitably meant that questions of gender and race and ethnicity were relegated to a secondary status. (Shortly before he died, Hall re-emphasized this very point quite forcefully in a discussion with David Harvey.)[8]

We can glean this move in Hall's writings from those scholars he references from the early 1990s—in particular, Derrida and Judith Butler, both of whom also helped in his arguments against the dangers inscribed within the fixity of identity politics. In a sense, Hall found himself constantly embattled; for the political economists, his Marxism was compromised by his refusal to pledge allegiance to the primacy of class and the economic determinism of classical Marxism, but he was also looked to for support by those who wanted him to sign up to an idea of essential blackness in struggle. One of the key terms (again, drawn from Mouffe and Laclau) in Hall's vocabulary, deployed frequently in his analyses of political culture, was *articulation*. He used this term to show how, often within the terrain of popular culture, hegemonic power was sought by stitching together diverse interest groups to create a field of consent—with Thatcher being particularly adept at this undertaking. In effect, these processes of articulation also had the capacity to interpellate new political constituencies, to create new categories of persons who, until that point, had not recognised themselves as such. One salient example I recall in discussion with Hall in the context of a series of articles for *Marxism Today* was the calling into being of 'parents' as a group of persons (or consumers of education on behalf of their children) to be mobilised for change.[9] Prior to this there were simply voters, or the electorate or, for that matter, the people. Thatcher wanted to reduce the power of entrenched interests, in this case teachers as professionals and as trade unionists. She invented this category of persons (parents) in order to 'go over the heads' of the teachers. This was a successful move, one that has stood the test of time, to the point that the term 'parent power' has become a political cliché across all political parties.

Conversely, articulation was also a potential tool for radical democracy, as Laclau and Mouffe put it, creating a *chain of equivalence*, in which, depending on historical circumstances, one struggle may well take precedence over another (e.g., LGBTQ campaigns) but could find support from other social groups (e.g. feminists or trade unionists) by stitching together interests into a particular and contingent field of unity in struggle. In his analysis of Thatcherism and the 'new times', Hall deployed his own politics of articulation. He made the point that new players had entered the game, such as gays and lesbians, and their interests could not be wholly subsumed under those of class. However, that did not mean he could not foresee strong alliances and coalitions. A focus on the minutiae of language, image and text also suggested that Hall was constantly producing a rough template for the future of cultural studies by referring, for example, to a key stock phrase used so repetitively in the *Daily Mail* such as council tenants' 'right to buy' thus allowing them to not just join the ranks of the 'property-owning democracy' but able to enjoy small things such as 'painting their front doors whatever colour they wanted'. Throughout the Thatcher years, he would look closely at Thatcher's chosen vocabulary, the kind of phrases with which she littered her speeches. Although he did not extend these often abbreviated *Marxism Today* articles into full-blown academic studies, we can say with some justification that Hall's research *oeuvre* lay in dissecting the power of images and texts and genres. He preferred not to overlook the significance of key television programmes (we might imagine him looking closely at *The Apprentice* in its US format fronted by Donald Trump) or in the style of coverage given to particularly resonant items of news; a pertinent example of the latter might be the kind of images used to portray 'benefit scroungers' on the pages of popular right-wing newspapers like the *Daily Express*.

For these reasons, Hall arguably remained wholly within the kind of cultural studies framework that he had established during his years in Birmingham. Even when he conceded that the realm of economics had been perhaps unduly marginalised (in response to questions about the recent recession, banking crisis and austerity regime), one could glean that this approach to economics would not mean embracing, late in life, a conventional political economy model of ownership and control of media, of the type associated with the founding fathers of mass communications theory. Had he been able to, Hall surely would have wanted to investigate the stock phrases, the common-sense framework that came to define the way in which the economic crisis of 2008 was spoken about—the insistence, for example, on the part of George Osborne that 'we are all in this together'. In an article co-written with Alan O'Shea, not long before his death, Hall and O'Shea dissect the everyday vocabularies of neoliberalism as littered across the pages and online comment sections of *The Sun* newspaper.[10]

Mediated Anti-welfarism

Let me continue this commentary, then, by focusing on some key moments in contemporary anti-welfare discourse. I would draw attention to the way in which the word *welfare*, as in the *welfare state*, has come into disrepute. It once designated a panoply of public goods (in effect a 'good thing' for the whole population), particularly associated with the post-war period in countries of Western Europe where there was a social democratic presence that was vocal even if not necessarily in government. However, the word welfare found itself laden with negative qualities quite suddenly, when Bill Clinton in his first term of office indicated his commitment to get rid of 'welfare as we know it'. Although anti-welfarism had long been a defining mark of the right—indeed, as Melinda Cooper has recently shown, a flagship of the US Republican Party—the decisive shift that has proved to have had real historical weight has been the embracing of this stance by social democratic parties: the US Democrats, New Labour in the United Kingdom and the SPD in Germany under Gerhard Schroeder.[11] These parties hitherto had all been supportive of the redistributive function of welfare. The inaugurating moment came into being around the derogatory term *welfare queen*, which entered the everyday vocabulary of the popular press, first in the United States and then also in the United Kingdom.[12] Eventually, attention was drawn to the racial underpinnings of the term, and it was dropped from the vocabulary of popular and serious political debate. However, there is a direct line of connection between this stigmatising image, and its more recent inceptions that appear so regularly in the UK media. Indeed, a whole genre of television programming designed to expose what has been called *dependency culture* has come into being, expanding and intensifying the derogatory meaning of *welfare*.

Although there is nothing new about having embedded political meanings attached to questions of poverty (we need only think about the famous differentiation between the so-called deserving and undeserving poor from the early nineteenth century on), what transpires now is a *dispositif* of 'multimediated anti-welfarism'—that is, a set of instruments and devices including catchphrases, and rehearsed images, generated within and disseminated by media and social media, that have the capacity to transform misfortune, events that befall an individual through no fault of his or her own, into an entirely individual situation, disconnected or disarticulated from the wider social responsibilities to protect vulnerable populations. The denigratory images, as well as phrases such as *deadbeat dads* and *council house single mums*, find concretisation then in the kind of policies pushed through by governments aiming precisely to punish people for not being self-responsible or 'aspirational'. Such people are designated as incapable of self-help and they become abject populations.[13] The media construct this new common sense, as Hall would put it, and this then becomes a dominant discourse with agenda-setting powers that be. In neoliberalism, the social is eviscerated, and sociological explanations, as Loïc Wacquant has shown with such perspicacity, are derided and invalidated.[14] After all, who needs sociology? Instead, individuals are called upon to self-improve, to become individually responsible and to refuse the status of being dependent. For doing this, they might then find themselves congratulated as a good example to others.

Herein lies the moral climate for a post-social society of individuals. For instance, the *Daily Mail* often will run a story about a single mother who, in the face of difficult circumstances, nevertheless showed strength of character, refused welfare benefits and with hard work and strong parenting skills, created a better environment for herself and her children. The family will be photographed looking clean and well turned out, sitting in a tidy house. The woman will be 'well groomed', thus confirming once again Skeggs's famous argument that poverty for women also nowadays means failed femininity, a kind of chastisement meted out to women who do not 'make an effort'.[15] Again, it is the small detail that is so important, precise instances of the microphysics of power. These individualising tropes are a key element of the *dispositif* in action. Poverty comes then to be associated with shame and victimhood and with an inability or an unwillingness to make the effort to lift oneself out of such circumstances. It is a *situation* (not a structural effect within a social field) from which everyone with a shred of self-respect will make huge efforts to escape at the earliest possible opportunity. Various sociologists and media studies academics have discussed the phenomenon of *poverty porn*, a genre of televisual programming that panders to a seeming desire on the part of a projected audience to witness people in various states of misfortune. Sociologically speaking, it is important to investigate the editorial terrain and conditions of production within the TV channels that commission these programmes.

The key factor, however, is the way in which the media can assist in performing the work of politicians. There is no space here to reflect in detail on two salient examples of the effectivity of these anti-welfarist programmes and news coverage, but for the sake of illustration, I will mention them briefly. First, let me refer to the recent studies of significant numbers of young people who, despite high degrees of tolerance for issues such as sexuality and immigration, nevertheless showed no particular support for the welfare state as such—indeed, quite the opposite.[16] Their main sources of information were mainstream and social media.

The second interesting case is the recently reported dramatic drop in teenage pregnancy rates in the United Kingdom. Although government public health policies have long attempted to reduce Britain's high rate of teen motherhood, successfully in the most recent times, it also seems that the power of peer pressure and social media, along with press and TV, on the question of teen motherhood, also prevails; as one commentator said, 'Now it's considered totally uncool.'[17] The recent drop in teenage pregnancy in the United Kingdom warrants a closer look, particularly at the role played by media images directed specifically at young women.

Let me conclude this chapter by reading a little more into this avoidance of early motherhood. The logic of the female individualisation process I referred to earlier is to view teenage pregnancy as a mark of abject or failed femininity and to link it with poverty, it is the direct opposite of the idealised neoliberal female 'subject of capacity' analysed in *The Aftermath of Feminism*.[18] And this abject status of the teenage mother is compounded by the seemingly pro-feminist stance now endorsed more or less across the political parties of the United Kingdom. For women to succeed and to be able to pursue an independent life, they cannot be trammelled by having babies too young. Indeed, such a situation is nowadays associated with what Wendy Brown, in her influential critique of neoliberalism, describes as the casting of such women as having 'mismanaged lives.'[19] In an era in which the ideas of life planning and calculation are deeply embedded norms, even incorporated into the school curriculum, single motherhood occurring too early is associated with making the wrong choices and failing to be personally responsible. But more specifically a young single woman pushing a buggy, now, in the public imagination, signifies poverty, which in turn means personal failure. If young women now take more active steps to avoid pregnancy, we can see this paradoxically as both feminist success *and* something connected to the wider, more punitive culture of shaming that is such a key feature of social media in the landscape of popular neoliberalism. There is also a widening of the gap of empathy between those who make the right calculations and avoid pregnancy, and those who fail in this respect. Going back to what makes Hall's contributions so valuable, we can point to his emphasis on the potency of single words, phrases and seemingly mundane images that constitute, in these current times, the moral climate, the background noise and the wider cultural environment for the disarticulation of welfare from ideas of the public good, and the denigration of 'dependency.'

1. Stuart Hall et al., *Policing the Crisis* (Basingstoke: Macmillan, 1978); Stuart Hall and Martin Jacques, *The Politics of Thatcherism* (London: Lawrence and Wishart, 1983); Stuart Hall, 'New Labour's Double-Shuffle', *Soundings: A Journal of Politics and Culture*, no. 24 (Summer 2003): 10–24; Stuart Hall, 'The Neo-liberal Revolution', *Cultural Studies* 6, no. 25 (2011): 705–728; Stuart Hall and Alan O'Shea, 'Common-sense Neoliberalism', *Soundings: A Journal of Politics and Culture*, no. 55 (Winter 2013): 8–24.

2. Michel Foucault, *The Birth of Biopolitics: Lectures at the Collège de France 1978–79* (Basingstoke: Palgrave, 2008).

3. Angela McRobbie, 'The End of the Social and the Denigration of Democracy: Wendy Brown and Michel Foucault: A Review Essay', *Soundings: A Journal of Politics and Culture*, no. 61 (Winter 2015): 117–123.

4. Jeremy Gilbert, *Anti-capitalism and Culture* (London: Berg, 2008); Gilles Deleuze, *Foucault* (London: Continuum, 2006).

5. Stuart Hall, 'Cultural Studies: Two Paradigms', *Media, Culture and Society* 2 (1980): 57–77.

6. Jacques Derrida, *Writing and Difference* (New York: Routledge, 1987).

7. Chantal Mouffe and Ernesto Laclau, *Hegemony and Socialist Strategy* (London: Verso, 1985).

8. Isaac Julien, *dir Kapital* (2014), www.isaacjulien.com.

9. Stuart Hall, 'Blue Election, Election Blues', *Marxism Today*, no. 25 (July 1987): 30–35; Angela McRobbie, 'Parent Power at the Chalkface', *Marxism Today*, no. 29 (May 1987): 24–27, http://www.unz.org/Pub/MarxismToday.

10. Hall and O'Shea, 'Common-sense Neo-liberalism'.

11. Melinda Cooper, *Family Values: Between Neoliberalism and the New Social Conservatism* (Cambridge, MA: MIT Press, 2016).

12. Cooper, *Family Values*.

13. Imogen Tyler, *Revolting Subjects: Social Abjection in Neoliberal Britain* (London: Zed Books, 2013).

14. Loïc Wacquant, *Punishing the Poor: The Neoliberal Condition of Social Insecurity* (Durham, NC: Duke University Press, 2009).

15. Beverley Skeggs, *Formations of Class and Gender* (London: Sage, 1987).

16. Horizon Scanning Paper, 'Social Attitudes of Young People' (HMI, 2014), https://www.gov.uk/government/uploads/system/uploads/attachment_data/file/389086/Horizon_Scanning_-_Social_Attutudes_of_Young_People_report.pdf.

17. A. Hill, 'How the UK Halved Its Teenage Pregnancy Rate', *Guardian*, July 18, 2016.

18. Angela McRobbie, *The Aftermath of Feminism: Gender, Culture and Social Change* (London: Sage, 2008).

19. W. Brown, *Edgework: Critical Essays on Knowledge and Politics* (Princeton, NJ: Princeton University Press, 2005).

Right: Stuart Hall speaking at a Campaign for Nuclear
Disarmament demonstration in Trafalgar Square, London, 1958.

Part II
The Politics
of Conjuncture

The Politics of Conjuncture

Beyond the academy, Stuart Hall was very much a public intellectual, who helped to shape debates about not only the rise of Thatcherism and the politics of neoliberalism but also the dynamics and problems of multiculturalism. In performing this work of 'applied theory', he consistently advocated the necessity of what he described as conjunctural forms of analysis, addressing specific contexts and constellations of issues. It is the politics of conjuncture—and how to analyse them—that are the principal concern of this section.

We begin with John Clarke's exploration in chapter 5 of the specific nature of the forms of conjunctural analysis in which Hall was involved—and with what Clarke argues to be their institutional foundations—in the forms of collective debate, dialogic practice and interdisciplinarity. These foundations, depending as they do on the building and sustenance of various forms of collaboration, were at the heart of the CCCS project—and, as Clarke argues, they represent, if anything, the exact opposite of the dominant modalities produced by the contemporary pressures of academic institutional life. Those pressures continually induce competitive forms of academic careerism, characteristically involving forms of self-promotion in which to advance (or even just sustain) their careers, individuals must claim to have made ever more exciting and definitive intellectual breakthroughs. Clarke's argument is pitched against the grain of the (often bombastic) claims of these new orthodoxies.

His further concern is with the need to resist the temptations of various forms of lazy theoretical reductionism (whether in the modes of fundamentalist Marxism or technological determinism) to, as he puts it, more carefully trace the different determinations to their specific sites and try to specify the precise way in which general factors play out in specific circumstances. As he notes, it is also crucial here to consider the various possibilities at stake in a given conjuncture and, rather than fall into the trap of believing that everything is necessarily predetermined, recognize that our task is also to identify and pursue the specific forms of marginal, residual and emergent cultures that may offer progressive prospects for the future. However, Clarke trenchantly concludes that this task is not something that can be undertaken readily alone; it is a form of work that depends on the creation and sustenance of long-term modes of collaboration.

Doreen Massey offers a valuable account of the work of the *Soundings* journal in chapter 6—as an example of exactly that kind of long-term, collective, intellectual collaboration. Indeed, following his years of involvement in collaborative work at the CCCS and subsequently at the Open University, *Soundings: A Journal of Politics and Culture* (along with his work in the Visual Arts at Rivington Place and elsewhere, discussed in part IV) was perhaps the project that occupied the most of Stuart's time in his retirement. Massey carefully traces Stuart's distinctive, long-term contribution to the development of that project, from its launch— at what is now clear was a time of historic opportunity—in the interregnum between the collapse of high Thatcherism and the arrival of New Labour in the mid-1990s—through to its most significant recent engagements, in the wake of the financial implosion of 2007 and the subsequent travails of neoliberalism.

As Massey makes clear, what Stuart did on so many occasions was to provide both a historical overview, which placed contemporary events in a more revealing historical perspective, and a clear perception of the urgency to figure out exactly what was at stake in each conjuncture. In doing so, Massey notes, Stuart characteristically paid close attention to the important role of economic dynamics—and most recently to the dynamics of financialization—but nonetheless, he always refused any simple recourse to economic determinism, insisting that our political interventions must also address the ideological and discursive dimensions of the conjuncture that we face. As he made clear, in the case of neoliberalism, it often has been the continuing hegemony of neoliberal ideology 'sedimented into the habitus of everyday life, common sense and popular consciousness' that has shored up the manifest fragility of its economic project, narrowly conceived (and thoroughly dramatised in recent years by the banking crisis and its aftermath). In all of this, as Massey demonstrates, the *Soundings* project has been alert to questions of what is now referred to as the *inter-sectionality* of divisions of class, gender, race and generation, but also to the positive glimpses of the (long-denied) alternatives to neoliberalism. In the last year or two, these alternatives have found voice in the anti-austerity movements in Spain, Greece and elsewhere; as Stuart always insisted, they are the kind of 'vital signs' for which conjunctural analysis must continually scan the horizon, in search of potential avenues of intervention, in the hope of constructing a better political future.

In a similar spirit to Doreen Massey's contribution, David Edgar in chapter 7 focuses on Stuart's involvement in two further collective intellectual and political projects—*New Left Review* and *Marxism Today*—which could each be said to characterize a particular political moment: the former, the initial conjuncture of the non-Communist left of the 1960s and the latter as the herald of the New Times movement of post-Fordist consumerism that characterised the 1980s. Evidently, the participation of Hall and David Edgar as non-party members on the editorial board of *Marxism Today* was a significant indicator of the degree to which that nexus of collaborations had, at least for a period, opened its doors to a wide variety of contributors; in so doing, it created a vibrant intellectual sounding board against which many of today's ideas about globalisation, technology and politics were first developed.

Notably, it was in *Marxism Today* that Stuart first published 'The Great Moving Right Show', in which, even before Thatcher's election, he defined the politics of Thatcherism and its particularly rich mix of neoliberal anti-statism and no-nonsense authoritarian populism. If ever an article can be said to have been prescient, then this clearly was a leading case; despite the scepticism with which some people greeted Hall's formulations concerning the specificity of Thatcherism as a mode of political authority, it manifestly was one that subsequently installed its hegemony, with only slight variations in the 'New Labour' period, over the last thirty-five years. It was not for nothing that Margaret Thatcher once described Tony Blair's New Labour as her greatest invention—and it was Stuart, working in collaboration with

Martin Jacques in the context of the *Marxism Today* project, who first articulated its political significance.

However, to return to John Clarke's formulation of how conjunctural analysis is often (and necessarily) a form of dirty work, Edgar's account of his own falling out with his erstwhile comrades at the Institute of Race Relations (IRR) over their rejection of what they saw as Stuart's 'consumerist revisionism' shows how contentious conjunctural politics can be. Edgar usefully demonstrates how one can now easily see that Ambalavaner Sivanandan's analysis of the *Silicon Age* (1979)[1] was, in fact, very similar to Hall's own analysis of globalisation. However, as he rightly observes, at the time, the urgency of the political questions at stake produced disabling fissures among those who might otherwise have been allies. Edgar's conclusion is also instructive in this respect, when he notes that if much of this is now no more than conventional wisdom, readily accepted by many different sectors of the left, then it was by no means always so. As he argues, Stuart in particular must be credited with having produced the analytical tools and concepts that have built—even in and through moments of deadly serious contention such as those he describes here—what has now become much of the accepted political common sense of our age.

As one of Stuart's longest standing collaborators, Michael Rustin in chapter 8 takes us back to their joint work in the period of the *Universities and Left Review* and the New Left Clubs, the *New Left Review* and the May Day Manifesto in the late 1950s and early 1960s—and from there traces the route of Stuart's extra-academic collaborations right through to *Soundings* and the Kilburn Manifesto of recent years. As Rustin notes, that earlier agenda was very wide—and for a considerable period very much addressed to the politics of the Cold War, not least through an involvement with the Campaign for Nuclear Disarmament (CND). The width of that agenda was, he notes, crucial as a way of challenging the patronising and complacent hegemonic ideologies of the day on as many fronts as possible.

Notable for Rustin is the fact that Stuart's work around *New Left Review* in this period already involved an early engagement with questions of consumerism, identity and youth culture (gained not least via the experience of secondary school teaching). There is a clear link here to some of his early work at the CCCS, such as 'The Hippies: An American Moment',[2] in which Stuart offers early versions of his analysis of the complex dynamics of youth/consumer culture, linking the hippies' 'progressive' modes of individualism to their later incarnation in the quite different political valences of Thatcherite entrepreneurialism (a trajectory for which the name Richard Branson will perhaps serve as a convenient shorthand). All this then finds fuller and more developed expression in Stuart's work with Tony Jefferson, John Clarke, and others in relation to youth cultures in the 1970s and in his later collaborations with *Marxism Today* around questions of New Times.

However, here again we must return to the sometimes divisive and politically contentious dimensions of these analytical debates. Just as David Edgar recounts the IRR's dismissal of *Marxism Today* for its supposed revisionist consumerism, so too in the earlier period of which Rustin speaks were cultural studies perspectives on consumerism and identity roundly denounced by Stuart's erstwhile comrades, Edward Thompson and Ralph Samuels. As noted earlier, what is perhaps most remarkable here is the extent to which these (once) seemingly heretical views have now come to be so widely recognised as the necessary premises from which our contemporary political differences and debates must be further articulated; however, it is instructive to consider Rustin's account of how far back in the trajectory of Stuart's work their roots can be traced.

When confronted with debates about the defining qualities of cultural studies, Stuart himself always walked a fine line, refusing so far as possible to be responsible for policing the boundaries of analytical or methodological permissibility—while at the same time insisting that to engage in cultural studies does involve stipulatory commitments. It is the methodological commitment to the necessarily provisional and concrete application of theory to the analysis of conjunctures that Lawrence Grossberg in chapter 9 argues is the most important defining quality of Hall's variety of cultural studies. In parallel with Doreen Massey's comments on the forms of conjunctural analysis developed in the *Soundings* journal, Grossberg usefully explores the issues involved in defining a conjuncture, along with its limits and boundaries. The insistence on the investigation of dynamic contexts, not disciplinary fixed or stable objects—and the commitment to open-ended and necessarily incomplete forms of interdisciplinary analysis—is, as Grossberg trenchantly argues, what distinguishes the specificity of cultural studies.

Grossberg's approach here works in close parallel with Michel Serres's rejection of the inadequacy of the more abstracted forms of political or theoretical certainty (whether Marxist or otherwise). As Grossberg rightly argues, approaches that, in their search for disciplinary legitimation or political certainty, often abandon the necessary provisionality of conjunctural analysis ultimately illuminate nothing more than a new form of over-theorised political pessimism (which is what Doreen Massey herself believed was represented at international conferences where people fly halfway around the world to confirm to each other that all is already lost). As Grossberg says, this form of theoretical pessimism not only abandons the necessary search for points of political intervention, as reflected in Gramsci's belief in the necessity for an optimism of the will, but also abandons the theoretical commitment to openness—and to the possibility (in an almost Popperian sense) of being prepared to be proved wrong—a commitment to which cultural studies must always remain attached.

Finally, Tony Jefferson in chapter 10 returns us directly to the present conjuncture by addressing the crucial and deeply problematic role played by matters of race and immigration in contemporary British politics. Jefferson here attempts to deconstruct the simplistic terminologies of racism, which have long provided the principal terminology for discussions of questions of envy, hatred and prejudice. These unwelcome forms of negativity have been noted to be principally displayed by what have come to be called the *left behind* or *neglected* sections of the United Kingdom's impoverished, white working class. The attempt to court these voters has clearly been crucial in recent elections, and it is this issue that remains at the heart of electoral strategy for the future—not only for parties that have long courted the racist vote, such as UKIP and the BNP, but also for the mainstream parties, which now feel that they must compete on this treacherous ground.

Rather than dismissing all those who display any tendency to stereotype others as necessarily ignorant or morally inferior, Jefferson attempts instead to deconstruct the category of racism into its differing component parts. Thus, he insists that the tendency to categorise experience—and others—into 'types' of one kind or another is an inevitable aspect of all our cognitive procedures. What he then attempts to do is distinguish among hatred, prejudice, 'othering' and racism and, in so doing, pay attention to the material conditions that tend to generate problematic emotions such as envy or hatred.

To this end, Jefferson in some ways comes close to the terrain on which Stuart Hall and Paddy Whannel worked very early on in producing *The Popular Arts*. In parallel with their insistence on the importance of popular cultural forms in representing the key ideological currents of a culture, Jefferson makes a close and detailed textual analysis of a set of films (produced by Shane Meadows) that offer an empathetic psychosocial representation of the role of everyday practices and discourses in the learning (and, crucially, unlearning) of the performative modes of prejudice and racism. In doing so, Jefferson offers an imaginative mode of integration of the forms of textual analysis conventionally associated with the humanities with a thoroughgoing sociological grasp of the larger structures within which these discourses find their place. Here, then, we are offered an insightful and productive way of returning to many of the key issues of the politics of race in the United Kingdom—as originally identified in the CCCS mugging project (which Jefferson himself helped to articulate more fully in the now canonical *Policing the Crisis*). As you will see, these are also the questions to which, in the North American context, Angela Davis returned in the conference's keynote speech (see chapter 23).

Notes

1. A. Sivanandan, 'Imperialism in the Silicon Age', *Monthly Review* 32, no. 3 (July–August 1980).
2. Stuart Hall, 'The Hippies: An American "Moment"', CCCS Stencilled Paper, University of Birmingham, 1968.

5 Doing the Dirty Work: The Challenges of Conjunctural Analysis

John Clarke

Conjunctural analysis is, I think, one of Stuart Hall's great gifts to cultural studies and beyond.[1] Despite the unfinished discussions about how to engage in it, conjunctural analysis provides an orientation, an approach or a way of thinking about and looking at social formations that is both distinctive and urgently needed. That sense of urgency is intensified by the combined and ugly pressures of contemporary academic life, of career making and of the increasingly commodified processes of publishing that lead almost entirely in the opposite direction from conjunctural analysis. On the one hand, as David Morley said in chapter 2, these pressures lead to a desperate desire for grand theory with a capital G and a capital T. On the other hand, they lead to a temptation to make epochal announcements. Books increasingly have been promising the 'end of . . .' or the discovery of a 'beyond the . . .' or 'post-(something)' as ways of announcing a distinctive—and presumably marketable—claim to new knowledge. This compulsion to tell the time feels unnerving. The announcement of 'ends' breaks historical analysis into separate segments; typically, such distinctions separate the past (not very interesting or complicated) and the new (exciting, mobile, dynamic).

The idea of conjunctural analysis involves an insistence—and I can hear Stuart saying it—that *we can do better than that*. Not just that we *can* do better, but that we *must* do better. Conjunctural analysis carries the promise that we can avoid the temptations of theoretical reductionism: the belief that because we have the theory, we know what the world is like and how it works. It also offers the possibility of escaping from epochal thinking: the belief that because this is late capitalism, we know what time it is. However, the promise of conjunctural analysis also brings with a price to be paid: the hard work of actually doing it.

In a conversation with Doreen Massey in 2010, Stuart articulated some of the issues at stake in thinking conjuncturally:

> It's partly about periodisation. A conjuncture is a period during which the different social, political, economic and ideological contradictions that are at work in society come together to give it a specific and distinctive shape. The post-war period, dominated by the welfare state, public ownership and wealth redistribution through taxation was one conjuncture; the neoliberal, market-forces era unleashed by Thatcher and Reagan was another. These are two distinct conjunctures, separated by the crisis of the 1970s. A conjuncture can be long or short: it's not defined by time or by simple things like a change of regime-though these have their own effects. As I see it, history moves from one conjuncture to another rather than being an evolutionary flow. And what drives it forward is usually a crisis, when the contradictions that are always at play in any historical moment are condensed, or, as Althusser said, 'fuse in a ruptural unity'. Crises are moments of potential change, but the nature of their resolution is not given.[2]

I will turn to questions of time and space later, but first I want to concentrate on the challenge posed by Hall's opening comments about the 'different social, political, economic and ideological contradictions that are at work'. Here we see a characteristic refusal to think that contradictions are only economic; instead, they are multiple, at play in different domains and only come together at specific points. Therefore, this is the first demand for hard work: to trace the different contradictions with attention to their specific sites, characters and effectivities. Only then can we track the ways in which they come together to reinforce, inflect, displace and intensify each other in the point of condensation that is a conjuncture. Later in the same conversation, Hall and Massey discuss the importance of resisting the seduction of economic reduction—particularly when the crisis appears to us as primarily, if not exclusively, economic in character.[3] Instead, they argue for the importance of thinking of the specific crisis—this conjuncture—in its 'over-determined' form, in which social, ideological and political contradictions play distinctive parts. Indeed, the conjuncture may be formed of multiple, intersecting crises of different sorts.[4]

With this insistence on the condensation of contradictions in mind, I want to take a step back and reflect on what feels like the relative decline or disappearance of the notion of contradiction. Much of what passes for critical work (including that which claims Marxist lineage) has apparently given up the idea of contradiction. The common outcome of this surrender is an account of capital's ever-increasing rule, domination and colonisation of the world and its destruction of everything that once stood in its way. The effect of this contradiction-free way of seeing is an accumulation of depressing narratives, each paying its tribute to the apparently uninterrupted power of capital.

This seems a strange—and unlikely—form of capital: a fantasy of an ever-expanding, smoothly functioning force that is free of contradiction, antagonism and disruption. This feels like the pessimistic inversion of the fantasy promulgated by capital's own advocates. Other forms of critique also tend to operate without the concept of contradiction—making it harder to identify the spaces, cracks, fissures and antagonisms that might demand our attention and resist depressive assumptions about the power and effectivity of dominant formations. Nor, in passing, is the last-page or last-paragraph gesture to resistance an adequate compensation; unless the conditions of resistance, contestation or mobilisation are grounded in the analysis, they are merely romantic bolt-ons.

Conjunctural analysis demands that we pay attention to these problems, inviting us to work with the present as a conjuncture formed out of multiple, heterogeneous and contradictory forces, tendencies and trajectories. In this way, we might consider the different forces that are in play in a conjuncture rather than assume any present moment is merely the expression of a single force. This also creates the possibility of paying attention to what possibilities are at stake in the conjuncture. What different lines of development may be available in this here and now? Therefore, my view of conjunctural analysis stresses multiplicity, heterogeneity and the condensed dynamics of over-determination. Such a mode of analysis is demanding in many ways—not least through the question of how we are to know all of these things, much less respond to them. Confronted by the challenge of the complexity of the present moment, I tend to reach for a simplifying shortcut, because I am not as good as I ought to be (and this mode of analysis is not easily accomplished by the lone scholar).

Thus, I turn regularly to Raymond Williams's useful distinction between what he called *epochal analysis* and *actual historical analysis.*[5] He suggested that epochal analysis is necessarily focused on the dominant (e.g., the transition from feudalism to capitalism). However, he argued that actual historical analysis must look beyond the dominant; one must know that the dominant is there, but must explore the dominant in its entangled relationships with the residual and the emergent. For Williams, the residual was never 'merely' residual, just an unfortunate leftover of an earlier formation. For him, the residual contains and articulates those social issues and questions that cannot be posed or answered within the framework of the current dominant. One of the interesting echoes for me from Angela McRobbie's contribution in chapter 4 is that welfare looks like one of those residual elements. It poses questions of needs and problems, and of sociality and mutuality, that cannot be answered in the terms of the current anti-welfarist and anti-statist dominant formation.[6]

Nevertheless, I think identifying the 'residual' is the easy part of working with Williams's distinction between dominant, residual and emergent formations, given that the 'dominant' is a mobile and adaptive formation, while the 'emergent' is harder to identify. I suspect that the emergent rarely looks like the cultural or political forms that we imagine or expect. It never quite takes the form of what we think we will see, but it is critical for any analysis of the conjuncture. However, Williams insists that it is not enough just to trace the three different strands; it is the dynamics of their inter-relationship that matters. For example, the dominant is always engaged in a struggle to make the residual merely residual and a struggle to incorporate, suppress or even ventriloquise the emergent, borrowing new voices.

There is not the space here to develop arguments about conjunctural analysis fully, but I will raise two problems for further consideration. The first, and most obvious, is this: What's a conjuncture? The discussion between Hall and Massey hints at questions of periodisation and points to the difficult relationship between conjunctures and crises.[7] There is an important refusal to define the length of a conjuncture, but I suspect this glosses over a more complex question about the different temporalities that are condensed in the formation of a specific conjuncture. What are the different sorts of time, temporality and temporal rhythms that are brought together in the present moment? How are they condensed in ugly relationships in this conjuncture? How do some of the long histories and the slow rhythms of change come to be accented or animated by the shifting political forces? How are they given a new significance or urgency by their encounter with more immediate pressures, shorter rhythms, or faster, more urgent political demands? More specifically, I wonder if one of the political struggles within a conjuncture might be about the capacity to 'tell the time': the ability to define what is 'modern' and what can be safely consigned to the past. This is a key element in being able to lay claim to constructing the *way forward*—the line of development that needs to be followed to escape from the present crisis, however that crisis is constructed.[8]

There is a parallel set of questions to be posed about the spaces of a conjuncture, rather than presuming that there is a singular 'here' (in parallel with a singular 'now'); this is a conversation that I will one day get to have with Doreen Massey. In *Policing the Crisis*,[9] we got away with talking about Britain, British capitalism and the British social formation. We certainly knew that Britain had a colonial history, and we knew that this history was consequential for the conjuncture—and specifically for the racialised inscription of crisis that the book explored. However, no one could say that the book offered a richly spatialised view of a British social formation that was constituted through spatial relationships. At the least, there is a case for thinking about the emergence of that conjuncture—and its crisis-ridden development into the present—through a set of spatial relationships in which Britain is complexly articulated with Empire, America and Europe. Those relationships are both real and imagined; each involves material and cultural dynamics. In cultural terms, each carries a strong sense of ambivalence, involving poles of attraction and repulsion. *America, Europe* and *Empire* are the 'imagined' others of Britishness—bound up in complicated connections of desire, loss, anxiety and fear. These orientations continue to shape ideas about who 'we' (the British) are, who 'we' were—and who 'we' might become. In passing, it is worth noting that this orientation implies a different way of thinking about space from the national/global binary that still dominates much of social science. In sum, both the space and time of the conjuncture—and their implications for conducting conjunctural analysis—remain unresolved but pressing issues.

In conclusion, let me return to my starting point: that conjunctural analysis is one of Stuart Hall's great gifts to cultural studies. What a gift it is—and what an unbearable demand it is. Performing conjunctural analysis, even in the skimpy, slipshod way that I attempt it, is not an easy thing to do. More pointedly, it is not something that should be undertaken alone: No one scholar can grasp the multiplicity of forces, pressures, tendencies, tensions, antagonisms and contradictions that make up a conjuncture; it is excessive. However, to repeat what I argued earlier, the current dominant forms of the academy run in exactly the opposite direction. They fetishise individual work, individual careers and individual outputs. In particular, they fetishise the heroic great scholar. As Mikko Lehtonen[10] has recently argued, this is one of the critical conditions that underpins the surprisingly rare incidence of conjunctural analysis within cultural studies (and elsewhere). In contrast, I think conjunctural analysis is one of those processes that is collaborative. I do not wish to fetishise or romanticise *Policing the Crisis*, but its attempt at conjunctural analysis relied on collective labour (and constant argument, discussion and revision). This is indeed the hard labour—or dirty work—of doing conjunctural analysis. This dirty work is best done collaboratively and in dialogical forms, and for such work we at least need friends. If I may claim one last message from Stuart Hall, it is that the building of friendship, dialogue and collaboration matters.

Notes

1. John Clarke, 'Conjunctures, Crises, and Cultures: Valuing Stuart Hall', *Focaal: Journal of Global and Historical Anthropology*, no. 70 (2014): 113–122.
2. Stuart Hall and Doreen Massey, 'Interpreting the Crisis', in *The Neoliberal Crisis: A Soundings Collection*, ed. Sally Davison and Katherine Harris (London: Lawrence and Wishart, 2015), 60–74, 62–63. First published in *Soundings: A Journal of Politics and Culture*, no. 44 (Spring 2010): 57–71.
3. Hall and Massey, 'Interpreting the Crisis', 62–63.
4. John Clarke, 'Of Crises and Conjunctures: The Problem of the Present', *Journal of Communication Inquiry*, no. 34 (October 2010): 337–354.
5. Raymond Williams, *Marxism and Literature* (Oxford: Oxford University Press, 1977), 121–122.
6. See also John Clarke, *Changing Welfare, Changing States: New Directions in Social Policy* (London: Sage Publications, 2004).
7. See also Larry Grossberg, *Cultural Studies in the Future Tense* (Durham, NC: Duke University Press, 2010).
8. Clarke, 'Of Crises and Conjunctures'.
9. Stuart Hall, Chas Critcher, Tony Jefferson, John Clarke and Brian Roberts, *Policing the Crisis: Mugging, the State and Law and Order* (Basingstoke: Macmillan, 1978).
10. Mikko Lehtonen, '"What's Going On?" in Finland: Employing Stuart Hall for a Conjunctural Analysis', *International Journal of Cultural Studies* 19, no. 1 (2016): 71–84.

The Soundings Conjuncture Projects: The Challenge Right Now

6

Doreen Massey

The journal *Soundings* ('a journal of politics and culture', we subtitled it) launched in 1995. It was a conscious response to the political moment. High Thatcherism had wound down into the John Major years. In the journal's opening issue, Stuart Hall wrote of a sense of exhaustion pervading the country. There was also a stench of corruption and widespread unease at deepening international inequality and environmental degradation. It was clear that Labour was going to win the next election. It was a historic opportunity.

It was equally clear that Labour (now New Labour) would not take advantage of the opportunity. (It later emerged of course that the party would take it, but in quite the wrong direction—a fact that Stuart analysed in his searing piece 'New Labour's Double-Shuffle'.[1]) We (myself, Stuart and Michael Rustin) founded *Soundings* to provide a forum for discussion of what it might mean to seize such an opportunity, but by issue 5—still before the election—Stuart could already write that 'a historic opportunity has been let slip'.[2]

Soundings continued, and in his analyses over fifteen years starting in 1995, Stuart's arguments cut to the core of things: the continuing exasperation with the Labour party, yet the recognition that it had to be addressed; the resolute refusal of economic determinism; the (related) insistence on the significance of other instances of society and on the need to *create* political constituencies; the idea that individual policies should be vehicles for the dissemination of a bigger politics. All these elements—in both method of analysis and manner of political diagnosis—are central to thinking conjuncturally.

Then came the financial implosion, beginning in 2007. It had the potential to rock to their foundations the pillars of the neo-liberal project—yet by 2010, a Conservative/Lib Dem coalition was settling into office. Stuart's immediate diagnosis was proven correct: that it would last a while[3] and that it had 'seized the opportunity to launch the most radical, far-reaching and irreversible social revolution since the war'.[4] (This gives real pause for thought now, after the 2015 elections and the unleashing of a fully Tory government.)

During a gloomy time, in 2011, Stuart contributed two things of real importance. First, he stood back from the immediacy of day-to-day politics and produced a sweeping survey of the historical roots and geographical scope of neoliberalism (the neoliberal revolution). Here we find the essential continuities, which are also 'antinomies and ambiguities',[5] through the shifts of (neo)liberalism's evolution. Here too we find the astonishing persistence of the old aristocratic, financial and landed interests, and the periodic upwellings of radical currents of protest, engendering new accommodations and articulations. Stuart argued in 2011 that 'the neoliberal project is several stages further on'.[6] (Again, four years later, we may feel this conclusion has been reinforced.)

However, in the same paragraphs, Stuart reminds us that neoliberalism is certainly a powerful hegemonic project, but no hegemony is ever complete or completed. Hegemony must constantly be worked on and maintained: 'Excluded social forces, whose consent has not been won, whose interests have not been taken into account, form the basis of counter-movements, resistance, alternative strategies and visions . . . and the struggle over a hegemonic system starts anew'.[7] (Yet again I wonder, is this what we are witness to now?)

Characteristically, this long historical and theoretical exploration was triggered by a question about the current political moment. 'What sort of crisis is this?' Stuart asked in the opening paragraph. In fact, this issue of the definition of a crisis was his second major contribution at this moment. He also argued that although this was 'another unresolved rupture of that conjuncture which we can define as "the long march of the Neoliberal Revolution"',[8] there was still the question of whether it would presage business as usual, a deepening of the neoliberal project, 'or the mobilisation of social forces for a radical change of direction . . . Is this the start of a new conjuncture?'[9]

These are crucial distinctions that were critical to the work we went on to do. At that moment of economic crisis, Stuart insisted, we must not fall back on economic determinism. If the crisis was going to be (or was going to be made to be) one that marked a shift between conjunctures, one that would bring about a real change in the balance of social forces, then there needed to be a coming together of economic crisis with crises in other aspects of society (he writes here in particular of the ideological, the political, the social). Referring to Gramsci and to Althusser, Stuart argued that these different levels both have their own relatively autonomous dynamics and provide the conditions of existence for each other, including the economic. 'The definition of a conjunctural crisis is when these "relatively autonomous" sites—which have different origins, are driven by different contradictions, and develop according to their own temporalities—are nevertheless "convened" or condensed in the same moment. Then there is [conjunctural] crisis, a break, a ruptural fusion'.[10] In 2011, it was evident that though there had been a massive economic crisis, there had been *no* serious unsettling of political and ideological hegemony.

In a sense, then, and given this approach, the moment presented itself in conjunctural form. It was impossible to fall back on economism or to evade the evident relative autonomy of the ideological and the political. Here, precisely, the continuing hegemony of neoliberal ideology and its political forces were providing the conditions for the continuing existence of an economic model that, purely in its own terms and without the state help that had been poured in to prop it up, was both extremely fragile and riven by contradictions. Here, there was clearly no ruptural fusion of crises in interlocking instances of society—and that analytical holding apart from the distinct instances is essential to exploring how the left might have a better idea of how/where to intervene effectively. 'So', wrote Stuart, 'is this crisis about a real shift in the balance of social forces?' (Clearly, it was not.) 'Or', he continued, 'if not, how can we push the crisis from a compromise ending to a more radical rupture, or even a revolutionary rupture?' 'But first', he concluded, 'you have to analyse ruthlessly what sort of a crisis it is'.[11]

It was in this context that *Soundings* launched a programme of seminars, papers and discussion on the meaning and nature of conjunctural analysis ('The Neoliberal Crisis', in which two of the pieces referred to here are included) as a lead-up to what became known as *The Kilburn Manifesto*. The aims of the latter were (1) to layout the structural nature of the crisis at that point; (2) argue that, given this structure, a priority for political intervention must be the ideological—that the aim must be to challenge accepted understandings and to attempt to shift the dominant terms of debate (Stuart's own written contribution—with Alan O'Shea—is 'Common-sense Neoliberalism'[12]); and (3) to instantiate that broad argument in different spheres of society (the state, feminism, the economy, energy) with some 'ruthless analysis' and an indication of what 'changing the terms of debate' might mean in concrete terms.

What Stuart most obviously brought to this work was his long engagement with this kind of thinking, from *Policing the Crisis* to his analyses of Thatcherism. However, each moment was different. *Policing the Crisis* had taken a specific phenomenon and used it to bring to light the wider structure of the conjuncture in which it was set. The analyses of Thatcherism insisted on the depth and revolutionary nature of a new hegemony coming into its pomp—one that inaugurated a new conjuncture. Now, however, that conjunctural settlement was showing fractures. What could be done to open these fractures further?

Throughout, the Manifesto project tried to live up to Stuart's constant double insistence on the one hand on the need for rigorous theoretical thinking (of the sort that did not easily come to conclusions but always seemed to have another awkward question to raise) and on the other hand on a total refusal of theoretical deduction. I remember moments of real intellectual and political exhilaration, sitting in Stuart's front room, as he made connections between the here and now and profound questions of, say, conceptualisation.

There was also his insistence on complexity at play. When Stuart was on a roll, addressing an audience, he didn't just *tell us* about the complexity of things (and of the importance of our paying due attention to the same); he *inhabited* it. He brought a meticulous logic and rigour together with a rich evocation of whatever it was he was talking about; you got the real feel and smell of it.

This approach to analysis brought out several things, just a few of which it is possible to mention here. There is the importance of the longer historical view, both nationally and globally. The housing crisis in the United Kingdom, for instance, is not only a product of an economic strategy that prioritises finance and assets (though it is that); it is also at a far longer, deeper level a symptom of the latest articulation of two historic pillars of this country's class structure—landed capital and finance. Understanding this makes a difference politically. It means that in the end, as they say, it is at this level that it must be addressed. Building more houses may be fine, but in the end it is the background structure of ownership, and the (unearned) profit from that ownership—especially of land—that must be tackled. Moreover, it is a help politically (both inspiring and depressing, for the battle has been so long) to set individual protests today in the context of centuries-long struggles against those who own the bulk of 'our country'. Or again, as Stuart pointed out, neoliberalism 'is able to do its dis-articulating and re-articulating work because these ideas have long been inscribed in social practices and institutions, and sedimented into the "habitus" of everyday life, common sense and popular consciousness—"traces without an inventory"'.[13] Such differential, intersecting temporalities deserve more recognition.

Also central to this approach to analysis is close attention to the structures of social division. Class remains crucial, but the rise of the rentier society means that class relations and the locations of expropriation have shifted and multiplied, which means in turn that the sites and lines of conflict have also proliferated. Other lines of division intersect with class. In the Manifesto, we focused on gender, race and generation, not just to document the inequalities and exclusions but to analyse how these relatively autonomous systems of division and subordination articulate with those of neoliberalism. What we found is that each is distinct in the nature of its entanglement in the current settlement.

Running through everything is the centrality of finance and financialization—in the economic and geographic structure of the country, in the political iron hand across Europe, but also more intimately. *Financialization* has weaselled its way inside our heads, our imaginations, our identities, the language we use. It provides the structure of thought that underpins neoliberal common sense. Maybe it is also the central fulcrum of articulation of the different instances in the current settlement.

The analyses in the Manifesto[14] confirmed just how much European social democracy in its post-war form has been weakened—not maybe in terms of formal structures, but in spirit and political purpose, and in terms of the philosophy and understanding of society that lay behind it. The very temporal structure of the prevailing common sense has been overturned. *Then* (and to oversimplify grossly), there was a feeling of living in a longer history in which there would be 'progress' and to which we might contribute. Of course, the nature of the progress could be (and was) challenged, and the complacency that sometimes accompanied it could feel constraining (see the sixties), but nonetheless there was the feel of a bigger history, even if (perhaps because) its nature was disputed. That sense of social possibility seems now to have shrivelled, in the hegemonic common sense, into the small change of technology and fashion: constant change, but no real change at all. It's depressing, but at least this understanding forbids the temptations of nostalgia: We can't go back.

It is some years now since Stuart was writing of these issues, and a year even since the conference at Goldsmiths. Times have changed. Since 2011, neoliberalism has in some ways pushed on to yet another stage. In the United Kingdom, there is a fully Tory government; in Europe, we have witnessed the brutal imposition of neoliberal economic dogma. Yet there is still economic fragility, both locally and globally, though in the everyday this has been transmuted into seemingly endless austerity. There have been upwellings of discontent in Greece, Spain, Scotland and now even within the United Kingdom's Labour Party. Moreover, the anti-austerity message has put on the table the argument that the economic is political (that it is not has been a central tenet of the elites' assertion that there is no alternative). This is a challenge (only emerging, but significant) to neoliberalism's *ideological* hegemony. SYRIZA especially has been crucial in opening that crack. Perhaps most of all, there is a growing crisis of the *political*: The combination of the rightwards move of existing European social democracy with the innately anti-democratic formation of neoliberalism is producing a crisis of political authority and legitimacy, a crisis of representation. Those 'excluded social forces, whose consent has not been won', of which Stuart wrote, begin to make their voices heard.

We must, then, go back to what Stuart wrote about the structure of a specifically *conjunctural* crisis—one in which the balance of social forces might be changed and from which a new social settlement might emerge. In 2011, the economic crisis was sealed by the lack of fracture at the ideological and political levels. Is that so clearly true at the end of 2015? The present insurgencies reflect the changing articulation. They are economic in the sense of being a rage against austerity—against poverty, insecurity, spiralling inequality. However, they are also a specifically political response to the lack of representation. To talk of a 'ruptural fusion' would be overoptimistic, but is there here an emerging shift in the structure of the crisis that could be worked on? Could this be *made* into a conjunctural crisis?

In the contribution to the Manifesto that explores common sense, Stuart stresses the significance of the *healthy nucleus*—what Gramsci called 'good sense'—which 'provides a basis on which the left could develop a popular strategy for radical change.'[15] Here perhaps might be a way to spread the passion of new resistance to a wider, more circumspect population. The piece explores the good sense of *fairness*. Likewise, recent political language in the United Kingdom has talked of *kindness*, of the need for a less macho and manufactured politics, of a more popularly democratic politics. There is widespread silent unease and discontent that can be spoken to. It cries out for a means of popular articulation. The very last sentence of the contribution on common sense reflects on this: 'The left, and Labour in particular, must adopt a more courageous, innovative, "educative" and pathbreaking strategic approach if they are to gain ground.'[16] This is what Stuart, in this arena, was all about.

Two books came out of the project:

Sally Davison and Katherine Harris, eds., *The Neoliberal Crisis* (London: Lawrence and Wishart, 2015).

Stuart Hall, Doreen Massey and Michael Rustin, eds., *After Neoliberalism: The Kilburn Manifesto* (London: Lawrence and Wishart, 2015).

Notes

Doreen Massey sadly passed away in March 2016. This essay is the unaltered version of her original contribution to the conference.

1. Stuart Hall, 'New Labour's Double-Shuffle', *Soundings: A Journal of Politics and Culture*, no. 24 (Summer 2003): 10-24.

2. Stuart Hall and Doreen Massey, 'Questions Which Remain', *Soundings: A Journal of Politics and Culture*, no. 5 (Spring 1997): 7-19, 7.

3. Sally Davison et al., 'Labour in a Time of Coalition', *Soundings: A Journal of Politics and Culture*, no. 45 (Summer 2010): 20.

4. Stuart Hall, 'The Neoliberal Revolution', *Soundings: A Journal of Politics and Culture*, no. 48 (Summer 2011): 9-27, 23.

5. Ibid., 14.

6. Ibid., 27.

7. Ibid., 26.

8. Ibid., 9.

9. Ibid.

10. Stuart Hall and Doreen Massey, 'Interpreting the Crisis', *Soundings: A Journal of Politics and Culture*, no. 44 (Spring 2010): 57-71, 59-60.

11. Ibid., 58.

12. Stuart Hall and Alan O'Shea, 'Common-sense Neoliberalism', *Soundings: A Journal of Politics and Cultures*, no. 55 (Winter 2013): 8-24.

13. Hall, 'The Neoliberal Revolution', 16.

14. *The Kilburn Manifesto*, available online at https://www.lwbooks.co.uk/soundings/kilburn-manifesto.

15. Hall and O'Shea, 'Common-sense Neoliberalism', 10.

16. Ibid., 24.

The Politics of Conjuncture: The Stuart Hall Projects—Outcomes and Impacts

7

David Edgar

My presence in this book borders on the fraudulent and certainly involves an embarrassing confession. My initial conjuncture with Stuart was—to put it mildly—contingent. My late wife Eve Brook was studying for a PhD at the CCCS in Birmingham—like Stuart, she was to abandon her doctorate in favour of activism— and much of our social life revolved around that brilliantly fissile group of people. To tell the truth, it took me some time to pick up that the elegantly spoken Jamaican seated in Buddhist detachment on our and others' sofas—possessed even then of his unique talent for laughing *through* speech as opposed to before or after it—was indeed Stuart Hall. Even then, my interest in him would have been more as the founding editor of the *New Left Review* than as director of the CCCS. To have contributed so much to the creation of a viable, non-Communist Marxism, a Marxism open (among other things) to the wave of cultural change that was to break onto Britain and the world's coastline during the following fifteen years, was achievement enough for one lifetime. But in fact, it was just the start—well, not even that—of a succession of political and analytical achievements, detailed in John Akomfrah's remarkable film *The Stuart Hall Project* (2013), which could be perhaps more accurately titled *The Stuart Hall Projects* (hence this chapter's subtitle).

There are two projects in particular I want to talk about, both involving boards on which I sat with Stuart in the 1980s. As an instigator of a New Left defined by not being the Communist Party, it's an irony that Stuart (and I) share the distinction of being the first and indeed only two non-party members to serve on the editorial board of *Marxism Today*. This was not because of a sudden political shift on Stuart's part, but because, under Martin Jacques's inspired editorship, *Marxism Today* had become the most open and creative journal on the left (and was therefore described by the Workers' Revolutionary Party as the most inaptly named periodical in Britain). Stuart analysed Thatcherism first in the book *Policing the Crisis*,[1] then in the *Marxism Today* article 'The Great Moving Right Show'[2] and finally in a ground-breaking 1983 essay collection titled *The Politics of Thatcherism*,[3] co-edited with Martin. In summary, Stuart argued against the prevailing wisdom on the left that the Thatcher government was both a continuation of previous Tory governments and—like Heath's before it—a temporary phenomenon. Instead, Thatcherism was something new: a potent mix of neoliberal anti-statism and no-nonsense authoritarian populism on social issues like race, law and order, education and the family, a mix that had been prepared in Enoch Powell's kitchen a decade earlier. Stuart also argued effectively that the seeming contradiction between economic liberalism and social conservatism was not so contradictory after all: Friedmanite libertarianism could lead and was leading quite directly to the strong state via unemployment and protests against it (including in the coalfields) and the need to encourage black people to leave Britain and women to return to the home. Finally, he pointed out (to much left discomfiture), that Thatcherism was based on popular consent.

In the second half of the 1980s, Martin and Stuart sought to explain the economic background of Thatcherism through the concept of a post-Fordist New Times, in which the power of the producer had shifted to that of the consumer. As a book (edited by Stuart and Martin), *New Times*[4] was overtaken by its own event, published as it was in late 1989, during the collapse of the Soviet variety of Fordism in Eastern Europe. As an idea, of course, it was remarkably prescient. However, Stuart and his colleagues were not alone in observing epochal changes in capitalism in the 1980s (beyond but connected with its victory in the cold war). The other board I sat on with Stuart, though for a much shorter period, was that of a radical anti-racist think tank, the Institute of Race Relations.

In many senses, Stuart was an obvious candidate for the institute, then led by Ambalavaner Sivanandan. Following Stuart's death, he was described as the 'pioneer' or—less fortunately—the 'godfather' of multiculturalism, which seemed like a convenient journalistic label for a man whose huge importance was hard to explain to the general public. However, in an important sense it was true. Stuart represented multiculturalism, of course, because he thought and wrote about it as a government policy—but he also *was* it. The darkest person in a mixed-race family, a 1950s Caribbean immigrant, then an Oxford student, scholar, editor and activist, he was a hybrid from the start. He frequently made the point that, in the contemporary world, if you ask someone where they come from, the answer gets longer and longer.

Race was a central preoccupation of the CCCS, not least because of what was happening all around it in Birmingham: the 1964 Smethwick election campaign, Enoch Powell's 1968 Rivers of Blood speech, the 1974 Birmingham pub bombings and the 1977 anti–National Front demonstrations in Handsworth. In addition to its prediction of Thatcherism, *Policing the Crisis* analysed in equally prescient detail the way in which a non-problem was formatted racially, in a way that anticipated the treatment of Muslims today.

Sharing the institute's long-established concern with police racism, Stuart supported and contributed to the community report into the shooting of Colin Roach in Stoke Newington Police Station in 1983. Like Sivanandan, he was suspicious of black cultural nationalism (seeing it, as he put it in a 1992 lecture, as an example of defining difference in terms of closure). He was also always concerned to see race not as a free-standing identity, but in terms of its conjuncture with other social forces.

Stuart was thus a natural to contribute to an institute the journal of which was and is called *Race & Class*. However, the institute's critique of *Marxism Today* as irredeemably consumerist and revisionist—clearly the godfather to New Labour—meant the relationship was short-lived. This disagreement led to my own temporary departure from the board, though I'm glad to say I'm now back. However, even at the time, it was clear to me that Stuart's thinking about the new conditions ushered in by globalisation was closer to the institute's thinking than was generally credited. As early as 1979, Sivanandan identified a new Silicon Age,[5] which he would later define as 'an epochal change in capitalism—at least as significant as the transition from mercantile capitalism to industrial capitalism',[6] shifting the centre of exploitation to a new mobile working class either located in or sourced from the periphery. In Robin Blackburn's NLR obituary,[7] he quotes a paper Stuart wrote for UNESCO in 1986, which says almost exactly that.

Just for the record, Stuart accepted that there was a '"kernel of truth"' in the idea that *Marxism Today* invented New Labour, but he himself excoriated Blair's appropriation of neoliberalism in his article co-written with Martin Jacques *before* the 1997 election.[8]

I argue that Hall and Sivanandan's politics are closer than is generally supposed, partly to close the gap between two of the thinkers—one from the Caribbean, the other from the bottom tip of the Indian subcontinent—who mean the most to me. I also do it to point out that the thinking they share is now conventional wisdom. However, when Stuart argued in the 1950s that Stalinism was dead, in the 1960s that Labour had fallen prey to managerialism, in the 1970s that popular culture often masked the impulse to resistance, in the early 1980s that Thatcherism was a new phenomenon (and would outlive Thatcher) and in the late 1980s that new technology had fundamentally changed the means of production and the character of labour, he wasn't expressing conventional wisdom at all. The prescience of New Times is to be seen all around us; both concept and title were revived by Neal Lawson and Indra Adnan for their excellent 2014 essay on how horizontal communications are impacting political action and possibility now (the essay was dedicated to Stuart's memory).[9]

Despite his commitment to the optimistic will, Stuart ended his life in intellectual pessimism about the left projects to which he contributed so much. However, as he himself said in a 2011 radio interview, one should not confuse outcome with impact. He was talking about the (literal) failure of the May 1968 uprising in Paris, compared with its immense influence later. His own impact is immeasurable. Through a lifetime of conjecture as well as conjuncture, Stuart built much of the common sense of the age.

Notes

1. Stuart Hall et al., *Policing the Crisis: Mugging, the State and Law and Order* (London: Macmillan, 1978).

2. Stuart Hall, 'The Great Moving Right Show', *Marxism Today* (January 1979): 14–20.

3. Stuart Hall and Martin Jacques, eds., *The Politics of Thatcherism* (London: Lawrence and Wishart, 1983).

4. Stuart Hall and Martin Jacques, eds., *New Times: The Changing Face of Politics in the 1990s* (London: Lawrence and Wishart, 1989).

5. Ambalavaner Sivanandan, 'Imperialism and Disorganic Development in the Silicon Age', *Race & Class* 21 (Autumn 1979): 111–126.

6. Ambalavaner Sivanandan, 'Globalism and the Left', *Race & Class* 40 (October 1998–March 1999): 5–6.

7. Robin Blackburn, 'Stuart Hall 1932–2014', *New Left Review*, no. 86 (March–April 2014): 75–93.

8. Stuart Hall and Martin Jacques, 'Tony Blair: The Greatest Tory since Margaret Thatcher?', *Observer*, April 13, 1997.

9. Indra Adnan and Neal Lawson, *New Times: How a Politics of Networks and Relationship Can Deliver a Good Society* (London: Compass, 2014).

8 *Stuart Hall and the Early New Left*

Michael Rustin

I first encountered Stuart very early on, when I was still a sixth-former at a London grammar school, soon to do national service and then go on to university. I attended the meetings of the *Universities and Left Review* Club (ULR Club) in London, at which Stuart was one of the highly visible and youthful presiding spirits, together with Raphael Samuel and Charles Taylor. These meetings were a truly amazing initiation into socialist politics. They brought together almost everything an attendee could possibly be interested in. I saw and heard Isaac Deutscher, who appeared as a legendary revolutionary in this crowded, smoke-filled room, and Wal Hannington, veteran of the Jarrow March of 1936. There was Claude Bourdet, of *France Observateur* and the parallel French New Left, then engaged in the struggle over the Algerian War of Independence, from 1954 to 1962. There was an ongoing debate about the soul of the Labour Party, in arguments, for example, with Anthony Crosland's influential book, *The Future of Socialism* (1956).[1] There were presentations about town planning, about political commitment in literature, about cinema (Free Cinema), theatre and education. In short, the club presented almost everything a person would need in an energetic and determined project to form a political movement of thought and action—'a New Left'.

Then, each Easter, there were Aldermaston Marches of the Campaign for Nuclear Disarmament (1958–1963 at their peak), at the concluding rally of which in Trafalgar Square Stuart was often the most inspiring and thought-provoking of the speakers. Adding to the general buzz were the Partisan Coffee House (1958–1962) and the various socialist study groups that met there. Providing the intellectual substance for all this were the journals *Universities and Left Review* and the *New Reasoner*, the latter produced from Yorkshire, and then the result of their merger in 1959, *New Left Review*.[2] I became aware of other major figures in this remarkable constellation, such Edward Thompson, Raymond Williams and Richard Hoggart, and began to read them too.

This early movement was a renaissance of earlier socialist and indeed Communist traditions and the birth of new kinds of thinking at the same time. There was the sense that something was emerging from a political deep freeze, many things suddenly becoming alive. (The deep freeze came from the conjunction of 1950s conservatism in Britain and the Cold War.) This moment, both a revival and a new beginning, occurred prior to the emergence of the field of cultural studies, before the vast expansion of the universities in the 1960s and 1970s and before the academic segmentation of so many of the fields of work in which Stuart was interested into separate disciplines, many of which hardly talk to each other. Although what was going on seemed enormous at the time—there were so many people!—the reality was that the numbers involved must really have been quite small: probably just a few hundred active people in London, with some parallel New Left initiatives and socialist reunions in other towns and cities.[3] It was the moment's focus and energy and its response to its times—initially those of Suez and Hungary and of the campaign against the nuclear bomb—that gave it such immense life.[4]

Most of these elements became extended and spread out over years as the ongoing subjects of Stuart's later work and political commitment. The remarkable range of his writing: his ongoing critique of labourism; the development of cultural studies as, at its core, a political project; his reflections on and engagement with issues of race, deepening over time; his continuing exploration of the lasting effects of colonialism; even his later engagement with the visual arts—all are prefigured in this early New Left fermentation of ideas and experiences. There were significant omissions from this agenda, only repaired later; for example, at that moment prior to the rebirth of feminism, questions of gender and sexuality were largely unrecognised, and women participants often found the atmosphere of those settings antipathetic.

The *collective* style of this early movement—with many people contributing, in dialogue with one another—was also reflected in Stuart's later development. The CCCS was notable for the way it encouraged so many young graduate students to make creative contributions to its published writing, even at early stages of their development. Many forthcoming volumes will show Stuart's own written output to have been very large and distinguished in many areas—though many pieces of it, like the great study *Policing the Crisis*,[5] were written in the context of collaborations, not as individual projects of his own. Written monuments to himself were of no interest to Stuart. His was indeed a shared intellectual life, lived, among other ways, through a succession of journals (*Universities and Left Review, New Left Review, Marxism Today, Soundings* and others)[6] and institutions (the CCCS, the Open University, Institute for the International Visual Arts [INIVA] and Autograph ABP [Association of Black Photographers]) to which he was always loyal.

Stuart drew on and engaged with many different intellectual traditions and disciplines throughout his life. He began, after all, as a student of English literature, beginning a PhD thesis in Oxford on the novels of Henry James. In writing about his first book on popular culture,[7] he noted how influential the example of F. R. Leavis and his journal *Scrutiny* had been at that time; although Stuart disagreed with Leavis's disdain for popular culture and was committed to a quite different kind of politics, he admired Leavis's commitment to literature and the quality and intensity of his reading. Raymond Williams also observed, while taking his distance from Leavis, that on matters of reading and literature Leavis set a far better example than the Marxist literary critics of the 1930s.

At the CCCS, Stuart and his colleagues engaged energetically with many different traditions and methods of cultural analysis in pursuing their investigations of popular cultural forms and of different forms of media and communication, such as television, American symbolic interactionism (linked to the New Criminology and the National Deviance Symposium) and structural linguistics were relevant and useful. In the exploration of racialised cultural identities, the psychoanalytically informed writing of Fanon proved essential. Later, in understanding the formation of identities within the ascendancy of neoliberalism, Foucault became another important source of ideas. As a professor of sociology at the Open University, Stuart also set about clarifying his relationship to some of the great sociologist masters, such as Weber and Mannheim. In fact, because Stuart was working on the boundaries of what would conventionally be viewed as so many different disciplinary fields, he found himself needing to engage with whatever ideas had proved fertile in *their* analytic work. *Policing the Crisis*, after all, began its life as the study of the reported incidence of street crimes in an area of Birmingham and developed into a masterly holistic analysis of the crisis of the post-war welfare settlement in its corporatist phase and of Thatcherism in its incipient moment, before Thatcher even came to power.

However, notwithstanding this apparent eclecticism of theory and method, there was an intellectual principle of connectedness, or a conviction of its necessity, which bound all these interests together throughout Stuart's life. This was his complicated relationship to Marxism, which, as he wrote, he was initially drawn into backwards and reluctantly by the invasion of Hungary and the ensuing crisis of Soviet Communism. Stuart rejected the different mechanistic and one-dimensional versions of connectedness propounded in orthodox Marxist traditions. He was never a Leninist, always rejecting the idea of an enlightened political vanguard the role of which was to transform society through gaining control of the state. (Indeed, one of his arguments with labourism centred on its Fabian version of top-down leadership by the party.) Nor did he hold with economistic Marxism, the idea that an 'economic structure' could be understood as a causal 'base' that invariably determined the political, legal and cultural superstructure of society, as Marx had proclaimed in one famous—indeed, notorious—passage.[8] Stuart was committed to an idea of human agency, to the idea that men do indeed make their own history, even if in circumstances not of their own choosing.[9] He was deeply influenced by Raymond Williams's idea that processes of learning were fundamental to human society and to its progressive development, both in the past and, one hoped, in the future. Democracy, in Williams's view, was essentially the learned achievement of the working class. This idea of learning, which is expounded in the opening chapter of Williams's *Long Revolution*[10]—for Stuart, a formative book—is almost the philosophical anthropology that underpinned cultural studies.

In the 1970s, Gramsci's writings became substantially available in English translation, and Stuart found these an enormous resource in his search for a theoretical framework that could discover societal coherence and connectedness in ways that were not reductive or dogmatic. Essentially, culture is given a much larger explanatory role in Gramscian than in orthodox Marxism, making it possible to recognise a measure of indeterminacy and of local specificity in social formations while retaining the central idea that they are organised as systems of power in which the relations between classes are fundamental.[11] This was the methodological position Stuart came to after considerable theoretical struggle and largely retained from the 1970s onwards. The complexities (and indeterminacies) of Althusserian models of societies composed of partially autonomous 'levels and instances' were also found by Stuart to be a useful theoretical resource. His analysis first of Thatcherism, then of New Labour and finally of neoliberalism deployed this frame of analysis, acknowledging in all three formations the role of political initiative and performance and of ideology 'normalised' as common sense in maintaining a system in which the power of capital and its dependent classes remains fundamental. This argument took a more pessimistic turn in Stuart's last years, as neoliberalism seemed to have imposed its ascendancy so successfully. His 'Common-sense Neoliberalism', a chapter in *The Kilburn Manifesto*[12] written with Alan O'Shea, was his last major political article.

A crucial question raised when we reflects on Stuart's work is the significance of his lifelong commitment to Marxism, complicated and highly critical—and sometimes barely visible—as it was. It seems that there is a major divide in our culture between two perspectives: One of these is the essentially liberal view, which holds the different institutional spheres of society—centrally, its economy, polity and culture—to be discrete, each domain preferably operating with a minimum of interference from the others. Accompanying this separation of institutions is a theory of its intellectual life or ideology, which holds that disciplines are also intrinsically separate and distinct from one another, each corresponding to its own institutional object of study. The 'liberal' argument, upheld by Weberians, is that this separation of spheres and functions is essential to a free society, whereas their conjoining or unification represents an aspiration towards or a risk of totalitarian control. At the level of ideas, this was the crucial opposition defined in Goran Therborn's *Science, Class and Society*[13] and fought out intellectually over decades from the later years of the nineteenth century between 'bourgeois social science' and Marxism. One might say that both Daniel Bell's *The End of Ideology* and

Francis Fukuyama's *The End of History and the Last Man*[14] were declarations of the supposed liberal victory in this war. The idea of a 'value-free' social science is a crucial foundation of the liberal view, because it rejects the idea that values and aspirations are immanent in the theoretical positions one takes up in social and historical analysis and holds that they constitute a quite separate domain of moral evaluation, best restricted to judgements of discrete goods and ills and avoiding evaluations of the well-being (or otherwise) of entire societies.

The alternative view is a holistic one, holding that social formations are entities held together by unequal powers and that so far as capitalism is concerned, the forms of production and the class relations that follow from them are decisive. Stuart's work seems to have been located formally at the 'holistic' or Marxist end of this spectrum, even though he believed this position to need continual revision. He thought, for example, that in modern capitalism the relations of consumption had acquired an enhanced importance, so far as social aspirations and identifications were concerned. He took an evaluative or ethically informed view of the condition of entire societies—those of Britain and Jamaica, to take two examples important to him—and believed that their condition should be understood as the outcome of interrelated struggles for emancipation and well-being, of course changing in their participants and agendas over time, but nevertheless intelligible as common struggles. This perspective was broadly held in common by all the major figures of the early New Left: Raymond Williams, Edward Thompson, Raphael Samuel, Charles Taylor and Stuart Hall himself.

The remarkable connectedness I noted as a feature of the early New Left was not therefore merely or mainly a function of the fact that a rather small number of people had come together in a restricted space and time and could create and join in a shared, effervescent dialogue. Far more important was that they shared an underlying view of society and its development and a commitment to its improvement, through linked-up kinds of political, social and cultural action. In short, they shared a socialist view of the world, in various forms.

The kinds of discussions of many topics that were so exciting in the late 1950s in the ULR Club are now widely diffused throughout society, as literary festivals have multiplied, universities have expanded beyond measure, and publishers and broadcasters now maintain a ceaseless output of cultural products of all kinds.

There is now also the Internet and social media, bringing about an infinity of communications and exchanges of different kinds. This proliferation makes the construction of any kind of consensus concerning what is important rather difficult and seems to undermine the least attempt to give analytical or theoretical substance to the 'symptoms' of the present (the refugee crisis, the European Union Referendum Act 2015, and illegal operations of this or that corporation) as they occur. For Stuart, such symptoms were always the starting point for analysis in depth, offering glimpses into the real state of the larger system.

However, I want to suggest that the deeper problem here is a theoretical and ideological one. Stuart found in an endlessly revised and internally contested Marxism a framework of ideas in which it was possible to think politically, and connectedly, about everything. Can such thinking and its related politics occur without such a framework? If one believes, as I do, that it can't, then where does this leave us with regard to the Marxist tradition that, for all his arguments with it, Stuart did not abandon?

1. Anthony Crosland, *The Future of Socialism* (London: Jonathan Cape, 1956).

2. Stuart was its editor until 1962, when he resigned. *New Left Review* then evolved with a different though related frame of reference under its new editor, Perry Anderson, and has continued in that recognisable style until today.

3. However, *Universities and Left Review* did sell several thousand copies of each issue.

4. On the first New Left, see Michael Kenny, *The First New Left: British Intellectuals after Stalin* (London: Lawrence and Wishart, 1995); Oxford University Socialist Discussion Group, eds., *Out of Apathy: Voices of the New Left 30 Years On* (London: Verso, 1989); and Lin Chun, *The British New Left* (Edinburgh: Edinburgh University Press,1993).

5. Stuart Hall et al., *Policing the Crisis* (Basingstoke: Macmillan, 2013).

6. The entire published archive of *Universities and Left Review*, the *New Reasoner* and *Marxism Today* can be accessed at the Amiel-Melburn website, http://www.amielandmelburn.org.uk/, free of charge. Readers can rediscover these successive moments of the New Left for themselves.

7. Stuart Hall and Paddy Whannel, *The Popular Arts* (London: Hutchinson, 1964).

8. 'In the social production which men carry on they enter into definite relations that are indispensable and independent of their will; these relations of production correspond to a definite stage of development of their material forces of production. The sum total of these relations of production constitutes the economic structure of society-the real foundation, on which rises a legal and political superstructure and to which correspond definite forms of social consciousness. The mode of production in material life determines the social, political and intellectual life processes in general. It is not the consciousness of men that determines their being, but, on the contrary, their social being that determines their consciousness.' See Karl Marx, *Preface to the Critique of Political Economy* (1859).

9. *The 18th Brumaire of Louis Bonaparte* was his favourite of Marx's works: 'Men make their own history, but they do not make it as they please; they do not make it under self-selected circumstances, but under circumstances existing already, given and transmitted from the past.' Karl Marx, *The 18th Brumaire of Louis Bonaparte* (New York: Die Revolution, 1852), 10.

10. Raymond Williams, *The Long Revolution* (London: Chatto and Windus, 1961).

11. Sartre's *The Problem of Method*, published in English in 1963, is astonishingly parallel to the writing of the early New Left in its attempt to refashion a Marxist method in ways that take adequate account of specificities, complexity and human agency while holding to Marx's central ideas concerning modes of production and class relations.

12. Stuart Hall and Alan O'Shea, 'Common-sense Neoliberalism', in *After Neoliberalism? The Kilburn Manifesto*, ed. Stuart Hall, Doreen Massey and Michael Rustin (London: Lawrence and Wishart, 2015), 52–68.

13. Goran Therborn, *Science, Class and Society* (London: New Left Books, 1978).

14. Daniel Bell, *The End of Ideology* (Cambridge, MA: Harvard University Press, [1962] 2000); and Frances Fukuyama, *The End of History and the Last Man* (New York: Free Press, 1992).

9 *Wrestling with the Angels of Cultural Studies*

Lawrence Grossberg

Stuart Hall's death in 2014 challenges those committed to the 'project' of cultural studies to continue doing the sorts of work he valued, supported and produced. Although there is always the danger that this will mean that we end up wrestling with each other rather than engaging in the more important encounters that Hall referred to as 'wrestling with the angels',[1] by which cultural studies moves constantly into the present, I think Hall imagined this as a convivial agonism. In political terms, this means that cultural studies must engage not only with the organization of domination and subjugation but also with the failures of the existing oppositional struggles. It wrestles with both the right and the left in its effort to understand what's going on and to make visible the possibilities of other futures, other forms of relations, or what it imagines as, in Stuart Hall's terms, 'unities-in-difference'.[2] In theoretical terms, (Anglo) cultural studies has struggled with, within and against a series of theoretical positions that have repeatedly dismissed it: certain forms of humanism, for taking theory too seriously; phenomenology, for taking social structure too seriously; Marxism, for taking culture too seriously; structuralism, for taking human agency and experience too seriously; poststructuralism, for believing in structure; and postmodernism, for believing in the reality and even the necessity of both unities and differences.

Therefore, it is worth asking: What is this project, and how do we move it forward? First, *cultural studies* is a dialectics of political passion and intellectual rigor, operating in an unexpected direction; a deep pessimism has to be achieved through rigorous intellectual work before a person can find the grounds for an optimism that enables effective political struggle and social change. Second, it takes culture seriously in its political calculations—although admittedly, this is too vague to provide much guidance. For some people who describe their work as cultural studies, this would be enough.

It is not enough for me, and, I believe, it was not sufficient for Hall either. So third, like many modern critical practices, cultural studies approaches the world relationally, interrogating the forms, modalities and practices of articulating relations. But cultural studies differs from other relational theories because it understands relations as both contingent (constructed) and real (effective), constituting itself as a practice of radical contextuality. As such, it investigates contexts (rather than disciplinary objects), not as fixed and stable objects, but as always open, changing and porous, as strategic and temporary constructions. *Radical contextuality* means that one treats theories and concepts as disposable tools, judged by their ability to help (re)organize or re-narrate overdetermined (and potentially chaotic) empirical realities. It means that one cannot assume in advance the appropriate tools, the specific political struggles or stakes, or even the vital questions that have to be addressed. For some, this is enough to define the specificity of cultural studies.

However, I think there is more. Cultural studies embraces complexity, thinks with and through complexity and, therefore, rejects any and all forms of reductionism. If contextualism denies that everything can be analysed in the same terms, then anti-reductionism denies that anything can be analysed in singular terms. The harmonics resulting from the dual commitments to contextuality and complexity define the specific political and epistemic tone of cultural studies: provisional, uncertain, open-ended and happily incomplete. They demand that cultural studies see itself as a constant experimentation, exploring forms of collaboration and meta-interdisciplinarity,[3] that it seek out more humble and convivial forms of unities in difference, in both intellectual conversations and political struggles. They demand that cultural studies must transform itself according to the demands of its own context.

Is this enough? Maybe—but I think (given my own formation) there is yet one more element that must be added to the mix that is cultural studies. Cultural studies makes the choice—in the present context—to work at a particular 'level of abstraction', giving itself over to what Hall called 'the discipline of the conjuncture'.[4] Conjunctural analysis expresses a strategic political choice, defining both an effective site—perhaps the most effective site—for political intervention aimed at changing the tides of social change and the most propitious level at which intellectual and political analysis converge. Approaching social change at a more specific (lower) level of abstraction—what is variously referred to as the *moment*, the *event* or the *situation*—threatens the political intellectual with the chaos of overdetermination, with what Roland Barthes once called 'the impossible science of the unique being'.[5]

Approaching social change at higher levels of abstraction—in terms of epochs, for example—is likely to silence the complexities and over-determinations, the contradictions and struggles, and, consequently, make it all too easy to read historical change along a single vector (e.g., capitalism or biopolitics or coloniality). Cultural studies does not deny the value of intellectual and political work at these other levels of abstraction, but it does assert that work on the conjuncture—often but not necessarily understood at the level of the nation state—is crucial in the present context.[6] In fact, cultural studies often seems to suggest that abandoning a critical engagement with either national or state formations in the contemporary context, whatever certain theories might assert, would be disastrous.

The concept of the conjuncture has a long history[7] in Marxist theory, especially in the work of Lenin, Gramsci and Althusser; in this complex history, its meaning varies, referring sometimes to the surface phenomena as opposed to the structural essences, at other times to a specific historical moment, and at still others to the occasional event as opposed to organic forces. As I said, for Hall and cultural studies, a conjuncture is located somewhere between a particular situation and an epoch, but that covers an enormous space. Hall found in Gramsci a more specific, strategic and contextual understanding, in which the conjuncture refers to the terrain on which a struggle 'over a new reality'[8] is carried out. In fact, a conjuncture is not defined simply by its level of abstraction; it is defined—called into existence in the first instance—by the emergence of what Gramsci called an *organic crisis*.

I do not know if Hall would agree, but I think this is what he meant when he talked about his 'own kind of conjunctural thinking'.[9] Hall made the concept of conjuncture into a more specific, contextually grounded concept. An organic crisis is constituted by the articulation of multiple crises—material, discursive and phenomenological—across the various dimensions (political, economic, cultural, social, etc.) of the social formation. It calls into question a society's understanding and imagination of itself. It demands in response a vision both of the crisis and of what the society can become as it works through the organic crisis. Thus, a conjuncture is a particular kind of context, one that David Scott calls a *problem space*:[10] 'the outcome of an historical interruption and conceptual reconfiguration in which one field of arguments is displaced by another'.

That is, a conjuncture signals that the driving questions and political struggles have been transformed as a result not of a sudden historical rupture but of the efforts of both cultural and political actors to transform the ways people understand their lives and the challenges they face.[11] A conjuncture presents itself as the result of multiple determinations, contradictions and struggles, a variety of struggles to change the complex 'balance in the field of forces' that shape a society's present and future, to use Gramsci's term. Thus, a conjuncture is an historically emergent reality that is the product, simultaneously, of (1) material forces and struggles both producing and responding to an organic crisis and its various component crises, and (2) the narrative constructions of the crisis itself, offered by politicians, intellectuals, cultural workers and the like.

However, the demand of conjunctural analysis also presents challenges, for the concept of the conjuncture and its particular forms of articulation and organization remain under-theorized and leave many unanswered questions, especially as the context seems to change. Without a more rigorous theorization, the concept provides at best rather uncertain and even perplexing directions for a political-intellectual project. I want here only to take notice of these questions, without attempting to pursue them, although I do want to acknowledge that Hall was trying to think more rigorously about these twin concepts. Many of the questions we can raise involve how to think about the identity and difference of conjunctures/organic crises. How do we think about their spatial extension? If they are defined in relation to national formations (as they often are in cultural studies), how do we deal with the increasing power of transnational and global determinations? How do we think about their temporal extension? When does one conjuncture become another, one crisis another, due to changing struggles and contradictions and their relations or due to struggles that offer new settlements or balances in the field of forces? How do we think about the political stakes of conjunctural struggles? Do they always and only involve state formations, or can they (or even, must they) involve larger socio-ontological changes? How do we think about the relations between an organic crisis and the various narratives of it, especially those offered by intellectuals? Finally, if conjunctural analysis is linked to an organic crisis and cultural studies is called into existence as a response to the emergence of an organic crisis, that would seem to suggest that cultural studies' intellectual and political utility is dependent on such moments; if we can imagine the end of an organic crisis (which might seem difficult at the present moment but has presumably happened in the past; an organic crisis emerges and society moves on, not without further crises and contradictions, but without their articulation into a singular organic crisis), then we can imagine a context in which cultural studies might not be the most appropriate way of approaching intellectual and political challenges. In that way, cultural studies would avoid claiming any universality for itself.

Still, there is something paradoxical about the way cultural studies has been taken up and even flourished. Despite the growing visibility of cultural studies (if only in name) and the enormous influence (again, even if sometimes only in name) of Stuart Hall as its leading representative, the collective record of cultural studies, however modest our expectations, is somewhat disappointing—although not necessarily any less so than that of other politically inflected intellectual projects.[12] The fact is that we can find claims of cultural studies that ignore any or even many of the commitments I identified earlier.

Recently, my friend Mikko Lehtonen, a founding figure in Nordic cultural studies, asked me why so little of what is done in the name of cultural studies actually follows the sort of conjunctural analysis that defined the heart of Hall's practice and, in my description, the project of cultural studies. Yes, cultural studies has changed the ways some people perform their disciplinary and disciplined work and has expanded the ways we think about culture and the scope of the forms of culture and politics we can think about in the academy—but is that all there is? Is that the limit of cultural studies' imagination? It is of course possible that Lehtonen and I are misperceiving the situation, failing to see the whole in the part, the larger conversations and collaborations into which individuals attempt to insert their contributions, or failing to see the importance of the growth of alternative sites of intellectual work in more overtly political and aesthetic sites/movements. We also must keep in mind that there is no necessary form of conjunctural analysis, and how it is performed may itself vary with different contexts.

Nevertheless, I believe that much of what goes on under the sign of cultural studies in the U.S. academy (and that of much of the North Atlantic) has abandoned conjuncturalism in favour of two other models—the first a more disciplinary model of intellectual work with more discipline-defined objects. In this slide, the specificity of conjunctural analysis gives way to a weak—often very weak—sense of context, allowing the object of study (e.g., media or popular culture) and the pertinent questions to become more stable and permanent—as if the media and their modes of operation within and insertion into everyday life and social spaces did not need to be significantly reconstituted. The result is that concepts, models and practices that were developed as contextually specific interventions (e.g., encoding-decoding, subcultural studies, the circuit of culture, and even notions of representation and difference) are decontextualized and generalized and then identified with cultural studies. Such work is often too worried, as Raymond Williams once suggested,[13] about legitimating itself as a disciplined field of study accumulating knowledge about rather unproblematized fields of objects, rather than with the project of cultural studies. The second model lends a different kind of legitimation, because the work is determined in advance by political and/or theoretical certainties, without the same commitment to openness, to the possibility of being wrong, that characterizes cultural studies itself, if not academic responsibility in general.

There are many things we might say about the all too common abandonment of the contextuality and complexity of conjunctural analysis. It is not that such work does not exist, especially outside the North Atlantic academy, but it is certainly not the most common practice in the name of cultural studies. Of course, the reasons themselves will be contextually specific and more complicated than I can summarize here. In the North Atlantic, one can lay a good deal of the blame on changes in the academy, including changing definitions and measures of impact, importance and value (of both research and education); budget cuts that have resulted in the reassertion of disciplinary power; and the implosion of the academy as a viable space of rigorous intellectual experimentation. These changes (and others even more disconcerting) have put new pressures on individual teachers and scholars, who have unfortunately too often responded by avoiding risk and focusing on their own academic success. No doubt, the abandonment of contextuality and complexity has been shaped in part by what I have described elsewhere (as the *contemporary crises of knowledge*).[14] All too often, cultural studies appears to have abandoned its provisionality in favour of the very sorts of assertions of certainty—about theory, politics and historical change—that have become dominant expressions of the emergent structure of feeling, a particular organization of pessimism.

Sometimes, cultural studies is pushed aside by a sense of political pessimism and desperation that abandons any sense of complexity in order to rediscover the power of reductionism—whether the old (it's all about capitalism) or the new (it's all about the emergence of new ontological or material forms of power). In many cases, such work is based on theoretical innovations that, ironically, seem to have given up on critique, at least as Marx understood it. Marx criticized 'political economy' for mistaking appearances for reality, as the explanation rather than what must be explained. That is, it took the effects of complex relations as a simple given of economic realities. It treated the products of complex systems of social relations as natural and universal (abstract) truths.

Furthermore, all too often, when contemporary critical work claims to be discovering apparently radically new forms of power and capitalism, the new in fact sounds very old, and culture is once again folded into capitalism; for example, capitalism has commodified heretofore unreachable realms of experience (knowledge, attention, affect) into calculable, disembodied entities or quanta, or contemporary capitalism has introduced culture (in some form) as a new mediating term in the place of labour (e.g., semio-capitalism). No longer operating as ideology (because apparatuses of ideology, meaning, representation and so on have apparently become residual at best), culture becomes a new mode of (primitive?) accumulation or an abstract value form. There is an increasingly visible tendency to equate critical analyses with the assertion of theoretical positions, as if the latter could answer empirical questions in advance, as it were.

Whatever we think of these various deformations of cultural studies and however we think through the various questions cultural studies must face, cultural studies must continue to question and reshape itself in response to the changing configurations, settlements and struggles of the organic crisis, and in engaging with emergent theoretical possibilities. Now, how do we take up and extend the specific project of cultural studies, which defined so much of Hall's intellectual vitality and generosity? We can start by continuing to wrestle with the angels. Here, I can only point to some of those conversations in which we might begin to wrestle a bit not in an effort to find the right answers nor merely to go on theorizing, but to find better ways of working conjuncturally, to find ways of telling better stories, stories that both embrace complexity and provisionality and that seek to open the space of a popular politics.

For example, I believe cultural studies should wrestle with the advocates of both so-called horizontalist and verticalist politics to find a space in a popular transversal politics. I believe cultural studies scholars should enter institutional debates around the university to offer more conjunctural diagnoses of the specificity and contextuality of contemporary struggles and transformations and to offer compelling visions for a new—future-oriented—university, one in which the practice of cultural studies is celebrated rather than suppressed. If we cannot imagine a way to bring about a better university, then perhaps we should think about alternative spaces, not only for academic research and speculation, but also for enabling productive encounters between academics and the multiplicity of cultural workers and political activists.

However, it strikes me that there are two other, perhaps more pressing, tasks. The first is, at it were, philosophical: If cultural studies, like many other contemporary critical projects, is in part a response to the recognition that the history of European Enlightenment and modernity is as much a history of barbarity as it is of progress, then it has to wrestle with some of the more recent and more radical efforts to think outside the European Enlightenment, in a variety of anti-Kantian philosophies, under such signs as the new materialisms, the ontological turn, post-humanism, affect theory and so on. Although I believe such work is deeply problematic and often ends up undermining the very possibility of critique and erasing political struggle, it also carries with it some important lessons and theoretical tools. Some of those tools might help us address the second task and wrestle

with ourselves a little more, for I believe that one of the 'scandals'
of cultural studies is that it has rarely adequately theorized culture
itself, especially in terms of its multiplicities and articulations,
and its conjunctural complexities.[15] These problems suggest that
there is more wrestling to be done, remembering that this is the
very practice that called cultural studies into existence and that
defined Stuart Hall's vision of a political intellectual.

Notes

This chapter is a very shortened version of Lawrence Grossberg, 'Wrestling with
the Angels: Cultural Studies in Dark Times (Cultural Studies and Deleuze-
Guattari, part 3)', in *Cultural Studies Beyond Identity*, ed. Eric Maigret and
Martin Laurent (Lyon: Presses Universitaires de Lyon, forthcoming).
1. Stuart Hall, 'Cultural Studies and Its Theoretical Legacies', in *Cultural Studies*,
ed. Lawrence Grossberg, Cary Nelson and Paula Treichler (New York and
London: Routledge, 1992), 277–294.
2. Stuart Hall, *Cultural Studies 1983* (Durham, NC: Duke University Press,
2017).
3. By *meta-interdisciplinarity*, I mean that cultural studies is a conversation not
across disciplines, but among intellectual formations that have already been
made interdisciplinary.
4. Stuart Hall, *The Hard Road to Renewal: Thatcherism and the Crisis of the Left*
(London: Verso., 1982), 162.
5. Roland Barthes, *Camera Lucida* (New York: Hill and Wang, 1982), 71.

6. In the most common (empiricist?) narratives of the history of British cultural studies, this turn to conjunctural analysis and politics first appeared in the collaborative work that resulted in Stuart Hall, Chas Critcher, Tony Jefferson, John Clarke and Brian Roberts, *Policing the Crisis* (London: Macmillan,1978), often held up as the example par excellence of (British) cultural studies. (Of course, the fact that it 'predicted' the rise of Thatcherism helps here!) However, it was not alone, and it was supplemented and extended by many important works including Women's Studies Group Centre for Contemporary Cultural Studies, *Women Take Issue* (London: Hutchinson, 1978), Centre for Contemporary Cultural Studies, *The Empire Strikes Back* (London: Hutchinson, 1982), *The Politics of Thatcherism*, ed. Stuart Hall and Martin Jacques (London: Lawrence and Wishart, 1983), Stuart Hall, *The Hard Road to Renewal: Thatcherism and the Crisis of the Left* (London: Verso, 1988), *New Times: The Changing Face of Politics in the 1990s*, ed. Stuart Hall and Martin Jacques (London: Lawrence and Wishart, 1989) and Education Group II, *Education Limited* (London: Unwin Hyman, 1991). One would also need to include the extraordinary contributions of, for example, Paul Gilroy, John Clarke, Angela McRobbie and others. These efforts to understand the rise of a new conservative/pro-capitalist formation, the emergence of new forms of political struggle, including the ways they deployed matters of difference—of race, sex and gender—depended explicitly on a significant transplanting of Gramscian concepts—of hegemony, organic crisis and conjuncture—into this new context. This is perhaps why the history of the CCCS is widely read as an ongoing experiment to produce cultural studies.

7. Juha Koivisto and Mikko Lahtinen. 'Conjuncture, Political-Historical', *Historical Materialism* 20, no. 1 (2012): 267–277.

8. Ibid, 269.

9. Cited in Helen Davis, *Understanding Stuart Hall* (London: Sage, 2004).

10. David Scott, 'Stuart Hall's Ethics,' *Small Axe* 17 (2005): 1–16.

11. Organic crises, especially at specific moments when even proposed settlements appear to be scarce, are often marked by crises of knowledge and intensive (re)turns to and inventions of theoretical positions.

12. This is particularly depressing in the larger context of the very limited successes (in much of the North Atlantic world, especially) of both the intellectual and political lefts (without denying that there have been and continue to be important and sometimes highly visible advances, often local and sometimes regional).

13. Raymond Williams, 'The Future of Cultural Studies,' in *The Politics of Modernism* (London: Verso, 1989), 151–162.

14. Lawrence Grossberg, *We All Want to Change the World*, 2015, http://www.lwbooks.co.uk/ebooks/we_all_want_to_change_the_world.html.

15. For some guidance here, I have turned in my own work to the efforts of Deleuze and Guattari to open the field of what they call *hybrid collective assemblages of enunciation*, which are similar but not identical to Foucault's discursive formations. See Lawrence Grossberg and Bryan Behrenshausen, 'Cultural Studies and Deleuze-Guattari, 'Part 2: From Affect to Conjunctures,' *Cultural Studies*, 30:6 (2016): 1001–1028.

10 Race, Immigration and the Present Conjuncture

Tony Jefferson

Nearly 4 million people voted for UKIP at the last election. If they are dismissed as racists rather than working-class people who often have unanswered fears over jobs, housing, public services and the future of their children and grandchildren, they will be lost forever.
—Owen Jones[1]

The phenomenon of working class racism . . . has proved extraordinarily resistant to analysis.
—Stuart Hall[2]

Although Stuart Hall was always interested in the 'race question,' his writings in this area multiplied as his interests in his own biographical journey and questions of identity, subjectivity and the postcolonial assumed greater prominence for him. My last research project[3] was an attempt to understand contemporary racism better using a psychosocial approach (one alert to both its psychic and social dimensions and their simultaneous effectivity). With this serendipitous conjunction of interests as a springboard, I wish to use my contribution to this text to try to advance from the current 'common sense' that dismisses working class fears of immigration as racist towards a 'good sense' that enables a shift in the current paralysis of left thinking on race and immigration. To do so, I shall combine an analysis of Shane Meadows's brilliant film about skinheads and racism, *This Is England* (2006), with some of the findings from our interview-based research project, comparing some of Meadows's fictional characters with some of our participants as revealed in their interviews. Using a psychosocial approach in pursuit of Gramscian good sense, aided by popular culture and a concrete research project, enables both an intervention in a significant aspect of 'The Politics of Conjuncture' (my panel's title) and a way of remembering Stuart.

In broad terms, *This is England,* set in the Midlands in 1983, is the story of a small group of teenage skinheads led by Woody. They 'adopt' Shaun, aged 12, and transform him, via shaved head and new clothes, into a pint-sized skinhead. Their everyday vacation exploits—from dressing up and destroying an abandoned house to hanging out and partying—are interrupted one day by the reappearance of an older skinhead, Combo, returned after three years in prison, and his threatening-looking prison buddy, Banjo. Combo's racist invitation to Woody's group to join him and 'fight' for their country splits them; some stay with Woody, and the others side with Combo. Thereafter, we witness the various exploits of the Combo-led group (which includes Shaun): attending an National Front (NF) meeting, spray painting racist graffiti, abusing and threatening Pakistani youth, robbing an Asian owned corner shop and, in a sickeningly violent scene, Combo viciously assaulting the one mixed-race member, Milky—Woody's 'main man'. This turns Shaun against Combo, and the film ends with Shaun ritualistically throwing his Combo-gifted St George's flag into the sea.

However, it is in the detail that Meadows reveals the sophistication of his take on skinheads and racism. By reminding us that skinhead groups had mixed race members, he immediately complicates the simple equation *skinhead = racist*—but he does much more than this. He shows the role of biography and contingency in the making and unmaking of racists, and he also shows there are different kinds and degrees of racism. Take Woody: He is not racist, even though he fails to challenge Combo's first racist rant. His friendship with the mixed race Milky and his decisive break with Combo over racism secure this reading. Moreover, on their first meeting, Woody protects the upset Shaun from being teased over his flared trousers by some in his group. Such teasing is a version of exclusion, or 'othering', based on some mark of difference. However, as if to show that we are all contradictory subjects, Woody, too, is guilty of othering: treating Gadget differently and calling him a 'fat idiot', which is the reason Gadget gives for siding with Combo.

Take Shaun: When Woody takes him under his wing, protects him from the less sensitive group members and supervises (and finances) his transformation, Shaun's willingness to be adopted (the day he became a mini-skinhead was 'the best day of [his] life') suggests an identification with Woody's non-racist version of being a skinhead. However, things change with the arrival of

Combo. During the second of Combo's racist rants, he calls the Falklands 'Thatcher's phoney war', in which people died 'for nothing'. At this point, Shaun, whose father (with whom he strongly identified) died in the war, attacks Combo. When he realises the reason for the attack, Combo apologises—but adds that if Shaun didn't stand up for his country and fight (interlopers), his dad would have died for nothing. He then congratulates Shaun for his bravery, and invites all the group members to stay with him and fight—or leave. Shaun stays 'to make [his] Dad proud'. At this point, he identifies with Combo and his racist version of being a skinhead. This transformation is cemented by Combo's promise always to be there for him. Thereafter, we see the compassionate and feeling Shaun being taught to walk and talk like a little racist: learning to be racially prejudiced. Only when he witnesses the horror of Combo's racist assault on Milky does he come to dis-identify with him and his racism.

Combo demonstrates a hatefully violent form of racism. His relations with Shaun, Lol (Woody's girlfriend) and Milky provide the key to understanding its biographical and contingent nature. Shaun becomes Combo's favourite, not just because of his bravery, but because Shaun reminds Combo of his earlier self. Combo too knows what it is like to lose a loved one, as he tells Shaun. However, whereas Shaun has lost a much-loved father, Combo reveals that his loss was one of abandonment: 'People walk out on you'. His relationship with Lol is one of unrequited love. When telling her this, he confesses that their one night of sex prior to his prison sentence was the best night of his life and that he'd always loved her. Lol's reply was a bruising re-enactment of rejection: For her, it was the worst night of her life, a drunken night of sex she had tried to forget. After she has gone, he sobs and bangs his steering wheel violently. Not long after this, he attacks Milky.

The prelude to the attack is Combo's decision to get stoned after his rejection by Lol. He seeks out Milky and persuades him to get some weed for them to share, at which point they go to Combo's flat, where his small group is hanging out. They all proceed to get stoned. To the accompaniment of Percy Sledge's classic black soul track 'The Dark End of the Street', Milky says what a 'good geezer' Combo is, playing the music that he and his uncle listen to. Combo reminds Milky that he, Combo, was an original skinhead when there was racial unity: 'black and white together'. They declare themselves 'like brothers. . . for life' and hug each other. Combo then starts asking after Milky's family. On learning it is a big, united, happy family, in which the many different fathers stay in touch with their children, his mood begins to change. He declares (with barely suppressed anger) that Milky has got 'the whole lot: the whole fucking package'. He asks what Milky thinks make for a bad dad. When Milky returns the question, saying he doesn't know, Combo spits out, 'niggers'. Milky's surprised 'what's with the nigger' response is met with ''cos you are, aren't you. Fucking coon'. Milky smiles—a mixture of stoned incomprehension and challenge. Combo's 'don't fucking smile at me . . . you fucking cunt' has no effect, and the vicious attack follows, accompanied by constant screaming of 'I fucking hate you' and a torrent of racist abuse.

What we are witnessing in this extraordinarily powerful scene is the transformation of love into hate via envy. Milky's revelation of his loving family background is a painful reminder of what Combo has never had. In the context of his recent rejection by Lol, perhaps assisted by some marijuana-induced paranoia, his biographically specific angry hatred—with origins in his early abandonment—spills over. Racism has become one habitual channel, or discourse, for this hatred. It is not the only one. When Combo throws Pukey out of the car for challenging his beliefs about nationalism, he is incandescent with rage and tells him to 'fuck off back to Woody you fucking little queer'. When women run past calling them 'fucking bastards' for daubing racist graffiti, Combo screams, 'fucking little whore'. Homophobia and sexism are also discursive vehicles for his underlying hatred.[4] The fact that in this hateful state he attacks others indiscriminately—afterwards, he tells Shaun to 'fuck off' and assaults and throws out both Banjo and Megsy—further secures the point: Hatred is the main issue here. The fact that he distractedly tells himself 'to leave them two alone' (after attacking Banjo and Megsy) and says to Shaun when he returns, 'It's not my fault. I didn't mean it', is indicative that hatred is a contingent state of mind, not a permanent state of being (though it has become a characteristic response to painful feelings of vulnerability). One can only wonder what might have happened if Lol's response to his declaration of love had been different.

Turning to the parallels in our research, Combo's hatred is reminiscent of Stan's, a white man, aged 19, who we interviewed while he was serving a two-year custodial sentence for racially aggravated affray (and other violent offences).[5] Unlike Combo's opaque background (beyond the fact of his abandonment), many details of Stan's troubled past were revealed to us. He was brought up by a series of stepfathers who abused his mother, was sexually abused by a babysitter at the age of eight and would 'blow up like a volcano' in infant school. By his early teens, misbehaviour in and out of school led to suspensions, expulsion and a criminal record. By his mid-teens, violence had become endemic and racialised: 'whites versus Pakis'. He had become, he said, 'a proper little racist' who 'signed up for the NF' and enjoyed the violence. The only sign he gave of his vulnerability was the admission that his head was 'all over the place'. Nevertheless, it was not difficult to see that his abusive, violent and troubled upbringing was seriously implicated in his hatred, racism and current love of violence.

Belinda, aged 18, was a good example of someone who was racially prejudiced but not full of hate. A white woman from a small, still-intact family living in a nice area, she enjoyed a 'happy life' full of 'nice things' (although she had been a victim of bullying at school and had a conviction for assault following a fight over a boy). However, her 'really racist' views seemed to stem from her strong identification with her racist father: she had, she said, been 'brought up . . . racist' by her father, to whom she was 'a lot closer' than to her mother.

Frank, aged 44, is an example of shifting identifications, like Shaun. He reminds us of what might have happened to Combo's hatred had Lol loved him in return. Frank had a very violent upbringing, a criminal adolescence, a spell in Borstal and a history of fighting, including years as a racist, NF skinhead constantly fighting black and Asian men. Superficially, this resembles Stan's (and what we know of Combo's) story, but with an important difference: Frank strongly identified with his 'dead racist' father, despite his abusive punishments. Thus, like Belinda (and Shaun), his racism would appear to have developed through identification. Getting married, having children and staying happily married led to a promise to stay out of trouble—a promise he kept. However, attendance at a British National Party (BNP) meeting in his forties led to him standing for election as a BNP candidate, because everything the party said made sense to him. After his wife left the party because of its racism, Frank was forced to reconsider and came to the same conclusion, after a senior BNP figure proposed excluding people with black friends or relatives from full membership. Still concerned about immigration and a host of local issues, Frank decided to withdraw and stand either as an independent or as a Labour candidate.

Understanding these shifts away from his violent past and then the BNP seemed, once again, to involve identification: Now Frank desired to be like his wife, to whom he remained very 'close', and like his beloved children, whose lives were very different from his violent, racist upbringing—and Frank was determined to keep them that way. Frank's case is also an example of moving from hatred (in his younger days as a NF skinhead) to othering—which is where he seems to have ended up. Now, no longer full of hate, he still prefers his own community over immigrant groups, the 'others' who are seen as a threat to 'our' jobs and an added strain on 'our' public services.

These all too brief sketches reveal different ways of attracting the label 'racist'. There are those, like Combo and Stan, who are full of hate. This hate is projected onto all kinds of different groups (gays and women, as well as the racially or ethnically 'different'), depending on circumstance. Such individuals are capable of extreme violence, especially when the vulnerabilities underpinning their hatred become exposed. Then there are those, like Shaun (under Combo's tutelage) and Belinda, who are racially prejudiced. Anyone who has laughed at a joke made about a 'thick' Irish navvy, a mean Scotsman or a mother-in-law is guilty of prejudice—which means all of us, to some extent.

Prejudice is just what it sounds like: a form of *prejudging* based on a stock of common stereotypes. These are not always negative; categorizing data into types is part of the way we think. Racial prejudice (for historical reasons I have no space for) has come to embrace a stock of negative stereotypes connoting inferiority, even subhumanness. However, such prejudice unaccompanied by hatred is unlikely on its own to emanate in physically violent acts. Finally, there is othering: of Shaun over his flare-bottomed trousers, Gadget over his size, and immigrants, in the case of Frank. Like prejudice, othering is a universal phenomenon stemming from our preference for those nearest and dearest (our in-group) over others (or out-groups). In-group preference does not necessarily equate with hostility to out-groups—but it sometimes does, as is presently the case with the immigrant/refugee/asylum-seeker other. As with racial prejudice, it is not on its own usually associated with physical violence.

The current problem with all this is that we have only one term, *racism*, to cover these three rather different things—hatred, prejudice and othering—that have different origins and are not necessarily related (even though they have routinely become so in theoretical, political and common sense discourse). Unsurprisingly, those only guilty of othering immigrants or of using common, racial stereotypes become upset if they are treated as though they are racists who hate those who are racially or ethnically different. Knowing that racial hatred is not how they experience themselves (as we found with the majority of the 'racists' we interviewed) turns them away from those who dismiss their concerns as racist and into the arms of those who appear to understand them better, like United Kingdom Independence Party (UKIP). A small start in another direction, towards Gramscian good sense, would be to deconstruct the term *racism* along the lines I am suggesting here.[6]

Notes

1. Owen Jones, 'If Corbyn's Labour Is Going to Work, It Has to Communicate', *Guardian*, September 16, 2015, 37.

2. Stuart Hall, 'Gramsci's Relevance for the Study of Race and Ethnicity', *Journal of Communication Inquiry* 10, no. 2 (1986): 5–27, 27.

3. An ESRC-funded project (RES-000-23-0171) entitled 'Context and Motive in the Perpetration of Racially Motivated Violence and Harassment', led by David Gadd. See David Gadd, Bill Dixon and Tony Jefferson, *Why Do They Do It? Racial Harassment in North Staffordshire* (Keele: Centre for Criminological Research, Keele University, 2005). See also David Gadd and Bill Dixon, *Losing the Race: Thinking Psychosocially about Racially Motivated Crime* (London: Karnac, 2011).

4. For a theoretical argument linking racism, sexism, homophobia and antisemitism, see Elisabeth Young-Bruehl, *The Anatomy of Prejudices* (Cambridge, MA: Harvard University Press, 1998).

5. Thirteen men and two women, variously thought to be racist, were interviewed twice each (in one case, three times) using the free association narrative interview method from Hollway and Jefferson in a study of racism in Stoke-on-Trent conducted during 2004. The method is designed to elicit stories from 'defended' subjects. See Wendy Hollway and Tony Jefferson, *Doing Qualitative Research Differently: A Psychosocial Approach*, 2nd ed. (London: Sage, 2013).

6. More detailed arguments, including how hatred, prejudice and othering have become erroneously yoked together, can be found in Tony Jefferson, 'Racial Hatred and Racial Prejudice: A Difference That Makes a Difference', in *The Unhappy Divorce of Sociology and Psychoanalysis: Diverse Perspectives on the Psychosocial*, ed. Lynn Chancer and John Andrews (Houndmills: Palgrave Macmillan, 2014), 359–379; and Tony Jefferson, 'What Is Racism? Othering, Prejudice and Hate-Motivated Violence', *International Journal for Crime, Justice and Social Democracy*. 4, no. 4 (2015): 120–135.

Right: Stuart Hall at the Black Cultural Archive, Brixton, early 1980s.

K CULTURAL
S MUSEUM

Part III
Identities and the Redefinition of Politics

Identities and the Redefinition of Politics

Stuart Hall made a fundamental contribution to the redefinition of politics itself, so that rather than the classical terrain of either of Parliamentary or class politics, it has come to be understood in the much broader sense of *cultural politics*, involving questions of representation and identity, with all their troubling complexities. Some of these complexities are taken up in the four chapters in this section. These cover the different areas of popular culture, gay sexual politics and the media industries. In each case, Hall is drawn on to understand the live nature of these questions. The answers are never simple or straightforward, and the unsettled and unsettling nature of these complexities of identity are even referred to by some contributors in terms of their experience of unease and even embarrassment.

One of the striking features about Hall's work on what he called the *ever unfinished conversation* of identity in the 1970s and 1980s is how much it resonates with current issues of identity politics, described in terms of intersectionality and lesbian, gay, bisexual and transgender (LGBT) issues. In the same way that 1970s sexual politics was about coming out, today's highlights the fluid transitioning between genders. For example, the recent deaths of David Bowie and Prince provoked discussion about their androgyny, and Hari Nef became the first trans model to grace the front cover of a mainstream fashion magazine with the September 2016 issue of *Elle*. The Black Lives Matter (BLM) movement and more recently BLM UK have been gaining political traction, again echoing the race issues of the earlier era. The personal is once again political—but there are also significant differences between then and now. If Hall's generation saw culture as being politicized, succeeding ones have witnessed its continuing industrialization.

Some of these issues are taken up in Julian Henriques's contribution in chapter 11, using what must count as a classic type of phenomenon for cultural studies: the reggae dancehall sound system that is at the heart of the popular street culture of Jamaica, as well as having a growing impact in many other parts of the world. Through this local phenomenon—as a recurring characteristic of Hall's approach—Henriques puts Hall's ideas to work in terms of how 'thinking-through-sounding might also be a way of thinking-with-Stuart'. He finds that both the techniques and practices of the sound system popular culture and the nature of auditory propagation itself provide models for some of the complexities of identity that Hall never feared to tackle. As with several of the contributions in this section, it is not so much about taking Hall's ideas on board as about inhabiting them, often as part of longstanding friendships and collaborations. The personal nature of the political is one of the themes explored in this section.

As Frank Mort tells us in chapter 12, he writes as an historian of British society and culture, as a PhD student at the CCCS and as a political subject involved in the gay politics of the 1970s. Mort considers the emergence of cultural studies in the longer perspective than that of Hall's widely acknowledged intellectual lineage via Richard Hoggart and Raymond Williams. Mort identifies the precursors to Hall's approach to culture in the Mass Observation in the 1930s and the Institute of Community Studies in the 1950s. In contrast, the identity politics of the 1960s and 1970s, informed by second-wave feminism and postcolonial studies, was preoccupied with the individual rather than the collective or class subject of these earlier movements. The 1970s were the days of Tom Robinson's 'Sing If You're Glad to Be Gay' hit, the opening of Heaven as the first gay mega-club in the United Kingdom and the Gay Left Collective.

Mort deploys two key features of Hall's approach to cultural studies. One is to make use of his own experiences of the personal and political strategy of coming out in the 1970s. The other is to use the prism of a particular intervention to explore broader issues—in this case, a comparatively little-known paper, 'Reformism and the Legislation of Consent', in which Hall aimed 'to probe English social and sexual morality in flux'.[1] The 1960s was a period in which the old post-war order felt itself threatened by the assault of 'permissiveness' afforded by increased income and social welfare, and the legislative reform underway included the 1967 Sexual Offences Act that in part decriminalised male homosexuality. Thus, in the 1960s the debate was polarised between the radical criminologists of the National Deviance Symposium on the one hand, including John Clarke, Victoria Greenwood and Jock Young, and the reaction against such progressive developments on the other, spearheaded by Mary Whitehouse, the outspoken leader of the National Viewers and Listeners' Association and self-proclaimed guardian of the 'British way of life'. That was indeed a very different era from our own. Currently, the tables have turned; progressive politics is now often 'small c' conservative in that it aims to preserve the progress of past eras, such as the establishment of the National Health Service (NHS) and the value of public education, and the revolution comes from the right in the form of the austerity required of neoliberal financialised capitalism designed to demolish the strengths of the welfare state.

Charlotte Brunsdon, like Mort, was a PhD student at the CCCS in the 1970s. In chapter 13, she is concerned similarly with the way 'the post-war settlement shuddered and cracked' in that period and how it was represented in the media. Brunsdon's interest in the role of broadcast media in contemporary society is highlighted by an early article of Hall's, 'A World at One with Itself', published in 1970.[2] For her, the issue of identity at stake here incorporates a conception of national as well as individual identities. Indeed, she is at pains to argue that despite the many gains achieved by an identity-based politics, it is crucial to recognised the multifaceted (and always shifting) nature of identities, rather than to imagine that they can provide a secure foundation for a productive form of politics. What Brunsdon emphasises is the 'ceaseless labour of the production and reproduction of power'. She uses this example from Hall's work (and the functioning of BBC radio, in this case) to rectify what she sees as misreadings of the famous 'Encoding/Decoding' paper[3] that concentrates only on meaning production in general, rather than situating the analysis, as Hall always tried to do, in the context of the particular meanings at play in a given conjuncture.

In chapter 14, the last piece in this section, Caspar Melville speaks from a generation too young to have attended the CCCS as students; instead, he attended Goldsmiths, under the influence of those who had been students in Birmingham. In fact, like many others, his first meeting with Hall was via television. Once again, the theme of identity is taken up as Melville reflects autobiographically on his own positioning in and by the preceding generations of cultural theorists, several of whom were present at the conference. As Melville puts it: 'We're part of this amazing loop, the reverberations of cultural studies all around us, echoing in our ears'. A significant portion of Melville's professional life has been spent serving as editor of *New Humanist*, in which he was able to include two interviews with Hall. This gave him an understanding of politics through culture; thanks to Hall, he says, he no longer believes that even the natural world is in fact natural. Instead, like culture itself, it is 'a terrain of struggle between . . . tendencies and forces'. Melville is well aware that he has inherited a world in which popular culture had been politicised, but he's now working in a world in which it has been transformed into what we now call the *creative and cultural industries*. This can be described as a journey from protest to product.

Notes

1. Stuart Hall, 'Reformism and the Legislation of Consent', in *Permissiveness and Control: The Fate of the Sixties Legislation*, ed. National Deviance Symposium (London: Macmillan, 1980), 1–43.
2. Stuart Hall, 'A World at One with Itself', *New Society*, no. 403 (1970): 1056–1058.
3. Stuart Hall, 'Encoding and Decoding in the Television Discourse', CCCS Stencilled Paper 7, CCCS, University of Birmingham, 1973.

11 Sonic Identities and Conjunctures of Listening

Julian Henriques

In this chapter, I'd like to make a few remarks on what sound might tell us about identity and conjunctures. The idea is to use the embodied and technological musical practices of the Jamaican dancehall scene as an example of how *thinking-through-sounding* might also be a way of *thinking-with-Stuart*. This is my aim, rather than to try to use Stuart's concepts to investigate or explain features of Jamaican popular culture. In addition, I would also suggest that the propagation and performance of sounding might provide a *methodology* for investigating these same issues of identity, conjuncture and even representation.

My investigation of Jamaican popular culture both as a filmmaker and researcher is entirely in keeping with some of Stuart's preoccupations, as well as those of my father, Fernando, who began his work as a social anthropologist researching the popular culture of Jamaica.[1] The other lineage to which I must give respect when I speak about sound is the Jamaican sound system audio engineers from whom I have learnt most of what I know about sounding.

 Two remarks are often made concerning what could be described as Stuart's *musicality*. Jazz was evidently a critical component of Stuart's world, as he wrote: 'When I was about 19 or 20, Miles Davis put his finger on my soul.'[2] Less well known is that Stuart was an accomplished jazz pianist in his Oxford days; despite this, he wrote remarkably little about music as such.[3] The second remark, which is one of the themes of sounding in the following pages, is this: Anyone who ever heard Stuart speak, on radio, TV or in person, noticed the particular distinctive depth and tone of his speaking voice.

Conjunctures of Listening

We will return to voice and voicing shortly, but first I'd like to raise some issues about the nature of auditory phenomena and to claim that these are relevant 'to the particularity of the conjunction—and attention to its complexity' that John Clarke describes as characteristic of Stuart's work.[4] Auditory propagation itself can said to be conjunctural in that sound is continually in transformation; it is only ever an event in time, as are cultural and political phenomena. Sound making and the experience of listening always require specific embodiments, durations and places; these are the materialities of sounding.

The transient and ephemeral, not to mention ethereal, nature of auditory phenomena make them impossible to pin down as a fixed object of study, in the way that images and text lend themselves so to be. Consequently, thinking-through-sounding directs our attention to the means of production or mechanism of propagation—such as the apparatus of the dancehall sound system. The open-air dancehall sessions that take place on the streets of Kingston every night of the week are an entirely phonographic medium; they rely on already recorded music on vinyl, CD or mp3, rather than live performances from artists. However, the MCs (or DJs) chat, special sound effects and the selectors' techniques—such as 'pull-ups' or rewinds—amount to a live reperformance of the music.

In brief, the sound system apparatus consists of two or three stacks or columns of speakers, often several meters high. This setup allows sounding to be experienced by the crowd or audience at its most immersive, intensive and liminal, described elsewhere as 'sonic dominance.'[5] Such experiences can also be described as conjunctural in so far as a dancehall session is a unique and often memorable event, pinned down to a particular time and place, as it were; in the open-air dancehall with the speaker stacks connected to banks of powerful amplifiers delivering thousands of watts of body-thumping bass, there is literally no escape for those who volunteer to enjoy such somatic pleasures. The dancehall session is an embodied and embodying experience par excellence in which, through sounding, there is a merging of the senses of vision, touch, smell and movement. This result is achieved not primarily through the volume of the sound system set, but by the clarity in the separation of the five frequency bands, each with its own dedicated amplifiers. These frequency bands are also spatialized vertically, with the tweeters at the top of the stack, then the horns, and the upper and lower mids and then the bass bins at the bottom. The better the separation, the 'sweeter' and more pleasurable the crowd finds the mix to be.

Importantly, in the sound system session, the speaker stacks face inwards onto the crowd, making it the recipient of direct and forceful auditory impact. This contrasts with regular modes of listening in two respects. First, this positioning creates a bowl within which the crowd listens, rather than the source of the sound being a stage somewhere in front of it. The crowd members place *themselves inside* the sound. This is the opposite from a person placing the sound *inside them*, as with in-ear mobile listening, which Raymond Williams could well have used as an example of 'mobile privatization.'[6] Second, this distinctive phonographic configuration of direct auditory propagation also contrasts with the way we most often hear sound, as reflected off surfaces. The dancehall session leaves little room for reflection—in terms of either sound or thought. Dub music compensates for this lack of echo by providing its own. Once all but a snatch of the vocal line and the melody have been removed, the music is characterised by the echo or reverb applied to the remaining drum and bass. Indeed, as the instrument on which this music is designed to be played, it is the sound system session that must be credited as giving birth to this musical genre.

With dub, we are listening to and thinking and feeling through echo and reverberation; this re-sounding, redoubling, reflection or copying (which gave dub its name) is even more transitory, fragile and ephemeral than the original.[7] In ways of which Stuart might approve, echo makes a mockery of any fixed idea of identity, repeating what is no longer there, preserving the long tail of sound, postponing the inevitable passage of time for as long as possible—delay attempting to defy inevitable decay. This makes echo all the more appropriate as a way of describing the unfinished or always incomplete conception of identity; we are echoic subjects.[8] What is true of dub in particular is also the case with all auditory propagation. Sounding always has to present be to itself in a performance; a recording is a *re-presentation*, distinct from a *representation* or *reproduction*, as Lastra reminds us.[9] For me, this idea resonates with Stuart's investigation of the constructive complexities of representational systems in so far as it shatters the illusion of any simple correspondence between an object and its representation.[10]

It can be said that the absences or gaps in the melody and vocals in a dub track leave room for the listener to inhabit—especially when the listeners in the crowd in the dancehall session are familiar with the missing lyrics. This chimes with Stuart's conception of the necessarily incomplete nature of the conversation of identity. With dub, it gives the music an unusual depth, not only in terms of bass frequencies, but also in the phenomenological terms of the way Merleau-Ponty considers *depth* as being the primary or founding dimension from which the familiar Cartesian coordinates emerge—that is, the source of becoming.[11] Indeed, dub continues to be a hugely productive and influential example of Jamaican musical inventiveness. It deploys what can be called a *subtractive* minimalist aesthetic—that is, an identity based in the interval, a vanishing point or *absence*. In a complimentary fashion, the other is the equally influential *additive* process of toasting pioneered by U-Roy and others in the 1960s, adding lyrics on top of those already there in the song or adding special effects such as sirens or gunshots on top of the phonographic reproduction.

Besides its materialities, the other most important aspect of listening—distinct from mere hearing, to use Barthes's distinction—is that listening requires the listener to give attention to what or who he or she is listening to. Stuart was a notoriously good listener, giving his full attention and his respect to his interlocutor, whoever it was, whether young or old, distinguished or ordinary. As has been said, Stuart was one of the few people who could learn a lot from someone who knew a lot less than he did.

Distinctive Voicing

From the MC in the dancehall to the pastor in the church hall, voice and voicing play an especially important part in Jamaican society. Traditions of oral culture remain strong, and the spoken word can signify a stronger presence than the written word. This takes us from the particularities of a conjuncture to those of a person. Thinking of Stuart, his voicing was particularly distinctive and personal—that is, both personal to Stuart (distinctively *his*) and also personal to each member of his audience (distinctively *ours*). This reminds me of a remark made by the great reggae balladeer Beres Hammond, when he told me his art consisted of singing in such a way that every single member of the audience (especially the women) felt he that he was singing *just for her or him alone.*[12]

In addition, thinking-through-sounding gives further definition to the idea of the distinctive personality that each of us has through our speaking voice. As Steve Connor puts it: 'Nothing else about me defines me so intimately as my voice'. He continues: 'If my voice is mine because it comes from me, it can only be known because it also goes from me. My voice is, literally, my way of taking leave of my senses. What I say goes'.[13] Our voices certainly say maybe even more about us than what we look like, because it is this element that locates each of us in the class hierarchy of the society from which we come, nowhere more so than in Jamaica.[14] For me, when listening to one of Stuart's cousins, a nun who remained in Jamaica, she was instantly recognizable by her voice as a member of a brown, middle-class family. I imagine these cadences lingering on in Stuart's voice, too. However, the most remarkable characteristic of his tone of voice was not even its warmth and humour, but its inclusiveness—as with the kind of open invitation a dub track offers the listener. It was a voice that listened even when it was speaking. To listen to Stuart was to become a native of his person (to adapt George Lamming's memorable novel title, *Natives of My Person*).[15]

This mingling of voice with person is deeply engrained. Our sonic identity is our personal identity, an enunciation of what made us who we are, our *facticity*, as Sartre called it.[16] In the days before caller ID, we only had to say, 'it's me' to our loved ones. The etymology of the term '"person" [is] from Latin *persona* "human being, person, personage; a part in a drama, assumed character," originally "mask, false face" … Latin *personare* "to *sound through*" (i.e., the mask as something spoken through and perhaps amplifying the voice)'.[17] The distinctive tone or timbre (sound colour) and expression or prosody is derived only from the unique combination of the two elements of every auditory vibration: volume (amplitude) and pitch (frequency or wavelength). These are the auditory material from which the phonemes of language are built. Similarly, a musical instrument has its own unique sonic signature, or timbre, whether a Stradivarius violin or reggae recording studio.[18] To the trained ear of the connoisseur, each one has its own discernable feel, vibe or style.

The thinking-through-sounding that gives an understanding of fine-grained nuances and subtleties of the distinctive nature of voicing can also be extended further afield in a multi-sensorial fashion. Nothing is more important than style and pattern in the dancehall scene. Style and pattern are how you define your profile as an artist, dancehall queen, dance crew or sound system follower, expressed in terms of clothes, fashion, shoes, accessories or dance moves on the part of the crowd.[19] Every member of the crowd wants to be a 'somebody'. This profile is also expressed by the tunes the selector plays, the novelty of the special sound effects and the power and quality of sound system technology on which each sound system prides itself—all put to the test in a sound system 'clash' with another sound. Dub plate specials, in which an artist records a special version of a hit, altering the lyrics to 'big up' the sound system that paid them, are another example of the distinctiveness that has long been the staple ammunition of such clashes.

Style and pattern describe the form of *rhythmos*, its gestalt or configuration, to complement its energetic flow. This is always a relationship, ratio or arrangement between things—what Gregory Bateson calls 'the difference that makes a difference';[20] never can this be reduced to the materiality of mere things themselves. *Style and pattern*, in the lingo, are what make something cool. It is no surprise that a subaltern class with little in terms of material resources might invest in the cultural capital of such relationalities. Often in African traditions, these are articulated in an aesthetic that particularly values asymmetry.[21]

Sonic Identities

This distinctiveness of voicing provides a good access point into one of Stuart's key themes – identity. This is nothing if not distinctive; in fact, it can be defined as such, as what makes one person or group different from another. Thus, it gives a sense of belonging. If identity defined by thinking-though-sounding in this way is a personal matter, then it is a political matter equally. Recently, issues of identity politics and intersectionality have re-emerged with the kind of political saliency that some of us remember from the 1970s and 1980s, then cast in terms of black power and the women's movement and slogans such as 'the personal is political'. For the generation entering political action at university with campaigns such as 'I Too Am Oxford'. In this campaign, each student was photographed with his or her own slogan on a board in front of them: 'Are you here on an access course? . . . Why are only 4 percent of UK professors black? . . . I'm not being divisive; white supremacy is divisive . . . Valuing education does not make me less black and more white . . . I am not the voice of all black people'—and so on.[22] Political and personal aspects of identity are literally voiced through our embodiment, as is seen and heard with the Black Lives Matter campaigns on both sides of the Atlantic.[23] Indeed, as Angela Davis describes in chapter 23, she has been involved in a decades-long campaign against the commercialised prison system, which increasingly incarcerates a disproportionate number of African American males.

Another reason for the current appeal of Stuart's work on identity is that it offers a handle on what for the social sciences (given their positivist origins) has traditionally been an 'awkward customer' of unique distinctive instance and the individual subject.[24] Indeed, issues of identity have once again been taken up on the theoretical front line: There is a crisis of subjectivity for Michel Feher and Giorgio Agamben and the process of 'subjectification' for Felix Guattari and Maurizio Lazzarato, also described as a symptom of the neoliberal 'crisis' in Hall, Massey and Rustin's *Kilburn Manifesto*.[25] These themes of subjectivity and identity were also sustained through Foucault's concept of 'the care of the self'.[26] Such issues take me back to my own interest in subjectivity, discussed in *Changing the Subject*.[27] In the early 1980s, we saw ourselves as fighting against the dichotomy between the individual and society by way of an alchemical amalgam of Marx and Freud. Thinking-through-sounding and sonic identities provide a different route by which the notion of the essential subject can be undermined.

Identity is personal and political—both at the same time. As has been described elsewhere, Stuart's political and cultural preoccupations flowed from his personal experience of a colour-based caste system growing up in Jamaica and his recognition of himself as an immigrant in the eyes of others in the United Kingdom. Rewriting my conference speaking notes, I am sitting in a place that Stuart knew from his youth in Jamaica and where the two of us sat and chatted on at least one occasion: Frenchman's Cove. This is probably the most beautiful beach on the island, with its freshwater river running down from the verdant tropical foliage of the limestone hills behind, a few miles outside Port Antonio. That is where Stuart grew up, and where, he told me, his parents were friends with my grandparents (before they moved to Kingston and thence to England in 1919).[28]

One of Stuart's most poignant definitions of identity is as 'an ever-unfinished conversation'. Thinking-through-sounding gives emphasis to several features of this concept. One is simply the way in which the energetic propagation and diffusion of sound waves serves as such a telling illustration of the energetic propagation and diffusion behind the migration of peoples. As Stuart put it, 'I am a sort of diaspora person'.[29] The diffusion or energetic propagation of sound, circling outwards like the ripples from a stone thrown into still water, models the diffusion of people, the exodus—the movement of Jah people, as Marley famously sang.

Echo and reverberation also model another aspect of ourselves—that is, how our identity so often references some other time or place. This is particularly the case with diasporic peoples, whether remembering Trinidadian East Indians retaining Hindu rituals long-forgotten in the subcontinent or the popular music 'remembering' rhythms that the enslaved brought from Africa.[30] Thus, an echoic identity is a remembering of itself—that is, literally putting ourselves back together again—*re-membering* as distinct from *dis-membering*. Like an echo, our auditory past is reflected back to us off the walls of our habitation, folded into the present. It is always a repeating, rhythmic beat, as with the drum and bass of dub music. A sonic self is a processional ever unfinished; it's always a work in progress, giving an impression of continuity through the duration of becoming different.

In the dancehall scene, there are several striking examples of this processional, always provisional and unfinished experience of identity. One of the prevalent tropes is *antiphony*, or the call-and-response between MC and crowd, against what might be called the soliloquy of rationalism. In the dancehall, it is through the MC's voicing of this conversation that he or she performs the role of a guide for the crowd, as much pastor as entertainer.[31] This resonates with Stuart's characterization of identity as an exchange—but less so with the much more subtle ways in which he offered leadership. This reciprocal relationship between speaker and listener in a conversation exemplifies the dialogical relationship, as

Mikhail Bakhtin described it.[32] Stuart evidenced this methodologically in his famously collaborative way of working.[33]

Although it is important to note that this relationship between MC and crowd is not one of equality, as only the MC has his or her voice amplified, it does indicate one way in which we are always subject to negotiation—and indeed, subjects of conversation.[34] Such ideas of auditory identity go against the conventions that there must be something *essential* about identity, that it could be finished and can be fixed. Instead, the idea of identity becomes extrinsic to the subject, and indeed diasporic, calling for 'the end of the innocent notion of the essential black subject'.[35] With this idea of dialogical identity, Stuart frees the subject from being impaled on the fixed point of Cartesian rationalism or vanishing point of linear perspective, to circulate as a linguistic signifier born out of spoken conversation.

In conclusion, sounding through Stuart, I suggest that auditory propagation can be considered not only as a medium, but a *modality*, a sensibility, a way of being and understanding ourselves. As an alternative to the solipsism of the cogito—currently enacted through the selfie—thinking though sounding might help us move forward towards more convivial, embodied and shared ways of being with others. Sounding suggests, 'I *listen*, therefore I am', or even, 'I feel, therefore I am'. Thinking-with-Stuart helps us to *re-cognise* (another repeating) ourselves in the present conjuncture to a depth and with a complexity that might not otherwise be quite possible.

1. Fernando Henriques, *Family and Colour in Jamaica* (London: Eyre and Spottiswoode, 1953).

2. Stuart Hall, interview by Sue Lawley, *Desert Island Discs*, BBC Radio 4, February 18, 2000.

3. Besides Miles Davis, another favourite was pianist Archie Tatum; personal communication.

4. John Clarke, 'Conjuncture, Crises and Cultures: Valuing Stuart Hall', *Focaal—Journal of Global and Historical Anthropology*, no. 70 (2014): 115.

5. Julian Henriques, 'Sonic Dominance and the Reggae Sound System', in *Auditory Culture Reader*, ed. Michael Bull and Les Back (Oxford: Berg, 2003), 451–480.

6. Raymond Williams, *Television: Technology and Cultural Form* (London: Routledge, 1974).

7. See Julian Henriques and Hillegonda Rietveld, 'Echo', in *Companion to Sound Studies*, ed. Michael Bull (London: Routledge, forthcoming).

8. See, for example, Gayatri Chakravorty Spivak, 'Echo, New Literary History', *Culture and Everyday Life*, no. 24 (Winter 1993): 17–43; and Philippe Lacoue-Labarthe, 'The Echo of the Subject', in *Typography: Mimesis, Philosophy, Politics* (Stanford: Stanford University Press, 1998), 139–207.

9. James Lastra, 'Reading, Writing, and Representing Sound', in *Sound Theory/Sound Practice*, ed. Rick Altman (London: Routledge, 1992), 65–86, 72.

10. Stuart Hall, 'The Work of Representation', in *Representation: Cultural Representations and Signifying Practices*, ed. Stuart Hall (London: Sage, 1997), 13–74.

11. See Maurice Merleau-Ponty, 'Eye and Mind', in *The Primacy of Perception*, ed. James E. Edie, trans. Carleton Dallery (Evanston, IL: Northwestern University Press, 1964), 181. See also Steven Rosen, *Dimensions of Apeiron: A Topological Phenomenology of Space, Time, and Individuation* (Amsterdam: Editions Rodopi B.V., 2004), 143.

12. Personal conversation with Beres Hammond while making my feature film *Babymother* (1998).

13. Steven Connor, *Dumbstruck: A Cultural History of Ventriloquism* (Oxford: Oxford University Press, 2000), 7. See also http://www.dumbstruck.org/.

14. Fernando Henriques, *Family and Colour*.

15. Georges Lamming, *Natives of My Person* (London: Allison and Busby, [1972] 1986).

16. Jean-Paul Sartre, *Being and Nothingness*, trans. Hazel E. Barnes (London: Routledge, [1958] 2003), 97–98.

17. OED, emphasis added.

18. Personal conversation with the author while making my film *Babymother* (1998).

19. See, for example, Al Fingers, *Clarkes in Jamaica* (London: One Love Books, 2012).

20. Gregory Bateson, *Mind and Nature: A Necessary Unity* (London: Wildwood House. 1979), 99.

21. This idea of asymmetry contrasts with the symmetries that have dominated Western aesthetic since the ancient Greece; see Robert Farris Thompson, *Flash of the Spirit: African and Afro-American Art and Philosophy* (New York: Vantage Books, 1984).

22. Modelled on "I Too Am Harvard" and subsequently duplicated in other UK universities; see http://itooamoxford.tumblr.com/.

23. See http://blacklivesmatter.com/about/.

24. This all the more so and given the increasing impoverishment of the arts and humanities, as against scientific or professional so-called STEM subjects for which the distinctiveness of the individual case. The particular anecdote is completely lost, as Morley discusses in this volume.

25. Stuart Hall, Doreen Massey and Michael Rustin, eds. *After Neoliberalism? The Kilburn Manifesto* (London: Lawrence and Wishart, 2015).

26. Michel Foucault, *The Care of the Self,* vol. 3 of *History of Sexuality* (New York: Vintage Books, 1988).

27. Julian Henriques et al., *Changing the Subject: Psychology, Social Regulation and Subjectivity* (London: Routledge, 1984).

28. Mark Holland, *The Jippi-Jappa Hat Merchant: A Jamaican Family in Britain* (Oxford: Horsgate, 2014).

29. Hall, *Desert Island Discs.*

30. See Kenneth Bilby, 'Distant Drums: The Unsung Contribution of African-Jamaican Percussion to Popular Music at Home and Abroad,' *Caribbean Quarterly: A Journal of Caribbean Culture* 56, no. 4 (2010): 1–21; and Julian Henriques, 'Sonic Diaspora, Vibrations and Rhythm: Thinking through the Sounding of the Jamaican Dancehall Session,' *African and Black Diaspora*, no. 1 (July 2008), 215–236.

31. Julian Henriques, *Sonic Bodies: Reggae Sound Systems, Performance Techniques and Ways of Knowing* (London: Continuum, 2011).

32. Mikhail M. Bakhtin, *The Dialogic Imagination: Four Essays*, trans. Michael Holquist and Caryl Emerson (Austin: University of Texas Press, 1982).

33. John Akomfrah, *The Unfinished Conversation*, exhibition, 2013; see http://autograph-abp.co.uk/exhibitions/the-unfinished-conversation-berlin.

34. Human Microphone: Occupy Wall Street, September 30, 2011, day 14.

35. Stuart Hall, 'New Ethnicities,' in *Black Film, British Cinema* (*ICA Documents*), ed. Kobena Mercer (London: Institute of Contemporary Arts, 1989). Also in *The Post-colonial Studies Reader*, ed. Bill Ashcroft, Gareth Griffiths and Helen Tiffin (London: Routledge, 2006), 441–449.

Remembering Sex and Identity in the 1960s and 1970s

Frank Mort

In this chapter, I offer some reflections on the politics of sexual identity, its relationship to the project of cultural studies and the influence of Stuart's own work in this field. I frame these questions concretely in terms of the politico-intellectual context of Britain in the 1960s and 1970s and in terms of my own social memory of doing cultural studies at the CCCS towards the end of this period. I write as a historian of modern British society and culture, a historian who, along with several others of my generation, made the transition from cultural studies to cultural and gender history. I also write as someone who has been concerned to understand the sexual and moral consequences of the long 1960s, as a post-Victorian moment.[1] However, I also write as a political subject, as someone who was involved in gay politics in the 1970s and who 'came out' using one of the strategic forms of identity forged by the new social movements at that time. So my chapter is about the convergences and the disconnections between an intellectual project on the one hand and a form of political activism on the other, as that contradiction was lived by me. It endorses what Charlotte Brunsdon has argued about the 'labour of identity' (see chapter 13) and especially about the tension between the production of cultural knowledge and the grounded experience of those of us who produced it.[2]

However, let me reflect first on the historical genealogy of cultural studies, which is relevant to what I want to argue about the post-war years. The cultural studies enterprise, as read in a specifically British rather than international context, was intellectually exceptional but not unique. What do I mean? Seeing the emergence of cultural studies as part of a cultural *longue durée*, rather than as part of a shorter-term, conjunctural moment of the 1960s and 1970s, can reveal how others 'have been there before'—not on the same terms, but in ways that point to significant parallels across time. Denis Dworkin has urged us to see these connections in terms of the history of cultural Marxism in post-war Britain.[3] However, I would go further and place cultural studies as part of much broader interventions by left-leaning intellectual movements across the twentieth century, which aimed to redefine the sociocultural terrain in the interests of radical or progressive democracy. Mass Observation in the 1930s, dedicated to producing an 'anthropology of our people', in the words of its co-founder Charles Madge, springs to mind as one significant comparison, on account of both its interdisciplinary modernism and its popular ventriloquism—with cultural professionals claiming to speak on behalf of the people.[4] An equally significant precursor was the Institute of Community Studies in the 1950s, with Michael Young's ethnographic mapping of communities of the disenfranchised and the subordinated. The historical genesis of cultural studies could also be taken back even further, to the radicalized and often unpredictable twentieth-century outcomes of Victorian social reform as they have been mapped by historians of 'the social', like Patrick Joyce and Seth Koven.[5] The value of these historical comparisons is to show that radical intellectual projects for the study of and intervention in culture in Britain do have a substantial history, an awareness of which enables us to see what was both distinctive about the post-war period and what was part of much longer and broader movements for change.

When those earlier cultural interventions are examined for their versions of identity, it is the big collectivities—of class, the people and mass society—which set the terms of social and political debate. Identity as conceived at this collectivist moment was brought to order via structures that subsumed individual experience into much larger agglomerations of people and power. It was much less the case in the 1960s and 1970s, when the identity politics of the new social movements were key influences in the cultural field. Second-wave feminism, postcolonial struggles and the politics of sexuality not only challenged the established corporatism of mainstream British politics but also fed into the crisis in the humanities, the so-called culture wars of that time.[6] Stuart himself intervened in many of these debates later, mainly from the vantage point of the 1990s and beyond. There are his reflections on the eruption of the contemporary women's movement into cultural studies and his arguments about hybridity in relation to black and postcolonial identities, conceived by him as 'unstable points of identification' and 'not an essence but a positioning.'[7] Certainly, he was not adverse to the idea of a 'strategic essentialism', which preserved the political call to identity but conceived of it as contingent, fluid and malleable instead of fixed.

Rather than returning to these debates about identity politics theoretically, I pose them historically by returning to the formative 1960s moment as Stuart dissected it in a seminal and, to my mind, somewhat neglected essay, 'Reformism and the Legislation of Consent'. In this piece, he addressed head-on the implications of the moral and sexual attempts in the period to liberalize British society under that most slippery of terms, 'permissiveness'. The article was published in a book edited by the National Deviance Symposium, *Permissiveness and Control: The Fate of the Sixties Legislation* (1980), in which contributors including John Clarke, Victoria Greenwood and Jock Young, as well as Stuart, grappled with different aspects of the 1960s in terms of policy and practice—on drugs, race relations, youth delinquency, families and sexuality.[8] The intellectual pedigree of the conference is worth recalling in terms of the radicalism of the time. In the words of the book's editors: 'The NDC was set up in opposition to the arid, criminological conferences of the Institute of Criminology at Cambridge, sponsored by the Home Office, and will . . . provide a "space" for radical thought and discussion of the nature of the state and its welfare and criminal justice systems.'[9] The reply from Cambridge, in the person of Sir Leon Radzinowicz, éminence grise of the criminological profession, was equally telling: 'It [the NDC] reminded me of little naughty schoolboys playing a nasty game on their stern headmaster.'[10]

Stuart gave me his article to read in draft form in the summer of 1978, as one of his new intake of PhD students. I was inspired by the sweep and the historical depth of his arguments—for this is one of the most empirically nuanced of his published works. In retrospect, it also reads as profoundly English in its concerns. For example, the impact of Caribbean migration (and especially young West Indian men) on British sexual attitudes and behaviour, one of the emerging moral obsessions of the period for politicians and social commentators, hardly featured at all.[11] Stuart's aim here was to probe English social and sexual morality in flux as it was being recomposed during the long post-war moment under the combined impact of material affluence, increased social welfare and shifts in the criminal law.

National types and collective identities, distinguished primarily by gender and social class, featured prominently in the piece; some of them were very up to the minute, and some were very traditional indeed. There was a good deal about the 'pleasure-seeking women' of the 1960s, empowered by consumerism and on the lookout for new pleasures—a favourite subject/object of advertising men and contemporary women's magazines alike. Also present were the elite masculine personalities who were the doyens of liberal reform: Tony Crosland, Roy Jenkins, 'Rab' Butler and, above all, Sir John Wolfenden, chair of the influential committee on male homosexual offences and prostitution (1954–1957), which proposed a wholesale redrafting of the criminal law. Mary Whitehouse, the energetic leader of the National Viewers and Listeners' Association, resurgent voice of feminine moral rearmament and self-professed guardian of the 'British way of life', made an equally telling appearance. All these figures were deliciously handled by Stuart in a series of brief but wicked pen portraits. At the same time, we were taken deep inside the workings of the Home Office, where the new policies on sexuality were hatched. Stuart's conclusions about the break-up of consensus politics paralleled many of his arguments made in the Birmingham mugging project, while his attention to the resurgence of the moral right pointed forward to the series of major articles that appeared in *Marxism Today*, starting with 'The Great Moving Right Show' in 1979.[12]

In discussing his article with me, Stuart told me an anecdotal aside. He knew Sir John Wolfenden's son, Jeremy, at Oxford. He didn't warm to him ('brilliant but egoistical', I think he said), but Jeremy was gay and so there was, Stuart suggested, more to the father's knowledge of the subject than Sir John was letting on. A journalist, a possible spy, and a friend of Guy Burgess, Jeremy Wolfenden died in suspicious circumstances in Washington at the age of thirty-one, having drunk himself into oblivion. But in the late 1970s Jeremy Wolfenden was seen by my own generation as part of an older world of male homosexuality: tragic, abject and fatalistic, to cite Jeremy's biographer, the novelist Sebastian Faulks.[13]

In 1978, the year Stuart drafted his article, there was a dramatic speedup in gay men's politics. This was largely organized around defending and expanding a version of sexual identity opened up in the space created by the liberal reforms of the previous decade; the 1967 Sexual Offences Act had partly decriminalized male homosexuality in England and Wales. Coming out was a key part of contemporary gay politics. It centred on a public declaration of (homo)sexuality that was seen to have been hidden or suppressed. In 1978, Tom Robinson released his celebration single, 'Sing If You're Glad to Be Gay', which got into the charts and was predictably banned by the BBC, while London's first gay super club opened with the apt name Heaven, dedicated to sexual liberation as hedonism and sexual excess—a portent of things to come. There was an immediate conservative challenge. *Gay News*, the UK's gay paper with its roots in the Gay Liberation Front and the Campaign for Homosexual Equality, was put on trial at the Old Bailey for blasphemy in a case brought by Whitehouse.[14] About this time, I became involved with a London-based group, the Gay Left Collective (1975–1980), where the issue of identity was high on the agenda of a radical sexual politics that was equally striving to be socialist.

Coming out was extremely successful as a form of identity politics, but it was marked by the traces of its own genesis. With the benefit of hindsight, it was clear that it privileged a white, educated male activist who was more often than not shaped by a distinctive European moral legacy as it had been exported worldwide via religion, rationality and empire. At the time, I was something of a reluctant convert to coming out for different reasons. I had already read the first volume of Michel Foucault's *History of Sexuality* (translated into English in 1978 and referenced by Stuart in his article).[15] I was inspired by Foucault's critique of what he termed the 'repressive hypothesis'—the idea that modern Western societies were moving inexorably forward towards a progressive sexual future. His arguments about the confessional and the sexualized speaking subject, as they were part of modern disciplinary power, made me think critically about the liberationist strategy of radical gay politics. When Roy Peters and I interviewed

Foucault in Paris the following year, we pressed him on precisely these issues.[16]

Along with Stuart's analysis of permissiveness as regulation, Foucault's ideas made intellectual sense to me, but they sat uneasily with the more stable versions of identity politics that were common at the time. I couldn't resolve that tension—personally and politically. Times have changed, and much has been written and practised about sexuality as constructed, queerness as contingent and sex as performance. So, why am I telling you this? Because many of us worked through the contradictions of identity not only in theory but as lived—emotionally and psychically. This was part of the labour of identity, and it was messy, awkward and frequently unresolved.

1. See especially Frank Mort, *Capital Affairs: London and the Making of the Permissive Society* (New Haven and London: Yale University Press, 2010).

2. Charlotte Brunsdon, 'On Being Made History', *Cultural Studies* 29, no. 1 (2014): 1–12; and Charlotte Brunsdon, 'A Thief in the Night: Stories of Feminism in the 1970s at CCCS', in *Stuart Hall: Critical Dialogues in Cultural Studies*, ed. David Morley and Kuan-Hsing Chen (London: Routledge, 1996), 276–286.

3. Denis Dworkin, *Cultural Marxism in Post-war Britain: History, the New Left and the Origins of Cultural Studies* (London: Duke University Press, 1997).

4. Charles Madge, 'Anthropology at Home', Correspondence, *New Statesman and Nation*, January 2, 1937, 12.

5. Patrick Joyce, *The Rule of Freedom: Liberalism and the Modern City* (London: Verso, 2003); Seth Koven, *Slumming: Sexual and Social Politics in Victorian London* (Princeton: Princeton University Press, 2004).

6. See James Curran, Julian Petley and Ivor Gaber, *Culture Wars: The Media and the British Left* (Edinburgh: Edinburgh University Press, 2005).

7. Stuart Hall, 'The Emergence of Cultural Studies and the Crisis in the Humanities', *October*, no. 53 (1990): 11–23; and Stuart Hall, 'Cultural Identity and Diaspora', in *Identity: Community, Culture, Difference*, ed. Jonathan Rutherford (London: Lawrence and Wishart, 1990), 222–237.

8. Stuart Hall, 'Reformism and the Legislation of Consent', in *Permissiveness and Control: The Fate of the Sixties Legislation*, ed. National Deviance Symposium (London: Macmillan, 1980), 1–43.

9. 'Introduction', in *Permissiveness and Control*, viii.

10. Leon Radcinowicz, *Adventures in Criminology* (London: Routledge, 1999), 229.

11. See Marcus Collins, 'Pride and Prejudice: West Indian Men in Mid-Twentieth-Century Britain', *Journal of British Studies* 3, no. 40 (2001): 391–418.

12. Stuart Hall et al., *Policing the Crisis: Mugging, the State, and Law and Order* (Basingstoke: Macmillan, 1978); Stuart Hall, 'The Great Moving Right Show', *Marxism Today* (January 1979): 14–20.

13. Sebastian Faulks, *The Fatal Englishman: Three Short Lives* (London: Hutchinson, 1996).

14. In 1979, the House of Lords upheld the conviction of the editor of *Gay News* in 1977 for blasphemy; the editor had published a poem that described a centurion's homosexual fantasies about Christ crucified. See Paul Crane, *Gays and the Law* (London: Pluto, 1982), 93.

15. Michel Foucault, *The History of Sexuality, Vol. 1: An Introduction*, trans. Robert Hurley (London: Allen Lane, 1978).

16. Frank Mort and Roy Peters, 'Foucault Recalled: Interview with Michel Foucault', *New Formations*, no. 55 (2005): 9–22.

13 The Labour of Identity: 'A World at One with Itself'

Charlotte Brunsdon

Thank you for inviting me to contribute to this event, and may I start by saying how much I like its title, associating Stuart Hall with the terms *conversations*, *projects* and *legacies*, about which I want to say a little more. I like that sense of Stuart somehow still in the middle of things, in the middle of conversations with so many people about so many topics and, in my experience, ceaselessly interested in and curious about what is happening now and what it means and how we should understand it.

I went to the Centre for Contemporary Cultural Studies in the 1970s—partly because I wanted to perform collective intellectual work with other people, but also because, with the arrogance of youth, I wanted that work to be about what was happening now—contemporary culture. I wasn't interested in old things. It was my good fortune to be there, in that place, at that time, as the post-war settlement shuddered and cracked, and to be involved in projects through which we tried to understand that crisis. An understanding that, I learned, must always be historical.

Those cultural studies projects are only a part of the many projects with which Stuart Hall was involved, and many people here have been involved in others; it is not their particularity on which I want to pause, but instead their plurality, which is why I think it is so appropriate as the title of the conference. One of Stuart's great gifts was his ability to enable others to see both the complexity and the broader significance of what they were trying to apprehend, to enable others to envisage their work as a project and—usually—bring them to completion. Conversations, projects—and then the third term of the title, more difficult to handle, *legacies*, of which there are many. Many of these legacies other people will talk about here, but the term is more difficult, for it demands recognition that the conversations and the projects are mainly, for most of us, in the past.

Thus, there is a change of tense in the title of the conference, after *conversations* and *projects* to *legacies*, and it is attempting to come to terms with that change of tense which I see us as doing here together, as well as beginning to consider what these legacies might be. That change of tense is significant, for it is the conversations and the projects, the manner of the doing of the work, that it is important to remember. Stuart's legacy is not just what he thought, but how he 'did thinking'—with others, in constant dialogue, a practice of exploring, of learning, of teaching, of making thinking.

In contrast to really liking the conference title, my heart sank when I learned that the panel to which I had been invited to contribute was called 'Identity', particularly identity conceptualised through that very 1970s triumvirate of gender, race and class. However, I recognise what is called in television crime series 'a fair cop' and that I have what is called in those same series 'form' for speaking and writing about one of these in particular: gender. However, I've pretty much said what I have to say about these matters, and I've said most of it more than once, and finally published about it again after the June 2014 conference in Birmingham to mark fifty years since the founding of the CCCS by Richard Hoggart in 1964.[1] My almost comical dismay when I learned the name of this panel is not to deny the significance of the mobilizations round identity, nor my own part in them, but it is to resist being stuck there forever. Many people here have been involved in many different conversations with Stuart Hall about identity, but I think the importance of his legacy in this area has two aspects: first, that identity should always be thought of as plural to enable recognition of its multifaceted qualities; second, that though requiring recognition—and recognition and analysis as complex, shifting, historical psychic formations—identity is not the foundation on which a productive politics can be sustained. To use the biblical language that is an under-recognised source of some of Stuart's rhetoric, identity is sandy ground on which to build.

Instead of discussing the analytic triangle of the gender, race and class of this panel's title, I want to consider another sort of identity, one that Stuart Hall was brilliant at analysing: the identities of power. Stuart was much occupied with analysis of the media in the late 1960s and 1970s, and he was creative and subtle in the way he approached the question of what it was necessary to know about to understand the role of the media in contemporary culture. I think that his legacy here is in danger of being only partially remembered. I want to draw attention to his sensitivity to the modalities and processes of power, the ceaseless labour of the production of identities of power, of an us, or a we, with a world view that is so obvious that it can be taken for granted.

Here, I will take as my text a short article Stuart Hall wrote in 1970 about radio in Britain, eloquently titled 'A World at One with Itself', a title to which I will return. For those of you unfamiliar with the rituals of British radio, this is a reference to the BBC's flagship lunchtime radio news programme, which is still broadcast daily, 'The World at One'. Stuart's article, which was published in *New Society*, reflected on the potential development of radio news at a point of significant expansion.[2]

This short piece is characteristic in various ways. It is historically situated, and its first move is deconstructive, to dissent from 'the notion that news somehow discovers itself' and argue instead that news is a product—that it is made, 'a human construction.' This is a significant challenge to the pervasive contemporary ideology of the naturalness and obviousness of the newsworthy. Stuart then goes on to explore the interrelation of the categories of 'violence' and 'law and order' in recent news and to consider the difference between the address of British newspapers and radio. He sees a less class-bound potential in radio at that point (i.e., 1970). What Hall wants is broadcasting and a definition of news that combine 'both the foreground event and the background context' (1056), as opposed to what he sees as characteristic, which is 'actuality without context' (1057), and the construction of an unintelligible world 'out there' which is full of meaningless and violent acts.

My point is not actually to summarise Stuart's argument about radio news; it is to point out that in this argument, in its very title, there is an acute consciousness of the ceaseless labour of the production and reproduction of power. It is the double movement in his thought that is so characteristic. Current news values produce an incomprehensible, violent, out there—but equally significant, this threatening 'out there', produces and confirms an 'in here'— at one with itself.

The enormous influence of what is now known as the 'Encoding/ Decoding' paper to audience studies has led, paradoxically, to a retrospective rewriting of Hall's media research as if it concentrated on the circuit of meaning production itself, without interest in the particular meanings in play.[3] There is a danger of his media writings being reduced to abstract theorisation of the role of the media. However, when you return to his writings on the media from this period, and particularly the shorter, more journalistic pieces such as this, they bristle with contemporary reference and evoke vividly the historical period of the writing. In the piece I have been discussing, for example, there is an insistence on the importance of colour/caste in the West Indies to understanding recent riots in Trinidad. The hierarchies of West Indian colour and caste is a matter to which he will return in later writings, particularly in his own understanding of the formation of his own identity as a Jamaican. Here, though, it functions to contextualise and give explanatory texture to events which have hitherto been characterised as inexplicable.

'A World at One with Itself' provides an exemplary case of the method Stuart Hall used across such varied topics, bringing extensive knowledge across a range of fields to better illuminate a specific case and thus reveal the complex determination of seemingly insignificant events or objects or texts—to see the world in a grain of sand. This method is exemplified in the elegance of his title—with which I'd like to finish. 'A World at One with Itself' is a title that summarises Stuart's argument and characterises an identity from which he dissented for the whole of his life.

Notes

This short essay was originally presented at the Goldsmiths' conference 'Stuart Hall: Conversations, Projects + Legacies', November 28, 2014.
1. Charlotte Brunsdon, 'A Thief in the Night: Stories of Feminism in the 1970s at CCCS', in *Stuart Hall: Critical Dialogues in Cultural Studies*, ed. David Morley and Kuan-Hsing (London: Routledge, 1996), 276–286; Charlotte Brunsdon, *The Feminist, the Housewife and the Soap Opera* (Oxford: Clarendon Press, 2000), 5–10; Charlotte Brunsdon, 'On Being Made History', *Cultural Studies* 29, no. 1 (2015), 88–99.
2. Stuart Hall, 'A World at One with Itself', *New Society*, no. 403 (1970), 1056–1058.
3. Stuart Hall, 'Encoding and Decoding in the Television Discourse', CCCS Stencilled Paper 7, University of Birmingham, 1973.

14 *The Uses of Stuart Hall*

Caspar Melville

I hope you'll forgive me if I speak autobiographically. Stuart was always quite reluctant to speak about himself, but when he did it really mattered. I was always struck by what he said in his reflection on the theoretical legacies of cultural studies: 'Autobiography is usually thought of as seizing the authority of authenticity. But in order not to be authoritative, I've got to speak autobiographically.'[1]

He was talking here as the father of cultural studies, a role he did not much relish, whereas I speak as a child of cultural studies; there is hardly any danger of anyone thinking I speak authoritatively for the discipline. Nevertheless, in the spirit of Stuart's intellectual modesty, I'll be speaking autobiographically about my own uses of Stuart Hall's work.

I'm finding this quite an emotional occasion, for many reasons. Thinking and writing about black music and cultural studies has framed my academic life and work and been very important to me; to refer back to Julian Henriques's talk about the techniques of black music such as rewind and remix, I feel like this event is a kind of remix of my academic life. Therefore, I'll try and tell you why, and I'll try to fit Stuart into this.

But first I just want to say how thrilled I am to be in the same room as Angela Davis, let alone to be able to speak at the same event. I had my political awakening through music, through my exposure to black American music especially, and I found out about Black Panther politics and Angela Davis through Archie Shepp and Gil Scott-Heron and Nina Simone and Public Enemy; that was my political education. My interest in cultural politics isn't only an interest in the politics *of* culture, but it exists because I've learnt what I know about politics *through* culture. Of course, we all live politics through culture, as Stuart taught us.

Just before this panel, I saw a good friend of mine, Anamik Saha, who was my student in a popular music course I taught when I was a PhD student here at Goldsmiths. He introduced me to a friend by saying, 'I wouldn't be here if it wasn't for Caspar,' which I was very touched by—and I said to him, 'Well, I wouldn't be here if it wasn't for Paul Gilroy,' I came to Goldsmiths searching for Paul Gilroy, his books taught me you can write intelligently about black music and put it into critical dialogue with Western philosophy—Burning Spear cut and mixed with Hegel, Rakim cross-faded into Adorno. Of course Paul Gilroy wouldn't have been here at Goldsmiths if it hadn't been for Stuart—and the CCCS, where he got his start. Thus, we're part of this amazing loop, the reverberations of cultural studies all around us, echoing in our ears.

Here's another feedback loop: All the professors sitting on the first panel of this conference—James Curran, David Morley, Angela McRobbie, Bill Schwarz—were all my teachers when I was earning my MA here in media and communications back in the late 1990s. It was from these professors that I learned about the media's 'power without responsibility'; the ideological discourses embedded in media texts; the power of identity; the possibilities of an active audience; Enoch Powell's Rivers of Blood speech; and the racial politics of the 1960s and 1970s. I think there was a Stuart Hall text used in every one of these courses; such is the breadth of his work. I now realise that before today I'd never actually seen this group of intellectuals sitting together at the same table, which is another kind of testament to Stuart's ability to bring people and ideas together!

So, I'm back in a weird place, the crucible of my academic career—but being back is also about experiencing the difference, because of course this building in which we are sitting didn't exist then. Goldsmiths was rather more run down and musty in my day, a bit faded and post-imperial. I first saw Stuart speak in that old building; he was giving a guest lecture in a lecture room called, if I remember right, the Small Hall. Now, here we are in the splendid modern theatre that is being officially dedicated today—the Professor Stuart Hall Building. From Small Hall to Big Hall.

When I first saw Stuart lecture, I realised that I already knew him from the telly. I used to stay up watching late-night BBC Two, and sometimes they had these Open University programmes on with eccentric scientists and sociologists in bad jumpers, the kind of thing endlessly satirised on TV ever since. But this programme was different. Stuart Hall was out in the English countryside somewhere, standing on the ramparts of a stately home with a local historian. He was looking around and saying: 'Isn't this beautiful? The perfect image of English nature?' He turned to the historian, pointed down the hill and said: 'Look at that view, the trees, stretching down into the distance to the sea, the epitome of timeless natural beauty and order.' The historian turned to him and said: 'Well, actually, it's not that timeless or natural.' When this grand house was built, he said, there had been a town down the hill, obscuring the view to the sea, so the owners of the house arranged a better view: They had the town moved. At that moment, Stuart Hall denaturalised nature for me. It blew my mind. It opened everything up. If nature wasn't natural, then . . . well, the idea blew my mind. It seems typical of Stuart that he could make such a profound point so clearly and do it on TV, too.

This brings me to another kind of loop. To get to the Stuart Hall building, you have to pass through the Richard Hoggart Building. Therefore, my last theme is a nod to Hoggart's classic, cantankerous book, *The Uses of Literacy*,[2] which kick-started cultural studies. Here, I want to talk about the uses of *Stuart Hall*. I'll talk about how I have used him academically in a moment, but first I want to talk journalistically. I only came back to academia in 2013; for ten years before that, I was a journalist. For seven of those years, I edited a magazine, a slightly eccentric journal of humanism, secularism and rationalism called *New Humanist*. I was excited to be a magazine editor, and I loved the job, but it was a rather uncomfortable spot to be in because I had been a graduate student at Goldsmiths during the high Foucaultian days, with its strong strain of anti-humanism; in the academia of the late 1990s, *humanism* was a very dirty word indeed.

Yet here I was, suddenly, a professional humanist. What could I do about this? I didn't want to repudiate Foucault or critical theory or cultural studies, as many humanists and rationalists have done; it was once standard for self-styled rationalists to dismiss cultural studies as a Mickey Mouse subject and French theorists as, in the words of Jonathan Miller, 'simply salon posturing dandies.'[3] This was a political moment, a crisis around Islamic terrorism and 'new atheism', defined by the twin poles of 9/11 and Richard Dawkins's trenchant anti-religion book, *The God Delusion*.[4] I felt a bit caught between the devil and the deep blue sea. I wanted to find a way to negotiate between these two antagonistic positions—and I thought of Stuart, who was the master of negotiating contradiction.

At the time, our main interviewer was the sociologist and broadcaster Laurie Taylor, who usually interviewed people like Dawkins, Steven Pinker, Mary Warnock, Christopher Hitchens: the great and the good of the white liberal secular establishment. I commissioned Laurie to interview Stuart.[5] It was while he was quite ill, but Stuart was his usual charming self, inviting Laurie into his house and giving a fascinating interview about politics and culture and race, during which Laurie got him to admit that he was himself a child of the Enlightenment. I thought, if Stuart can say he's a child of the Enlightenment and that reason matters, then it was OK for me too. Afterwards, Stuart lent his name to support the magazine, the first Afro-Caribbean honorary associate of the Rationalist Association (which published *New Humanist*) in more than a hundred years.

A couple of years later, I sent Laurie back to interview Stuart,[6] because he always had so much more to say. He's the only person that that we interviewed twice during my tenure. I was especially proud that I had been able to lever into the debate a notion of 'critical humanism' that Stuart proposed and embodied. In that sense, I found him, his example and his generosity incredibly useful in trying to change a particular cultural formation, which is still reverberating; my replacement as *New Humanist* editor, Daniel Trilling, is still fighting the battle to ensure that criticism of religion and the celebration of reason doesn't tip over into racism and smug xenophobia—and Dawkins really doesn't like him, which is a good sign.

Now, to discuss the academic uses of Stuart Hall. I now teach at SOAS. (We call it SOAS, by the way—not the School of Oriental and African Studies—because we're very embarrassed by the word *oriental*. It's another slightly uncomfortable place to be, but that's okay; Stuart encourages us to live with that kind of embarrassment and to recognise that this sort of thing is part of the larger history of (post)colonial institutions, a small example of the larger contradictions of colonialism and capitalism.)

The MA course I teach is called Global Creative and Cultural Industries, and it's all potentially very whiz-bang and groovy, all about new digital media and entrepreneurs and creativity, hot topics like that. I thought, what can I do with Stuart Hall and with cultural studies in a course like this one? What cultural studies texts can I set that can inject some much-needed critical thinking into a course for students starry-eyed about start-ups and social media and careers at Google?

A couple of essays proved invaluable, and both are widely anthologised. The first is 'New Ethnicities'[7] (1988), in which Stuart talks about the 'end of innocence' in terms of how we conceptualise and think about identity. The challenge this poses to those who want to think through identity, and to politics based on innocent notions of identity, helps inoculate students against the lure of simplistic identity politics. The other is the brilliant 'Notes on Deconstructing the Popular'[8] in which Stuart makes the simple but profound point that popular culture is nether simply the voice of the people nor that which is imposed from above by the cultural industries, but a terrain of struggle between these tendencies and forces—and the stake in that struggle, too. He also says a wonderful thing that I think is one of the keys to Stuart's thinking and personality: He says popular culture is a struggle, and it's therefore deeply political, and if it weren't, he frankly wouldn't give a damn about it. I think that's kind of true because, as he revealed on Desert Island Disks,[9] in his taste he was really a high modernist. He acknowledges the cultural power of reggae and hip-hop, but really he preferred Miles Davis. It's a lovely irony that the father of the serious study of popular culture is no populist.

When Stuart died, I wrote an article in his honour that was published in *New Humanist.* I'm just going to read the final paragraph, which expresses what I think about how relevant Stuart and his work remains:

> For some people the idea of culture is a site of struggle probably seems anachronistic, carrying as it does such a strong whiff of the culture wars of the 1970s, all patchouli and crisis and sit-ins and futile calls for revolution. These people can now turn to wannabe intellectual brands like 'Creative Industries' that have ditched Cultural Studies' Marxism and its wariness of collaboration with policy makers and corporations, in favour of a cheery view of the progressive potential of new technologies and entrepreneurialism. But for those who are alive to the growing inequalities and inequities of the global economy, Hall's model of culture as a site of struggle makes more sense than ever. And the stakes in this struggle, as Hall reminds us time and again, couldn't be higher; nothing less than the conditions of possibility for human freedom.[10]

Notes

1. Stuart Hall, 'Cultural Studies and its Theoretical Legacies', in *Cultural Studies*, ed. Lawrence Grossberg, Cary Nelson and Paula Treichler (New York: Routledge, 1992), 277.
2. Richard Hoggart, *The Uses of Literacy* (London: Penguin, [1957] 2009).
3. Jonathan Miller, quoted in Laurie Taylor, 'Walking in the Dark: Laurie Taylor Interviews Jonathan Miller', *New Humanist* (Spring 2002), https://newhumanist.org.uk/articles/554/walking-in-the-dark-laurie-taylor-interviews-jonathan-miller.
4. Richard Dawkins, *The God Delusion* (London: Black Swan, 2007).
5. Laurie Taylor, 'Culture's Revenge: Laurie Taylor Interviews Stuart Hall', *New Humanist* (September/October, 2006), https://newhumanist.org.uk/articles/960/cultures-revenge-laurie-taylor-interviews-stuart-hall.
6. Laurie Taylor, 'Laurie Taylor Interviews Stuart Hall: Race, Relativism and Revolution', *New Humanist* (May/June 2011), https://newhumanist.org.uk/articles/2551/stuart-hall.
7. Stuart Hall, 'New Ethnicities', in *Stuart Hall: Critical Dialogues in Cultural Studies*, ed. David Morley and Kuan-Hsing Chen (New York: Routledge, 1996), 441–449.
8. Stuart Hall, 'Notes on Deconstructing the Popular', in *Cultural Theory and Popular Culture*, ed. John Storey (London: Pearson/Prentice Hall, 1998), 442–453.
9. Stuart Hall, 'Desert Island Disks', *BBC Radio 4* (February 18, 2000), http://www.bbc.co.uk/programmes/p0094b6r.
10. Caspar Melville, 'The Politics of Everyday Life', *New Humanist* (September 2014), https://newhumanist.org.uk/articles/4734/the-politics-of-everyday-life.

Right: (image copyright Janet Mendelsohn)

Centre for Contemporary
Cultural Studies
Annual Report: 1968-69

University of Birmingham
October 1969

Part IV
Policy, Practice and Creativity

Policy, Practice and Creativity

In the later part of his life, Stuart Hall was very involved in the field of creative practice in film and photography; this section explores such issues, most particularly in relation to questions of race and ethnicity, in the period of his involvement with Autograph ABP (Association of Black Photographers), and later with INIVA and the development of Rivington Place as a locus for innovative artistic practice and exhibition. Hall was chair of both these organizations until 2008, and he helped found Autograph ABP in 1988 and INIVA in 1994. As is described in this section, Hall's ideas inspired the work of these organizations, and through their exhibitions, events and publications they provided a unique space for conversation and discussion between succeeding generations of artists, photographers, creative practitioners and activists.

In chapter 15, Avtar Brah introduces some of the key concepts that Hall and others deployed for intervention in this area of policy and creative practice. Brah describes her encounter with Hall as a person and director of CCCS in the 1970s. For Brah, Hall's manner and intellect embodied both the 1970s feminist slogan 'the personal is political' and the intellectual trajectory that she was to follow throughout her work. Most important for Brah is the way in which Hall placed 'questions of race, ethnicity and identity at the heart of social and cultural analysis', characterising these not in terms of race as such, but rather racialization and, in the 1980s, diaspora.

With the example of the seminal collective work *Policing the Crisis: Mugging, the State and Law and Order*, Brah unpacks how Hall did this in terms of his non-reductive approach and the way in which the social formation was seen as 'relational and historically specific' as theorised through 'contextualism' or 'conjuncturalism'. Brah also admires Hall for his pragmatic and strategic approach in his critique of what he called the 'authoritarian populism' of Thatcherism. She goes on to outline the intellectual and political traditions from which Hall drew to develop the distinctive approach of cultural studies—notably, Antonio Gramsci's concept of hegemony and, in the 1980s, the postmodernist ideas of 'multiplacedness, of multiplicity and hybridity', which, for Brah, prefigured the current discourse of intersectionality.

In chapter 16, Lola Young describes the various ways in which Hall translated the theoretical sophistication of thinking on culture into a language in which it could have practical application across initiatives and interventions in the field of public policy in the arts. This is certainly one of the characteristics of his role and a contribution for which he was widely admired. It is also entirely indicative of what set Hall apart from most of his academic contemporaries and allowed him to fulfil the role—more commonplace in the United States than the United Kingdom—of a public intellectual. Young gives several examples of the way Hall adopted such as position, such as in relation to the Greater London Council (GLC) until it was abolished by Thatcher in 1984, a time when the idea of a black arts movement was at the cutting edge of the debates between creative practitioners and policy makers. Hall's contribution was never to simplify—in fact, the opposite, to recognise 'the fluidity of cultural identity and identification' in a non-essentialist manner.

The debates moved on to the issues of the archive in the 1980s; Young describes how it was 'difficult to think about such matters and the long tail of damaging historical stereotypes without reference to Stuart Hall's work in and on the heritage sector' and how Hall's engagement with history and heritage was 'a source of renewed energy for many of us', not least for those charged with 'the burden of representation'. Young gives several examples of Hall's contribution to the understanding of the history of the present, not by simplifying it, to redress what others might have seen as historical imbalances, but rather, identifying its complex and contradictory nature. The celebrations of the fiftieth anniversary of the arrival of the Windrush occurring at the same time as the official inquiry into the death of Stephen Lawrence would be an example of this. Young also points to Hall's many keynotes and his ongoing support for the Black and Asian Studies Association (BASA), the Black Cultural Archives (BCA), New Beacon Books, the George Padmore Institute, the African and Asian Visual Arts Archive (AAVAA) and, of course, INIVA.

In chapter 17, John Akomfrah speaks as a filmmaker and an artist who spent a period of five years researching and talking to people about Hall. Akomfrah transformed these researches into two major works, *The Stuart Hall Project* (2013) film and *The Unfinished Conversation* (2013) three-screen installation (that was installed in Goldsmiths for the conference). Akomfrah describes his own predicament as a black youth in Britain in the 1970s not recognizing himself in his 'doppelgänger' media image as an educationally subnormal mugger bent on the destruction of Little England. This sent him searching through Fanon, Malcolm and others until he came across Hall talking about ideology in an Open University programme. For Akomfrah, Hall's thinking provided a lifeline.

Akomfrah describes some of the surprises in his research process that concerned how early on in Hall's career the ideas for which he became known were already present in embryo, how the 'iceberg of "race" was always floating in the sea of Cultural Studies'. One was a 1964 radio programme that Hall presented, *Generation of Strangers*, about migrant children in the Midlands. For Akomfrah, the eclectic cluster of issues covered in the programme prefigured many of the theoretical issues that Hall was at that time already formulating—eventually emerging as *Policing the Crisis* in 1978—in his work at what was to become the CCCS in Birmingham. The generation discussed in this programme, Akomfrah realised much later, was the one to which the filmmaker himself belonged. This makes one of the points about the effects of Hall's work: It enables us to recognise ourselves, because he is actually talking about us. Another surprise for Akomfrah in his research process came from reading Hall's articles and editorials in *Universities and Left Review*, which he edited in the early 1960s. Here, Akomfrah was struck by his 'impeccable sense of vigilance' in relation to how these same issues of race, film and patterns of consumption also arose as rallying cries in the debates of the day.

When editing his first film, *Handsworth Songs*, in 1986, Akomfrah goes on to describe how he was emboldened to offer Hall an invitation to discuss the material with him on the inspiration of a speech Hall had given at The Black Experience at London's Commonwealth Institute several years earlier. 'We sat with him, in a black film space that we went out and got because he, amongst others, said it was "ours".' As is often remarked, one of the distinctive characteristics of Hall's interventions, both in private and in public, was to create precisely such spaces. Travelling with Hall over the years, the filmmaker also recognised the deeply personal nature of this journey. Hall was a 'protean presence' whose 'shape-shifting facility' attracted many different people in so many ways. However, there was one consistent source of attraction, maybe even above and beyond what Hall actually said. As Akomfrah puts it: 'Hall had the most beautiful smile I have ever seen'. (Angela Davis also remarks on this smile in chapter 23.) Akomfrah saw this smile at the Commonwealth Institute in 1982. Perhaps more surprisingly, he also found it in the television archive of a 1968 studio discussion of Enoch Powell's Rivers of Blood speech; in the discussion, Hall countered an audience member's remarks about black immigrants as uninvited guests being here by saying 'because you were there'—and then gave the smile. 'It was a beguiling and empathic smile, a smile that told you it understood things beyond the confines of the moment of its appearance.' It was this that for Akomfrah and many others helped to transform a mood of disaffection into one with the energy to stay, mount critiques and conduct the necessary fight.

In chapter 18, Mark Sealy describes how Hall provided the 'curatorial direction' for Autograph ABP, right from the initial discussions at the Photographers Gallery in 1988, to build 'a counter narrative around the black subject within photography'. Sealy charts some of the key essays through which Hall developed these arguments through the 1990s, starting with 'Black Narcissus' in the Autograph ABP newsletter of 1991. In his essay 'Reconstruction Work', Hall challenged the popular memory of West Indian emigrants, for instance. This essay was published in *Ten 8*, undoubtedly the key journal in this section, in 1992. Hall argued that the task of black photographers was to articulate 'how a people who have been objectified throughout history can enter their own subjectivity through making images and, literally, put themselves in the frame'. Identity, in short, is only ever expressed in negotiation with its representations.

Hall's work with Autograph ABP continued through the 1990s, both locally and internationally. Hall wrote the introduction to the work of the long-established Birmingham-based photographer

Vanley Burke.[1] According to Sealy, Hall recognised photographic practice as being made 'out of a desire, identification and love of community' that for Burke had begun in the mid-1960s. The publication by the Phaidon Press of *Different* in 1991, edited by Hall and Sealy and with Hall's framing introductory essay, presented the plurality and the plenitude of black experiences in an international arena. This marked the high point of a journey that Hall, Autograph ABP and black photography has made over a little more than two decades.

Note

1. Stuart Hall, 'Vanley Burke and the "Desire for Blackness"', in *Vanley Burke: A Retrospective,* ed. Vanley Burke and Mark Sealy (London: Lawrence & Wishart, 1993), 12–15.

Reflecting and Remembering the Work of Stuart Hall

15

Avtar Brah

I have often thought about the first time I met Stuart Hall. As students embarking on our PhDs at Bristol University in the late 1970s, three of us decided that we would visit Stuart Hall in Birmingham, where he was director of the Centre for Contemporary Cultural Studies (CCCS). Totally in awe of him, and intimidated by the prospect of meeting such a renowned figure, we were not sure when—or, indeed, whether—we would succeed in getting an appointment with him. Of course, we needn't have worried; despite his immensely busy schedule, Hall made time for an early appointment with us. Our visit to the CCCS was memorable not only because of the excitement generated by holding a conversation with Hall, but also because of the warmth with which he greeted us and the encouragement he gave to our fledgling ideas. He asked us questions and listened to us carefully, as if we were some well-established scholars. Few intellectuals of his stature are that generous with their time and willing to share ideas and insight.

Hall genuinely respected and valued all individuals equally for their uniqueness, even when he might have disagreed with them intellectually or politically. This respect for the individual resonated well with the feminist slogan of the 1970s: 'Personal is political.' It is important to bear in mind that the individual—in whom Hall evinced such interest—was not conceived as an isolated entity but rather understood as a subject constituted within the economic, political, cultural and psychosocial contexts of the life and times of the person. He was interested in social relations of the everyday, of how ordinary lives are lived. It is perhaps this outlook of Stuart Hall that focused his analytical and political optic on the subaltern, the marginalised, the Othered. It is why respect for the person was so central to his vision of a better world. Contrary to the stereotypical image of an 'ivory tower' academic, Hall was first and foremost committed to academic collaboration and conversation. Indeed, many of the works published under his directorship of the CCCS at Birmingham University were undertaken collaboratively. Such collaborative approaches are somewhat rare in the neoliberal universities of today.

The controversies surrounding the feminist construct 'personal is political' were hugely productive and posed novel questions about the subject, subjectivity, identity and politics. Hall has contributed massively to theorising and analysing all these concepts. As is well known, feminist attempts at working through entanglements of the personal with the political resulted in changing the very basis of the modernist binary between the private and public spheres of life. Feminism laid bare the constructed nature of this seemingly natural binary and at the same time, foregrounded the diverse ways in which the various axes of power—gender, class, race, sexuality and so on—are implicated in differentiating culture and society. This perspective that drew attention to the articulations of different forms of inequality came later to be known as *intersectionality*. Intersectionality has not been a stranger to Hall's work, although he never used the term. During the 1970s, when class was seen in social sciences as the primary axis of power to address, Hall argued for the importance of race, ethnicity and age alongside class.

Hall is known as one of the leading figures in British—indeed, international—intellectual life. Stuart Hall's towering intellect and his powerful political imagination produced some of the most incisive analysis of the workings of postcolonial Britain and the impact of globalisation on culture and politics. What seemed to matter a great deal to him was that everything in a social formation was relational and historically specific, so it had to be analysed accordingly. He was a social theorist of *contextualism* or *conjuncturalism*—how, for instance, different dimensions of power, multiple forces, social solidarities as well as conflicts—all the contradictions—articulate and are played out in the struggles for social hegemony.

Although always critical of economic determinism, he emphasized the importance of understanding the centrality of economy to global capitalist social relations that shape our lives. He was relentlessly non-reductive in his approach. This is what made his particular type of cultural studies, a field in the development of which he was a central figure, stand out from others. The world was not only complicated, but it was changing all the time, and this change was contingent. No single theory or subject discipline or analytical perspective was up to the task of examining and studying, for all time, all relational and contingent facets of a society. A theory relevant for understanding one set of circumstances may not always be suitable for another when the conjuncture has changed.

Although a theoretician of note who did a great deal of theoretical work, Hall approached theory pragmatically, never making a fetish of it. What seemed important to him was the extent to which a specific theory could provide appropriate tools for analysing a specific problematic at hand. The problematic was critical: to be analysed not just for the sake of an intellectual exercise, but to understand it so as to change the world for a better future. In other words, he was not enamoured of a variety of 'high theory' that evacuated politics. Because his use of theory was strategic, depending upon what issues and problems he was tackling, he was, to my mind, usefully and judicially eclectic in the use of theoretical concepts—drawing from Marxist thought, especially the work of Althusser and Gramsci, as much as from poststructuralism, and drawing upon the conceptual repertoire of intellectuals such as Foucault, Derrida and Judith Butler. However, he was always deeply concerned about making his work accessible to as wide a range of people as was possible without compromising on complexity. He was a renowned theoretician who did not resort to obtuse and unnecessarily esoteric language. His exposition was one of the most lucid that one comes across. He was a brilliant teacher, galvanizing his students with incisive analysis mixed with a good dose of wit and humour. It therefore is not surprising that his work was as avidly read by teachers as much as by their students.

Stuart Hall was an astute analyst of social class. His early work on class was written during the late 1950s and the 1960s, and it charted changes in class identities. This was followed in 1978 by the monumental study *Policing the Crisis*, co-written with four writers who were then students at the CCCS and who later became eminent in their own right.[1] This tome is a conjunctural analysis par excellence, and it addressed what the authors termed 'the crisis of the social order' of pre-Thatcherite years.

In a lecture televised on BBC in 1978, Hall identified the salient features of this crisis.[2] It was, he argued, a crisis that was simultaneously economic, political and ideological, and one that was represented through moral panics about race, youth and class. Addressing the ideological formation often known as Powellism—with its dominant discourse consisting of the infamous Rivers of Blood speech and Enoch Powell's contention that minority ethnic groups could be 'in' Britain but could never become 'of' Britain—Hall's lecture anticipates the imminent emergence of *Thatcherism*—a term he is said to have coined for the phenomenon he analysed in detail.[3] Thatcherism, according to his analysis, emerges out of the social contradictions and crisis of the previous two decades. Hall understood Thatcherism as a singularly significant and successful economic, political and ideological project, promoting what he called 'authoritarian populism' and accompanied by a massive political swing to the right. This project was underpinned by discourses of mugging, law and order, social discipline, permissive society and social anarchy. It conjured images of racial dilution of national character through the presence of people of colour.

On the economic front, Thatcherism was characterised by monetarism, deregulation, privatisation of key national industries and a commitment to flexible labour markets. It mounted an onslaught on trade unions and argued for a minimalist local and national state. This formed a political agenda for free markets, cuts in state funding and cuts in taxes. It spawned a variety of nationalism that harked back to imperial glories and spoke of contemporary social threats to Britishness from 'enemies within'. As Hall pointed out, Thatcherism deployed the discourses of 'nation' and 'people' against 'class' and 'unions' to give voice to its anti-statism and anti-collectivism. Hall says that although Powell's political career might have floundered early, his ideas, views and perspectives came to exercise a long-term influence over British society and could be said to have been transmuted into a social terrain upon which Thatcherism came to flourish. Thatcherism, in turn, came to exercise a very significant impact on the Blair period. Indeed, it is arguable that the current period is deeply marked by these preceding social formations.

Although I admire all aspects of Hall's work, I am particularly attracted by the way in which he places questions of race, ethnicity and identity at the heart of social and cultural analysis. What is important is that he does not regard racism as a stand-alone, single dimension separate from others; instead, he examines its relation to other structures and social forces. Indeed, he has said that his interest lies less in race, per se, and more in the processes of racialization. How, why and in what form do processes of racialization articulate with other features, such as class or gender, in a particular historical context?

In the late 1970s and 1980s, Hall's work on issues of racism drew upon Marxist conceptual repertoire, especially the frameworks of Gramsci. In the article 'The Relevance of Gramsci for the Study of Race and Ethnicity', Hall draws attention away from thinking about racism as if it is always the same, though it may certainly have certain common features over a period.[4] He argues that it is important to think of *racisms* in the plural. Different racisms have different histories, take variable shapes and forms, and change over time. Hall strongly favours a non-reductive approach to the study of racism and class, eschewing both those views that privilege class as the only critical feature of society and those that emphasize the centrality of racism and ethnicity at the expense of class structuration.

The 'class subject' is heterogeneous; it is simultaneously racialized, gendered and sexualised. It is intersectionally produced. There is no one-to-one correspondence, Hall emphasizes, between economic, political and ideological levels; they all have their specific effectivity, and they articulate in complex ways. Race as a discourse and racism as an economic and political practice thus operate in multifarious ways. Key Gramscian concepts such as common-sense and hegemony, Hall writes, can extend conceptual horizons in the analysis of race and racism. Racialised discourses play a formative role in constructing the common-sense of social groups and in the processes of securing consent for hegemonic projects. The relationship between state and civil society in Gramsci is complex, and the relations between the state and different dimensions of civil society, such as education, family and cultural organizations, can be analysed in and through the workings of race.

Throughout the 1970s and up until about 1986, the Marxist influence on Hall's writings on race and ethnicity remained marked. However, the 1980s also saw a turn towards poststructuralist paradigms. Hall's work on diaspora and what he termed *new ethnicities* was path-breaking, critiquing essentialism without dismissing out of court all forms of what detractors often call *identity politics*. As I have suggested elsewhere, the argument in this article would seem to articulate three features: analysis of intergenerational change, shifts in how to conceptualise cultural politics, and a move in theoretical perspective from structural/materialist to poststructuralist.[5] The valorisation of the concept of ethnicity posed serious challenges to the biological concept of racism as an inherent and immutable property of social groups, and the use of the concept of diaspora was a critique of the racialised discourse of 'immigrants' and of an over-emphasis on the nation state.

Diaspora for Hall is a global phenomenon marked by the histories of slavery, colonialism, imperialism and holocausts. In a late modern or postmodern context, diasporic experience emerges as one of multiplacedness, of multiplicity and hybridity. In 'New Ethnicities', Hall espoused the politics of resistance mounted by the post-war black migrants to Britain but argues that though common historical experiences do make for the *specificity* of experience, they did not mean that there was an *essentialist Black subject*.[6] Prefiguring intersectionality discourse, Hall contended that race and racism always appear 'historically in articulation, in a formation, with other categories and divisions' of class, gender and ethnicity and sexuality. In this essay, culture comes to assume a highly significant affectivity in and of itself. Culture is seen to play a constitutive role rather than merely a reflexive role.

This intellectual shift in thinking led Hall to produce some extremely complex, innovative and nuanced work on the concept of identity. How do we see the relationship between his Marxist and poststructuralist phases? Does one displace or replace the other? I would suggest that it is the former; that is, the later thinking displaces but does not replace the importance of neo-Marxist (as opposed to orthodox Marxist) insights in Hall's work. The two are distinct but not unrelated phases. Indeed, his later work should be *read under erasure*—as, perhaps, he would say.

At a festschrift held for me in 2009, Stuart Hall spoke of how our work was marked by the 'moment of the diasporic' and the 'moment of the problematic of the subject'.[7] Today, there is the ascendancy of the 'affective turn' that raises questions about 'the subject'. Jasbir Puar, for instance, has indicated that 'affect entails not only a dissolution of the subject, but more significantly, a dissolution of the stable contours of the organic body, as forces of energy are transmitted, shared, circulated'.[8] Such critiques of perhaps an undue emphasis on the subject in previous studies are suggestive, although the subject was never purely a sign for the organic body; it centrally entailed the psychic dimension. Of course, affect is critical to the psychic dimensions of existence, and the 'nonhuman'—both organic and inorganic—remains crucially important. The 'affective turn' comprises a complex conceptual repertoire. Yet I would argue that the subject does not disappear, though it may need rethinking within and through the affective turn and post-humanism. It may need to be displaced, but not replaced.

Stuart Hall's legacy is not only intellectual but equally political. He was generous to a fault. His intellectual and political project was dedicated to equality and justice. That is the great legacy of his work and life.

Notes

1. Stuart Hall et al., *Policing the Crisis: Mugging, the State, and Law and Order* (London: Macmillan, 1978).
2. Stuart Hall, 'Racism and Reaction', in *Five Views of Multi-racial Britain* (London: CRE with BBC Television, 1978).
3. Stuart Hall, 'The Great Moving Right Show', *Marxism Today* (January 1979).
4. Stuart Hall, 'Gramsci's Relevance for the Study of Race and Ethnicity', in *Stuart Hall: Critical Dialogues in Cultural Studies*, ed. David Morley and Kuan-Hsing Chen (New York: Routledge, 1996), 411–440.
5. Leslie Roman and Annette Henry, 'Diasporic Reasoning, Affect, Memory and Cultural Politics: An Interview with Avtar Brah', *Discourse: Studies in the Cultural Politics of Education* 2, no. 36 (2015): 243–263.
6. Stuart Hall, 'New Ethnicities', in *Stuart Hall: Critical Dialogues in Cultural Studies*, ed. David Morley and Kuan-Hsing Chen (New York: Routledge, 1996), 441–449.
7. Stuart Hall, 'Avtar Brah's Cartographies: Moment, Method, Meaning', *Feminist Review*, no. 100 (2012): 27–38.
8. Jasbir Kaur Puar, 'Coda: The Cost of Getting Better: Suicide, Sensation, Switchpoints', *GLQ: A Journal of Lesbian and Gay Studies* 1, no. 18 (2012): 154.

16 *Policy, Politics, Practice and Theory*

Lola Young

During the late 1980s and early 1990s, there was a moment when the adoption of the politics of race and culture in the academy represented a fresh, invigorating space for ideas and debates about identity and representation. Critiques, research and ethno-historical studies of black style, music, beauty, history and hairstyles became if not abundant, then at least visible in places where previously they had been excluded. Alongside the exploration of these themes, there was a keenness to explore and reveal what were seen as the inherent contradictions of the term *black British*. The often-heated public debates and ideological spats that took place during this period were my introduction to cultural studies and Stuart Hall.

While I was working in arts development in Harringey in the 1980s, the national political context was no less alarming than it is now. Contradictions and tensions were evident as Bernie Grant became the first black leader of a local authority in Europe even while the impact of the previous decade's rise of the far right made itself felt; newspapers carried made-up stories about 'the loony left'; civil disturbances took place in several major cities, as well as racist attacks and anti-racist demonstrations; and Margaret Thatcher abolished the elected Metropolitan and Greater London Authorities. Against this backdrop, it was particularly important that a black intellectual from Jamaica was recognised as one of the most astute and challenging analysts of contemporary political culture and the politics of culture of the time.

Stuart reached prominence at a time when to invoke 'the black experience' was to testify to the numerous ways in which communities were under physical and verbal attack from politicians, the police, the education system, the media and the extreme right.

Too many black people were living under siege-like conditions, and there were few paths open for cultural practitioners to express those experiences on their own terms. Yet where invocations of the (singular, authentic) black experience sometimes led to closed, quasi-essentialist positions, Stuart's engagement gave rise to an altogether more fluid, more inclusive, more *interesting* way of thinking through our predicament as diaspora peoples.

Although some of us enthusiastically engaged with the rapidly evolving body of cultural theory and creative practices that became bound up with a small but significant 'black arts movement', many others did not. I experienced on numerous occasions how difficult these concepts were for some cultural activists to discuss, let alone accept. What was perceived as the intellectual elitism located in and emanating from an academy dominated by Eurocentric cultural theory was seen as remote from everyday experiences of racism and could be profoundly alienating. Cultural theorists argued that the notion of a single 'black community' was inherently undermined by the fractures of ethnicity, sexuality, gender, social class, age and so on. If that were so, then what were the implications for community-based activism?

Having been an activist himself, Stuart acknowledged the importance of grass-roots struggles over history, representation and cultural ownership. However, his privileged access to the corridors of the academy and his mode of articulation marked him as different from many of the campaigners involved in setting up organisations that represented an alternative to official, 'mainstream' arts and cultural bodies.

Therefore, though lived experience, memory, positive images and authentic voices—often captured in oral history projects with community elders—were seen by community-based organisations as essential to fill the gaps created by racist versions of history, for those schooled in the labyrinthine abstractions of cultural theory, authenticity and lived experience were trumped by cultural hybridity. The picture wasn't simply about the binaries of black and white but about the fluidity of cultural identity and identification. Ethnic and racial certainties were flushed out by the fragility of conceptions of self and other. The difference between negative and positive imagery was spurious; what mattered was the struggle for the power/hegemony to represent self and other.

The 1980s/1990s phase of the history of black artists and arts in the United Kingdom was one during which Stuart made numerous decisive interventions, bringing his robust political and intellectual analyses to bear on the interplay between the state and its agencies' politics and policy-making on the one hand, and the cultural practices of black artists and their work on the other. However, for many of us with an interest in identity, history and heritage, policy and practice, it's difficult to think about such matters and the long tail of damaging historical stereotypes without reference to Stuart Hall's work in and on the heritage sector.

For decades, community-based movements struggled to assert the place of black people of African and Asian descent in British history. This was seen as an essential component of the fight against a racist society that was unable to recognize black people as having been productive, creative members of British society for centuries. Heritage institutions' executives and their boards of trustees, as well as funding/policy-making bodies, worked in discriminatory ways to deny black people's place in British heritage.

The movement for change in the heritage sector gathered momentum towards the end of the 1990s, thanks to those activists that sensed new opportunities due to a Labour government trumpeting access and inclusion and massive funding coming on stream via the various lotteries. Stuart's engagement with struggles over history and heritage was also a source of renewed energy for many of us. Thus, during the mid- to late 1990s, the ways in which the archives, museums and historic environment sector—Britain's heritage institutions—had contrived to disregard the history of colonialism, enslavement and indentured labour were subject to intensified scrutiny.

At the same time, more keenly than at any other moment, I felt that the 'burden of representation' had settled on our shoulders as cultural and academic practitioners with an interest in the largely ignored black and Asian presence in British history. As heritage sector organisations gradually began to grasp the arguments and evidence from, for example, the Black and Asian Studies Association (BASA), the Black Cultural Archives (BCA), Naseem Khan, Nima Poovaya Smith, Rachel Hasted, John La Rose and New Beacon Books, and many others, so demands for expertise and knowledge grew—often in the form of unpaid 'advisors' to boards of trustees or local authorities.

The individuals and organisations mentioned previously worked diligently for decades to press the 'mainstream' of the UK heritage sector to come to terms with its past, whether that be the entangled histories of enslavement and art collections and

182 the English country house or ethnographic collections and their crude primitivism. With this body of knowledge and experience at hand, there was no excuse for the 'historical amnesia' identified by Stuart as a key component of the professional baggage of those cultural institutions that re-present the past for national and local consumption.

Stuart's interventions in this sector were so compelling because he was brilliant at making connections between what appeared to be abstract ideas developed in an aloof, exclusive academy that too often looked down upon mere policymakers. Linking the intellectual work of those institutions to cultural policy—not only discussing it, but also actually delivering that work and bearing the responsibilities and the consequences of doing so—was a large part of what differentiated Stuart from so many other cultural theorists. In his foreword to an edition of *Soundings* commemorating fifty years since the landing of the *Empire Windrush*, Stuart Hall identified the root of the problem of our place in British history—and thus the nation's take on heritage: 'Asian and African communities [who were] in different ways central actors in the drama [of the official *Windrush* narrative] which has unfolded but who, in the event, tended to be somewhat de-centred.'[1] The 'decentring' came about because the authority and power to represent and to define was located outside of those communities, even—or perhaps especially—in the telling and retelling of the story of the *Windrush* as a narrative exemplifying British open-mindedness and tolerance towards 'strangers'.

There is the hint of a methodology here for approaching the past, contained in Stuart's comment in the same essay. It entails connecting 'the event irrevocably to the present, to our current situation: writing it as a "history of the present", not a nostalgic revisiting of the past'.[2] It is a mode of working that avoids being overwhelmed by an urgent desire to redress previous historical imbalances or to gloss over problematical—embarrassing/divisive—subjects, exposing tensions and contradictions within and between official accounts of the past.

As an example of the always-present contradictions that may arise, while the various celebratory *Windrush* events were taking place, 'the Official Inquiry into the death of Stephen Lawrence was being convened . . . *The fact is that neither the one nor the other represents the "true face" of multicultural Britain*'.[3] Not long after the *Windrush* celebrations ended, there were two major conferences, each of which challenged museum and archive practitioners and policy makers to engage in a thorough rethink. The first took place in early 1999 and was organised by the BASA, relating to black and Asian peoples' participation in the archive sector.

Later in the same year, *Whose Heritage?*[4] set out to insert race, ethnicity and identities at the heart of debates on British heritage and its associated 'industries'. Hall's keynote address at *Whose Heritage?* was delivered in typical challenging and inspirational style. I can't, of course, speak for others, but I recall a familiar frisson of delight when Stuart Hall took to the lectern to deliver 'Unsettling "the Heritage": Re-imagining the Post-nation' to museum curators, archivists and funders. At these and other significant events, organisations such as BASA, the George Padmore Institute, the African and Asian Visual Arts Archive (AAVAA), Panchayat, the BCA and the Black Environment Network (BEN) all demanded a better service from funders and strategic bodies in order that this under-resourced, rapidly developing field could take its rightful place in the construction of historical narratives and new national identities.

The sector known as *black or ethnic minority arts* has changed in the intervening years since the 1980s/1990s. As new, younger players enter the field and as the creative potential of new technologies makes itself felt, there have been some notable successes: Turner prizes, literary successes, music awards, Venice biennale pavilions, Oscars, honours and so on. Nonetheless, some people claim that there has been no progress, that nothing has changed. Indeed, it is argued that on many levels, there has been a loss of ground, with 'the struggle for black arts' depoliticised, made bland and labelled 'diversity' and with an anti-racism movement neither recognised nor prioritised. Here, I return to Stuart's earlier suggestion that it's possible for two seemingly contradictory statements to hold true at the same time.

Stuart never confined himself to a purely theoretical engagement with black cultural practices, whether through his critique of Salman Rushdie's interpretation of Black Audio Film Collective's *Handsworth Songs*; or his narration on Sankofa's cinematic meditation on the Harlem Renaissance, *Looking for Langston*; or his position as chair of both the Institute for the International Visual Arts (INIVA) and Autograph ABP (Association of Black Photographers); or his keynote addresses to cultural practitioners. An unusual combination of astute intellectual, friend, mentor, critic and generous donor of practical help, he continues to inspire heritage sector practitioners, as well as artists and other cultural workers around the world.

Notes

1. Stuart Hall, 'Postscript', in *Soundings: A Journal of Politics and Culture—Windrush Echoes*, ed. Gail Lewis and Lola Young (London: Lawrence & Wishart Limited, 1998), 188.
2. Ibid.
3. Ibid; italics added.
4. G-Max, November 1, 1999, Manchester, UK. The conference was funded by Arts Council England (ACE), the Heritage Lottery Fund (HLF), the Museums Association (MA) and what was then known as the North West Arts Board.

17 *The Partisan's Prophecy: Handsworth Songs and Its Silent Partners*

John Akomfrah

I've spent the last five years or so talking about Stuart Hall to many people across the world,[1] and like most conversations, much of the discussion has been in the anecdotal realm. It's been as if, having met him largely through his writings, many of my discussants felt this compelling need to know something more, something 'intimate'—more 'local', if you will—about the man behind the texts. I therefore want to continue in this anecdotal vein, because it feels like the best way to answer the overriding question most felt compelled to seek an answer for—namely, in what ways did Stuart's influence shape the emergence of the black arts movement in eighties Britain.

I want to stay with anecdotes too because I believe that what they reveal and say about me and my experiences with Stuart can somehow also stand in for and be seen as emblematic of a larger set of relations; mine is an almost generational leitmotif in which a figure admired from afar because he made many symbolic and intellectual openings possible goes on to become first an inspiration, then an ally and finally a friend. This was by no means one-way traffic, and because of that the extraordinary routes by which such a relation became possible at all need some spelling out.

From the offset, it goes without saying that the politics of relation implied by this 'coming together' are complex and multi-faceted. All genealogies and biographies are necessarily unique because they always imply many distinct locations and temporalities. Yet what always surprised me about 'our' connections with Stuart was that you couldn't speak about this seemingly improbable set of elective affinities between a charismatic public intellectual and a bunch of nerdy black British kids, all born sometime between the late fifties and early sixties, without also raising a question about familiar spectres—without saying something about the similarity of the phantoms that organised these affinities.

Speak to curator David A. Bailey or artists Isaac Julien and Sonia Boyce and you'll hear the same thing: We all 'came' to Stuart Hall with a baggage of ghosts; we arrived at his symbolic door, if you like, as a set of discreet fragments, never quite whole and as selves haunted by the ghosts of other, already existing encounters and relations. What he gave us all was the assurance this was not only legitimate baggage but desirable, too; to be everywhere, sometimes at the same time, was a condition or a state of 'disaffection' to be embraced, he seemed to say, simply because it may well be the precondition for a 'somewhere' more fascinating, more engaging and ultimately more rewarding.

Speak also to founding director of the Institute for the International Visual Arts (INIVA) Gilane Tawadros or to cultural critic Kobena Mercer and you'll recognise something else, too: You always encountered several Stuart Halls, and because of that, you never quite knew which Stuart you were speaking to. Yet for many of us, it was precisely this protean presence, this shape-shifting facility that he possessed in abundance that made him such a source of attraction.

Why? Because in what we experienced as a ceaseless movement and traffic of thought, in that almost permanent 'war of position' between questions and enquiries that all meetings with him seemed to become, one always glimpsed something else, too, something the great writer and photographer Valerie Wilmer caught in the title of one of her books: In Stuart, one encountered an impeccable sense of vigilance, a weariness with complacency and a steely determination to always find room for the telling question, the question that always said to you that this encounter, always this encounter, this moment, was *as serious as your life.*[2] To spend time with him always meant not simply being told this in many different ways, but also arriving at this conclusion yourself in the answering of many such questions.

Over the years, a few commentators will see this ceaseless movement on his part and its implied questing as a character flaw. In time, it will also become clear to us that knowing him also meant acknowledging that there were many others who saw these nomadic questionings as overly modish, 'trendy' or band-wagon-hopping. What those critics would never fully grasp was why these so called 'failings' then became the fertile, almost phantasmatic grounds of his appeal for us. To fully comprehend that involved not simply 'repositioning' these so-called 'defective wanderings' but also coming to a whole other set of conclusions about what they symbolised and stood for outside the space of the alleged defects.

In the absence of that more generous perception of him, you also knew that what was being misunderstood was why for a group of young people who had gone from *coloured* to *black*, and many other derogatory epithets in between in their very short lives, these alleged shortcomings would become precisely the basis of Stuart's appeal; why a figure whose very existence seemed an embodiment of the manifold transitions that had overdetermined our lives, a figure of montage with a diversity of interests, identities and orientations, seemed to hold clues as to what an alternative could literally be like. In the misunderstanding about such a figure of migrations—in the outline of whose life one sensed a groping for a 'beyond' that was a key yearning in our lives—what would elude his critics is why he would become the symbolic flag bearer for our manifold ambitions and aspirations. Many of these critics, in effect, had not sufficiently understood the darkness—that space termed the *Not Yet Become* by Ernst Bloch—of our lives.[3] Because they hadn't seen that void, they could hardly see why we were journeying toward that light, towards the promise of hope that Stuart Hall would come to represent in our eyes.

Given the foregoing, what can we say now about that darkness and about some of the phantoms that populated it, stalking our lives, usually in very surreal, very 'gothic' ways? It's a very difficult thing to explain without recourse to a Fanonian metaphor, but one way of formulating it would go something like this: Growing up black in seventies Britain involved living a Wagnerian dramaturgy with the doppelgänger. You were aware from very early on that there was this abject and anarchic figure, loosed on the world, as Yeats described it, 'educationally sub-normal', unclubbable and on the rampage. Rootless, caught between two cultures, turning whole cities into carnivals of mugging and lawlessness, this 'double' was an emblem of trouble, an unreasonable figure whose modus operandi seemed to be characterised by an 'alien unreason', a figure of psychosis hell-bent on burdening something called *the nation* with behaviour and demands that were beyond reason, understanding and, importantly, amelioration.

For a while, you assumed and hoped that this figure was elsewhere, but you had suspicions to the contrary. Occasionally, you were aware that this thing—which bore a faint resemblance to you—was in fact stalking your every move, endlessly threatening to name and shame you as someone complicit in its manoeuvres. In those moments, you were also aware that you were in flight from it, making moves of ever-increasing complexity to avoid what seemed a predestined encounter. At a certain moment, something absolutely unexpected happens, something so devastating that everything else appears in a new light. Usually in public but occasionally privately, you have this moment of epiphany, this mirror scene when you realise that this doppelgänger is, in fact, you; you are the mugger, the trouble, the nightmare from which others are trying to wake.

For a while, you are deeply confused about how this terrifying reversal has been engineered, and with the confusion comes a plague of questions: Why are you in this tormenting scenario of 'becoming'? What is the nature of this convoluted mimetic ruse that has now choreographed into being this swapping in positions of 'presence' with the doppelgänger? What is your 'agency' in this pas de deux between you and the shadow, this depositing of your self in the space of the Other? Worse still, something else too began in that moment. Teachers, neighbours, friends and former babysitters all now seem to look at you in a new light. Because you don't understand how this process of morphing and transfiguration has come about, because you don't know how you became the embodiment of this mirage and how this condition solidified into a truth, you are at a loss to explain how everyone around you suddenly came to believe in the veracity of this fiction. In this space of uncertainties, there is one glaring certainty: that you now explain your existence in a space of spectatorship, a place from which you now watch a surreal Sturm und Drang in which you are clearly a central actor, but without a speaking part—an unfolding narrative in which you have a major role but no *agency*.

Thus begins the death of another innocence in your short life and the search for speech, with which will come, in time, the will and the wish for another transfiguration: You delve into all the books on great black civilizations, read everything by and about Malcolm X and the Black Panthers. Fanon is an immense help, but still the questions remain and the phantom sits on your shoulder, taking the occasional bite—until one day, you watch this man, Stuart Hall, talk about something called *ideology* on an Open University program one Saturday afternoon. From that point on, you begin to piece it together; you start to understand how you and that phantom became fused into this monstrously unfamiliar whole, this new figure of abjection. Later still, Reading *Policing the Crisis*[4] and coming across the 'race as the lens for crisis' formulation for the first time, you begin to understand the processes by which this 'ventriloquizing' of you by that double became—amongst many things—also possible. At that point, you also learn the importance of a very valuable distinction: You've always understood *racism*, but now you also need to understand *racialization*. You start to grasp the full reach and breath of how the doppelgänger became your silent partner in this contact zone of unbecoming. You grasp the immense lifeline of new thinking that you have been thrown by this man, this Stuart Hall fellow. Why would you then not fall in love with such a figure? Why would that love not become 'the declaration of [that which] marks the transition from chance to destiny', as Alain Badiou so eloquently put it?[5]

Much of my dissatisfaction with the modishness criticism was due to its persistent refusal to see something else too, and this has to do with the complex ways in which Stuart wrestled with the many varieties of the doppelgänger throughout his work. Listen to him talking about the new migrants from Kosovo in one of his last television appearances, which we used at the end of *The Stuart Hall Project*, and you will see what I mean. And don't just listen: Watch the impatience with which he listens to the puerile racist bile, the look in his eye that simply says, oh dear, here we go again. On the many occasions in which we heard the 'trendy' criticism, we were aware that it was always a refusal to truly see these moments, always a refusal to recognise how often earlier projects, projects deemed more legitimate areas of concern (the Suez crisis, the French in Indochina, the anticolonial eruptions in Kenya and Southeast Asia, the Cuban revolution) led him inexorably to confront many versions of that doppelgänger and why it would therefore always remain the elephant in the room for many of his seemingly unrelated pronouncements.

Far from signs of modishness, these multiple projects of naming the conditions and the spirit of the doppelgänger had considerable staying power in Stuart's thinking and were present for far longer both in their intensity and duration than many of the things he was accused of 'deserting' in order to 'embrace' them (classical Marxism, class politics, etc.).

One further factor that connects Stuart's thinking on the doppelgänger and many of my generation is this: Once you see that proverbial elephant in the 'living room' of his work, you never again hear the modishness criticism without somehow feeling implicated in its attendant accusation of a heresy. Once you learn to see the outlines of its perennial grip on him, you never again read that criticism without feeling an accusation is being made, which, by means of circumlocution, basically says that you were somehow responsible for his 'deviation', because what was always implicit in that critique is the idea that Stuart was on the 'right' road until he got waylaid by that siren call of your 'epiphenomenal' questions, your 'superstructural' identity obsessions. Because that is the case, or because my feeling is that it is the case, let me give you a few examples of why that critique is both misplaced and historically inaccurate.

While performing archive research for *The Unfinished Conversation*, I came across a BBC radio programme called *Generation of Strangers* that changed my thinking on many things to do with Stuart's work. Made in 1964, the key question the documentary addressed was what the future of Britain's migrant children would be, especially in England's Midlands region.[6] Listening to it five years ago, I was struck by two things. First, Stuart not only introduced but concluded the programme, and this suggested to me that, in line with sixties radio convention and protocol, he was the author, the 'expert', the framing device for one of the earliest of sixties media motifs on 'race': migrant children and their futures. As I listened, it became clear too that he was in fact rehearsing in that programme many of the themes that would figure in his later work. The second important point, of which I'll say more in a minute, has to do with the year of that radio broadcast: 1964, the year Stuart moved to Birmingham to begin work with Richard Hoggart on the cultural studies project.

As more and more such programmes emerged from the sixties during our research, fragile deposits of things past from an array of sources, including both public and commercial broadcasting outlets, what became increasingly clear was that these were not unofficial or extracurricular presentations on race and migration—heretical wanderings, if you will, away from the 'true calling' of Stuart Hall. They were not—in other words—outlaw or pariah sentiments deviating somehow in their subject matter from a more substantial, more official cultural studies trajectory. Rather, they mostly felt like foundational ruminations in their own right, in many cases precursors to what would become the more renowned reflections on class and on subcultures that now define his work in classical cultural studies.

By the end of the research phase, we were confronted by so many such programmes that we felt compelled to use their existence as a foregrounding premise for *The Unfinished Conversation* and frame it as an artwork about *multiple becoming*—about the indisputable presence and coexistence of overlapping projects all within the same frame, each with its distinct trajectory and raison d'être and each bearing a singular testament to an ongoing set of unfinished conversations.

The one fragment that kept standing out for me throughout was the 1964 radio broadcast. What the coincidence of dates immediately suggested to me—and again, this was something that became a narrative device for *The Unfinished Conversation*—was that far from being a later supplement, an addendum to a hermetically sealed and self-contained cultural studies itinerary, questions pertaining to race were always already in place from the very beginning—and not always simply as a marginal field of operation. Race was a constituting space from which the nascent and now more familiar undertakings of the discipline would draw themes and narratives. Why? Because Stuart Hall was not in a radio studio in 1964 making this programme simply to pass time; his presence therefore presupposes some links between this seemingly extracurricular undertaking of radio presentation and the goings on at the new Centre.

Furthermore, and just as importantly, he appeared in that broadcast not simply because he volunteered for it. He was there in that moment, delivering the thesis of that broadcast, because those who had invited him in the first place felt that his new (Centre) appointment also 'qualified' him for the pronouncements they needed made on the racial question in their programme. Whatever else you might say about the BBC at the time, it was almost certainly no underground samizdat. Therefore, it is fair to say that this was as 'mainstream' a recognition as one could plausibly expect in 1964, that part of what would be 'new' about this new Centre was that what it had to say was new and would also be about the becoming of a 'new community'. Because this was happening in 1964, the year zero of cultural studies, what that conclusively meant was that though *Policing the Crisis* would become the largest visible tip of it in time, the iceberg of race was always floating in the sea of cultural studies. This was certainly the case for Stuart Hall and almost certainly for a group of radio producers at the BBC.

For a while, the fact that this 1964 radio programme existed at all would start me off on a train of thought that always seemed bound elsewhere, always seemed as if it was taking me in some unforeseen direction; yet at the point of arrival, I would find myself back at the same question: Given its existence, why did the modishness criticism ever become attached to Stuart at all? Didn't that programme's existence suggest that such a figure, with his prolonged interest in these epiphenomenal subjects and over this expanse of time, might be the very opposite of a dilettante? Also, placed alongside some of the work in the eighties and beyond, did not that radio broadcast also suggest that here was a figure who, from the very beginning, seemed wedded to a cluster of overlapping concerns that he would return to again and again, always sidestepping the hierarchies many would assume an interest in these would imply? Why, therefore, were accusations of bandwagon-hopping levelled at him? Why would a thinker in whose work in over fifty years one could glean 'a homeland of identity'[7] in which the coexistence of multiple themes was always the norm then be later criticised for displaying these very qualities—and in the name of a hierarchical modelling of these themes that the work, from the very beginning, disavowed? At first, my assumption was that this might simply be to do with the difference of media ontologies, the different personalities of the locations for his output: pronouncements on migrant life or ethnicity in broadcast media, reflections on class and culture in print media. Then, something else happened that disputed the neatness and symmetry even of that equation.

Six months into our research, Stuart put us in touch with a colleague from the Partisan Coffee House years with the hope that it might provide some 'material',[8] and Suzy Benghiat kindly loaned us her copies of the very first issues of *Universities and Left Review*. To complement those readings, we also found every copy Stuart

Christopher Hall, Marlon Riggs and Robert Shepard, Oakland, 1993 (image courtesy of Lyle Ashton Harris)

Sonia Boyce, Stuart Hall, and Isaac Julien, 2 Brydges Place, Covent Garden, London, 1992 (image courtesy of Lyle Ashton Harris)

Stuart Hall speaking at the Black Popular Culture Conference, Dia Art Foundation, New York, December 8-10, 1991 (image courtesy of Lyle Ashton Harris)

Stuart Hall and Cornel West, Black Popular Culture Conference, Dia Art Foundation, New York, December 8-10, 1991 (image courtesy of Lyle Ashton Harris)

edited of *The New Left Review* from 1960 to 1962. As we trawled through these materials, reading everything Stuart wrote between 1957 and 1962, something else begun to emerge that both surprised and confirmed many intuitions, something that told you 'things' about the hubris of a penniless young man from the Caribbean who had both the panache and the temerity to assume editorship of a new movement's journal, something that freed us from the guilt of tainting his otherwise impeccable credentials with our identity politics, but something too which would complicate our understandings of the charge of disloyalty and its origins. Artist and writer Kodwo Eshun has also read many of these articles, and in a recent conversation we were both surprised by their polymath range as well as the enduring presence of certain perennials in these writings: race, music, film, television, patterns of consumption, the transforming outlines of working-class identity and so on.

What surprised us was not so much their existence but the manner of their appearance. Every one of these articles and editorials seemed to always emerge as rallying cries, usually with Stuart arguing for their necessity and usually against a backdrop of disagreement with the importance he attached to them from others. Invariably, what would then follow their disagreement would be a polite but polemical response by Stuart, insisting on the legitimacy of the original formulation. This would in turn usually be met by further disagreement. In the end, not only did the existence of these writings help make sense of the genealogy of an intellectual, they also provided insights into the longue durée of some of the criticisms he faced throughout his life. For a man who seemed to be forever fighting somebody or other and for reasons that didn't seem to alter in profile or orientation, certainly on his part, the mystery deepened about how the dilettante label ever then managed to stick at all. What these pieces showed was that though there were changes of emphases, clarifications of the old as well as the occasional change of course, there were enduring and persistent obsessions with certain themes, and the stubbornness with which he defended his right to place them on the agenda seemed—even on a cursory reading—one of the key motifs in his life.

All this was surprising at first because Stuart seemed in many ways such an apostle of discontinuity that one would have expected otherwise. Yet looking at these earlier editorials and essays now, what are forcefully foregrounded are narratives of continuity that will join earlier insights to later 'provocations.' More than anything else, what you saw clearly were the germinations of many ideas, all on multiple, almost mutually exclusive paths of becoming, all laid bare to us in their embryonic forms as we read these pieces. Of course, many also remain necessarily moored to their moment; interventions now absolutely tied to then-current events and without those earlier ecologies now seemed without resonance. However, there was enough to suggest a remarkable persistence of visions, enough constant and familiar flickers on the retina to suggest that *stubborn* might have been a more fitting epithet than *modish*.

Looking at some of the earlier criticisms alongside the new ones by the likes of Alex Callinicos,[9] Terry Eagleton and Colin Sparks, we couldn't help but be struck by the incredible ironic reversals at play in this continuum. Here was a political project (the New Left), premised on unearthing the new, and, in the name of what Robert Frost called 'promises to keep', squirming in its seat as the full outline of what that 'new' might be is announced to it by one of its members. Here too is the irony of a political imaginary for which questions of the historical, both in its materialist and its vocational aspects, occupies a revered place, blundering into a space of critique wrapped in the clothes of amnesia, in garments of forgetting.

What also surprised me when reading some of the sixties disagreements was how much of early life they made me recall. Growing up in the Britain many of those early essays and editorials were written in, I was reminded of one of the 'primal scenes' with its familiar incantatory logic of British xenophobia you routinely encountered via the question, 'But where are you really from?' This would usually be a response to you describing yourself as British to someone, usually white. When you heard it, you knew you were listening to Little England's way of telling you that your appearance provided insufficient evidence for describing yourself thus. In its racially codified index of belonging, this was its way of telling you that it viewed with suspicion the 'slip' that you embodied, of telling you that it sensed a lack of alignment between you and its predefined map of belonging, and therefore the truth that now required verifying was whether the border crossing your appearance suggested was merely a troubling symptom (that you and your parents were from that threatening elsewhere) or the presence of a more irredeemably tragic narrative (that you, possibly your parents too, were born here). All this needed to be known in the entirety the question presupposed, because without that knowledge, the certainty of naming and the implied closure it seeks to affirm could not proceed.

All this came to me reading some of the early criticisms, and I can't help but sense echoes of it too in some of the later one. Not so much the question itself, but the impulse behind it, the desire to purge, to suture, to make plain and clear the borders of inscription—the sense too that a person's very existence in a certain space necessarily marked that territory as a space of miscegenation and defilement. What you were, first and foremost, was a harbinger of a certain conceptual untidiness, an emblem of asymmetry. Because that was the case, you were always operating in the shadows of an archaic patriarchal injunction in which you were seen but not heard, to exist but not have too many 'implications' for a preexisting symbolic order. All this came back to me reading those exchanges.

This has probably been said by many others in the past, but it is worth saying again because of what it says about the enduring power images, of charisma and its locations: Stuart Hall had the most beautiful smile I have ever seen. It was a beguiling and empathic smile, a smile that possessed and was possessed by a rare Weberian verstehen; a smile that told you it understood things beyond the confines of the moment of its appearance. The first time I saw it up close was when I explained my prodigal struggles with the doppelgänger to him. Then it appeared, flashed with ease and welcoming. In that moment of its appearance, I recognised something else, too, something to do with ghosts again—but it would take me another thirty years or so to fully grasp the secular hermeneutic of continuity that it would come to stand for in my dealings with Stuart.

The first time I saw that smile was in 1982, at the Commonwealth Institute in London; in 2012, I realised it wasn't always there. During our viewings, I remember noting the first time it appeared in any of Stuart's broadcasts. It was in 1968, in a Birmingham studio discussion about Enoch Powell's Rivers of Blood speech and the future of the city's migrant community,[10] the community he had been following closely since his arrival in the city in 1964. It appeared when an archetypal 'member of the public' taking part in the discussion suggested that Britain's host community should have been consulted about the invitation to 'them.' 'Why are they here anyway?' the man asks. At point, Stuart smiled for the first time on British television and said something like, 'They are here because you were there'. From that point on, I started to follow that smile, trying to figure out what it revealed about him and about the place he had chosen to call home, about the lessons it would teach me about becoming and the presence of the phantom in that.

'What all moments of visual culture have in common', Nick Mirzoeff tells us in a recent book, 'is that the "image" gives a visible form to time and thereby to change'.[11] The very first time I saw a phantom was in an image, and one of the reasons I don't see that ghost any longer is bound up with the changes that the absence of that image now signifies for me. As a child in the late 1960s—becoming in the moment of Stuart's essays and editorials—the only houses I went into were 'black' ones. I remember that now because there was always a sign on one of the walls that said something like, 'Christ is the head of this house, the unseen guest at every meal'. I remember thinking more than once, *wow, this Christ is the head of many houses. So how come he's always an unseen guest? What is he, a ghost or something?* For all I knew then, that Christ was the head of many 'white houses' too, but because I was never invited into those houses, I'll never know. Black houses, mixed heritage houses, those where the houses I knew as a child, and they were spaces of 'unseen guests'—uninvited ones, too, sometimes real, sometimes flickering outlines on the cathode ray tube that sat in the corner of every living room: spectral, uninvited presences who brought with them narratives that will frame our adventures with the doppelgänger. Insults, abuse and psychic violence always arrive uninvited, but like all other unwanted guests, making themselves at home in your life is their default.

I chanced upon many of those uninvited guests again during *The Unfinished Conversation* research, and they served to remind even more powerfully of the many reasons that seeing Stuart on that Cronenbergian box for the first time was such a revelation, why he was such a catalyst and force for banishing many of those uninvited figures from our midst. Thinking back now to the three years we spent talking with him about *The Unfinished Conversation*, I also realise that many of our discussions around his and Catherine's kitchen table were about coming to terms with some of those 'disinvitation letters' he helped to compose. Often, too, we spoke about the benevolent guests, probably more so by the end—those that required the memorial of acknowledgement. Sometimes, these were not necessarily figures but moments, not characters but events.

For instance, by January of 1986, Black Audio Film Collective had shot most of the material that would feature in our first narrative piece, *Handsworth Songs*, and we had commenced the process of trying to think through the form and direction that material would take us. I can't remember how now, but at some moment during that month, we wrote to Stuart, asking if he would come talk to us about this. Much to our initial surprise, he accepted our invitation.

Now, the very fact that we invited him at all presupposed the presence of several benevolent guests, and some of those are worth naming now. First, in 1982, Lina Gopaul—soon to be a member of the Black Audio Film Collective—invited Paul Gilroy and Errol Lawrence to talk about a book we were then blown away by: *The Empire Strikes Back*.[12] All future members of the collective were studying at Portsmouth Polytechnic at the time, and we were all in the hall that evening when Gilroy and Lawrence spoke. All of us remembered them namecheck Stuart Hall in a way that suggested an intimacy and a familiarity, and I can vividly recall us looking at them with a mixture of admiration and envy because of that. Nothing I can say now will help situate the envy, but to understand the admiration, you need to go back to another moment—in 1979, when, as further education students at Blackfriars (London) College, most of the future members of the collective saw the actress Maggie Steed with Stuart Hall in that seminal, anti-racist critique of mainstream media output, *It Ain't Half Racist, Mum* (1979), a BBC documentary. It was the first time that we saw someone forensically lay out the representational 'logic' for British racist (and racializing) discourse, and it would serve as an opening gambit in a move away from a distinct form of disaffection. Disaffection has always been for me the first act in the three-act narrative of falling out of love, and watching that programme that night forced many of us to reconsider our varying states of disaffection with this place of our birth and belonging.

It was one of the first things we watched together, and over the course of that evening many of us came to understand the full reach of a word and concept that will almost become shorthand for much of our work in the eighties: *representation*. To fully explain why watching that programme was so inspiring, I need to say something about the reasons for its unintended impact on our evolution. We were then all militant anti-imperialists, having already read the Black Panthers, Malcolm X, Fanon and Amílcar Cabral. All of us were seized by the fervour of a millenarian dream about joining the struggle in Angola, Mozambique or Guinea Bissau. All of us were caught in the whirlpool of disaffection with Britain and its place in our lives, filled with dreams for the elsewhere, dreams that would lead at least one young man I remember to join others with very different dreams, in the suicidal Spaghetti House siege of 1975.[13] What we had not completely grasped—and what that programme would help us grasp by providing that different navigational wind, that difference of orientation—was that there was a means by which one could turn our current space, that melancholy place of disaffection, into one of a representational critique that would have implications as far reaching in their impact as those of our initial war of liberation death wish.

As I recount this, I am aware too that this moment of our turning away from the beckoning of the elsewhere and the embrace of representation's allure is also, in retrospect, more the crystalizing of an already lingering resolution to stay and tough it out. I also am aware that the germination of this 'stay and fight here' credo was fertilised by other encounters, other moments that can also press their legitimate claims to be defining moments for this narrative of arrival. Yet it is also clear that a majority of those moments also bear some trace of Stuart's presence—like the moment when many of us crowded into a flat in Brixton (London) for an Althusserian reading group run by *The Black Liberator* editorial member Ricky Cambridge and found ourselves a few weeks later reading excerpts from the CCCS collection *On Ideology*, or when we attended a Campaign against Racism in the Media (CARM) meeting, and one of its organisers, Carl Gardner, told us to 'read the work of this man [Stuart Hall], because you'd like what he has to say'.

As it happens, Carl was a little late with that advice, because the first book most of us went out to buy immediately after watching *It Ain't Half Racist, Mum* was *Policing the Crisis*. Our close reading of that book would be equally central in that set of Damascene conversions that turned us from an outlaw bunch of (literally) woolly headed secessionists into representational activists committed to a fight on these shores. To paraphrase Valerie Wilmer's title again, that representation detour was as serious as our lives. As I watch young British Muslims respond to the fatal logic of those millenarian stirrings again, I am filled with sadness about the continuities that it implies in black British lives.

Looking back over those *Handsworth Songs* conversations with Stuart now, what is also interesting is how many other phantoms in his other lives prefigured that moment of our encounter. For instance, we were meeting in a Greater London Council–funded art space, and there we were with the figure who in 1982 made an inspiring speech at London's Commonwealth Institute in which he urged us 'to go out and get it [the funding for 'Ethnic Arts'] because it's ours.'[14] There we sat with him, in a black film space that we went out and got because he, amongst others, said it was ours.

Looking back at that moment now, I also realise that we were sitting in a space of destiny for other equally beautiful, equally resonating reasons: We were there with one of the few people whose prophetic soundings had made the very idea of fighting to occupy such a space a possibility at all. We were there, sitting with the figure who, along with Paddy Whannel, wrote *The Popular Arts* (1964),[15] the manifesto that quite literally 'licenses' the very idea of the existence of a such a space; the very figure who throughout the seventies championed in countless radio programmes the need and desire for the art centre. We were there with him in a place overwhelmed by all these coincidences to the point that I can't now think about that moment without somehow connecting it with that Indeep song from 1982, "Last Night a DJ Saved My Life."

Once you turn to the substance of our discussions, there too phantoms of earlier moments and lives loomed and hovered over our proceedings. Much of the discussion centred on images of race and the language of film—and of course this too, this language of film, was one of the things that Stuart, along with Paddy Whannel and Lindsey Anderson (as well as quite a few women, I might add), had been instrumental in pioneering during his time at the British Film Institute in the sixties. Moving into the basement of the institute and via a series of seminars, they began a cultural revolution, the implications of which are still with us fifty years later.

From those groundbreaking sessions, the teaching packs Stuart, Whannel and Anderson subsequently produced were disseminated across the country, inspiring and empowering others to follow in their wake. And this is how, in a roundabout way, I ended up in one of the first experimental O-level Film Studies courses in the country in the summer of 1976, learning that language of film and coming to the conclusion that I wanted to work in cinema.

The other hauntings of those *Handsworth Songs* meetings go back to the book I namechecked earlier, the one Angela Davis speaks so eloquently about in chapter 23: *Policing the Crisis.* Most of us had thoroughly read *Policing the Crisis* years before that meeting, but what we had perhaps forgotten by then was its connections with the central location of our film, with Birmingham. In revisiting the subject of the book again with Stuart, listening to him speak about moments in Birmingham's black political past, about the complexities involved in naming and separating those pasts from its insurrectionary present, we gradually chanced on the formulation that will be the key narrative devise of the film: There are no stories in the riots, only the ghosts of other stories.

I returned to *Policing the Crisis* again during the making of *The Unfinished Conversation*, and something else jumped at me, another unseen guest we could not have foreseen in 1986, because to see it then would have meant knowing something about *Generation of Strangers*, the BBC radio programme I spoke about earlier. Remember again that this radio documentary was made in 1964. One of the prophetic asides Stuart makes in it is that for the five- to seven-year-old migrant children who were the impetus for the programme, 'the problems' would only start as they entered their teenage years.

As I reread *Policing the Crisis*, I immediately saw a connection between *Policing the Crisis* and the documentary and this something unseen reading it in 1979. At that moment, a line of reasoning appeared that stretched from the now-forgotten radio documentary in 1964 to some of those celebrated essays in the 1980s and 1990s. To see that line, bear this in mind: The research for *Policing the Crisis* began in the early seventies, on Birmingham's black youth, and it began at precisely the moment when Stuart's five- to seven-year-olds of *Generation of Strangers* were entering that teenage problem space he had predicted a decade before. Ten years after Stuart encountered them, they were now the subjects of the moral panic over mugging and lawlessness that *Policing the Crisis* dissects and lays bare.

It was only after those two moments came together that I realised something else too, something so obvious that it had escaped my attention all along: That group of five- to seven-year-olds that Stuart met in Birmingham in 1964 was us—my generation. By the 1970s, we had become death, the destroyer of worlds, and the problem. I also realised something deeply moving: since 1964, Stuart had been watching us, waiting for us, waiting to see what our presence would say about the country he had chosen to call home.

Notes

1. These conversations started, in fact, with Stuart himself. In the winter of 2011, Mark Sealy, Lina Gopaul and myself started regular meetings with Catherine and Stuart Hall for a collaborative project on 'race, the image and twentieth century'; those talks were the genesis of both the three-screen artwork that I made, *The Unfinished Conversation* (2013), and the feature-length archival documentary *The Stuart Hall Project* (2013), dir. John Akomfrah.
2. Valerie Wilmer, *As Serious As Your Life: John Coltrane and Beyond* (London: Quartet Books, 1977).
3. See Ernst Bloch in *The Principle of Hope*, 3 vols. (Cambridge, MA: MIT Press, 1995), https://mitpress.mit.edu/books/principle-hope.
4. Stuart Hall et al., *Policing the Crisis: Mugging, the State, and Law and Order* (Basingstoke: Macmillan, 1978).
5. Alan Badiou, *In Praise of Love* (London: Serpent's Tail, 2012).
6. *Generation of Strangers*, BBC Home Service, August 23, 1964.
7. Bloch, *The Principle of Hope*.
8. The Partisan Coffee House was a venue of the New Left in the Soho district of London, established by historian Raphael Samuel in 1958 in the aftermath of the Suez Crisis and the Soviet invasion of Hungary. The group that founded the Partisan Coffee House initially came together in Oxford as editors and contributors of the *Universities and Left Review* magazine. In addition to Raphael Samuel, the group included Stuart Hall and Eric Hobsbawm.
9. For example, see Colin Sparks, 'Stuart Hall, Cultural Studies, and Marxism', in *Stuart Hall: Critical Dialogues in Cultural Studies*, ed. David Morley and Kuan-Hsing Chen (Abington: Routledge, 1996), 71–101; and Alex Callinicos, 'The Politics of Marxism Today', *International Socialism*, no. 29 (Summer 1985), https://www.marxists.org/history/etol/writers/callinicos/1985/xx/marxtoday.html.
10. Enoch Powell (1912–1998) was a right-wing populist British politician and conservative member of Parliament (1950–1974), who became an infamous national figure in 1968 for an address that became known as the Rivers of Blood speech. The speech criticized immigration into Britain from the Commonwealth nations and opposed the anti-discrimination legislation being discussed at the time.
11. Nicholas Mirzoeff, *How to See the World* (London: Pelican, 2015).
12. Centre for Contemporary Cultural Studies, *The Empire Strikes Back: Race and Racism in 70s Britain* (Birmingham: CCCS, 1982).
13. The Spaghetti House siege of 1975 was an attempted armed robbery of the Spaghetti House restaurant in Knightsbridge, London by three gunmen. When the robbery failed, nine Italian staff members were taken hostage and moved into the basement. A staff member escaped and raised the alarm, leading to a six-day siege.
14. A filmed excerpt of this speech appears in both *The Unfinished Conversation* (2013) and *The Stuart Hall Project* (2013), http://www.imdb.com/title/tt2578290/.
15. Stuart Hall and Paddy Whannel, *The Popular Arts* (London: Hutchinson Educational, 1964).

The Historical Conditions of Existence: On Stuart Hall and the Photographic Moment

18

Mark Sealy

In 1988, Professor Stuart Hall sat on a platform at the Photographers Gallery in London and addressed an assembled group of disaffected black photographers/artists and activists who were working within black cultural politics. He optimistically participated in the launching of Autograph ABP (Association of Black Photographers). The project had been seed funded by the Arts Council of England in recognition that there was no specific organisation in place to support the work of a growing constituency of black artists using photography. Debates concerning the condition of black arts in Britain had in previous years passed through the corridors of the Greater London Council and later through the hands of the policy makers at the Arts Council of England, who struggled through various and limited programmes to address the reality of black artists being historically marginalised and neglected by the state and its cultural institutions. In time, the history of Autograph ABP will be written through many different voices, but Hall's voice was and remains its intellectually and theoretically most prominent, respected and relevant. He became chair of Autograph ABP in 1991, and we worked closely together until 2008.

Within Britain's cultural landscape, 1991 was framed by debate and contestations surrounding the politics of race and representation, and within the context of black artists using photography, new ideas were being framed that were aimed at deconstructing long-held mainstream negative stereotypical media images of black people. In discussing the very first Autograph ABP touring exhibition, *Autoportraits*, which was shown at Camerawork in London in 1990, Stuart Hall addressed the complexity of how the photographic image and specifically images of the black subject were being opened to new articulations by black artists. His key essay *Black Narcissus*, published in an early Autograph ABP newsletter in 1991, was to foreground much of what was to come from the curatorial direction we would discuss at our catch-up meetings and calls, which generally took place on Fridays at around 4:00 p.m. It's in these meetings that Stuart would say things like, 'we forget the things that shape us and all the things that make us'. He often talked about history as a dead piece of knowledge, reclaiming robbed histories and reflections on the experiences that have passed, and we talked about making archives—archives that bring us back from a past-imagined place, that remind us of what has happened, in the then and in the now. We talked about heritage work and shifts in funding. We often discussed archives as a project to remember who we were and where we came from and why we came here. He spoke in 2008 at a symposium staged by Autograph ABP at Rivington Place in London titled 'Missing Chapter, Cultural Identity and the Photographic Archive', about the most important 'trope of memory being forgetting'. He considered the notion of 'forgetting an essential part of remembering', systematic forgetting, the making of invisible and visible marginalised histories. He talked often about the cultural mainstream in relation to our work and the margins in fact being the new centre.

What was framed in these moments was effectively a way of working with and against photographic discourses with the aim of building a counter narrative around the black subject within photography—not from the point of a photographic, historical, 'correct' perspective, but from the position or positions of being able to address, recontextualise and reposition historical images of the black subject and crucially provide a contemporary context for reading photographic works by black artists, which were being produced out of the desire to have a 'voice' and a sense of place in Britain and beyond. In "Black Narcissus" Hall stated: 'Photographic practises are always historically specific they belong to particular conjunctures. Black self-portraiture, in this historical moment, has broken many of its links with the dominant "western" humanist celebration of self and has become more the staking of a claim, a wager. Here, the black self image is, in a double sense, an exposure, a coming out. The self is caught emerging.'[1]

Throughout the 1980s, and early 1990s the photographic magazine *Ten 8* was produced out of Birmingham; it soon became a critical platform for what could then be called the independent photography sector throughout the United Kingdom. In 1992, volume 2, issue 3, of *Ten 8* was published, and it was in this issue, titled 'Critical Decade Black British Photography in the 80s' that Hall published one of his most influential photography essays on the image of post-war Britain and West Indian migration to the United Kingdom. The essay was titled 'Reconstruction Work', and in it Hall directly challenged the context in which early West Indian migrants had been portrayed in mainstream newspapers and magazines, such as *Picture Post*. The essay issued a direct challenge to contest 'the iconography of popular memory';[2] Hall's thoughts on 'Reconstruction Work' had a major influence on my work, helping to shape the necessary shifts I needed to make on the perception and receptions of the black subject in photography. It's within and through the essay 'Reconstruction Work' that we began to discuss what a black photographic archive might be and the necessary cultural work it might produce. Some critical issues to emerge were when and how we look back at photographs taken of black people when they first started arriving in Britain in substantial numbers, after the WWII and during the early 1950s, and what we might make of these images in the present. Hall stated in 'Reconstruction Work' that the photographs, of early West Indians arriving in the Britain,

'contradict our expectations. Why is everyone so formally dressed? Why does everyone wear a hat? Why do they look so respectable? Where are the ruffians, the rude boys, the rastas, the reggae? How can we resist the feeling of innocence which these photographs construct so powerfully? Because innocence is a dangerous, ambiguous construction for black people. These men and women are not simpletons, smiling country folk, just swinging down from the coconut trees . . . They have just survived the longest, hardest journey of their lives: the journey to another identity.[3]

Effectively, what Hall charted in 'Reconstruction Work' was that the arduous journey these people had made was not just about enduring distance and changes in location, but was also in effect the journey to a new becoming. In the same issue of *Ten 8*, Hall went on to stress that the work of the photographers presented showed the clear influence of the critique of documentary realism and notions of photographic 'truth' articulated by many black British photographers during the 1980s. Hall argued that traditional photographic practice represents Black people in a negative, stereotypical way because it is controlled by and serves the dominant white power structures. Hall also stated that many black photographers' works, especially in the 1980s, articulated how a people who have been objectified throughout history can enter their own subjectivity by making images and, literally, putting themselves in the frame. In the *Ten 8* issue, 'Critical Decade', Hall progressed his theories concerning the end of the essential black subject: that identities are floating and meanings cannot be fixed and universally true at all times for all people; that the subject is constructed through the unconscious as much in desire, fantasy and memory as it is in the political time of their making. Most importantly, though, Hall stated that 'the notion of representation is so important' and that 'identity can only be articulated as a set of representations'. The act of representation then becomes about not just decentring the subject but exploring the kaleidoscopic conditions of blackness.[4]

Making things new was important for Stuart. He always enabled thinking about the making of things and acting on things. Our conversations were always about acting. We worked in a way that was framed by certain questions: What are we going to do? How are we going to act? Where are we going to go, and what does it actually mean? Not only did we think and discourse about ideas; the most important thing I think we did at Autograph ABP together was to open different conduits and push open different spaces for artists' work to be read. This action was tied to the kaleidoscopic conditions of existence, which Stuart often talked about. At Autograph ABP, there was to be no one single position we would work through; our work carried many meanings and possible readings.

In 1993, in partnership with Lawrence and Wishart, I edited a retrospective photographic book on the works of Vanley Burke, a Birmingham-based photographer who had been taking photographs of his community since 1965. Burke at the time rejected the idea of captioning his photographic images. In his essay titled 'Vanley Burke and the "Desire for Blackness"' which accompanied the photographs, Hall addressed Burke's 'desire for a plenitude of blackness,'[5] which encapsulated and recognised the desire of black documentary photographers to produce images not necessarily out of a search for truth but out of a desire for, identification of and love of community—to reproduce the intimate life story that makes up the ordinary.

Throughout the 1990s and through very difficult funding rounds and agreements with our main sponsors, the Arts Council of England, Autograph ABP managed to sustain its profile locally and internationally to emerge as an important agency for the development and distribution of black photographic artists' work globally, with publishing being a core objective; the first black photographic monographs to occur on a regular basis were established in 1993, a major milestone for the organisation.

The winds of political change throughout the UK public funding system have a habit of going around in circles. What was *black or ethnic arts* twenty years ago is labelled *cultural diversity* today. It has been important for Autograph ABP and Stuart Hall to name these shifts and monitor these changes publicly as we advocated for the recognition of cultural difference and as we embraced the politics of human rights. As an agency, Autograph ABP needed to send clear and distinctive signals to policymakers, highlighting the shift in black artists' aspirations and the need to compete on an institutional level to consolidate the past and meaningfully develop the future ways of being.

In 2001, I brokered a collaboration with Phaidon Press to produce a detailed study of black photographers globally; this would highlight the international matrix of photographers that Autograph ABP was connected with. The book was titled *Different*; photographic artists from all over the world were to be discussed, and Stuart Hall was to provide the political context for the work to be read. *Different* was our attempt to engage with photographic history, and it was important that a major publisher like Phaidon was receptive to this theoretical and visual dialogue. This shift for Autograph ABP was significant because it signalled a phase of greater distribution for the organisation and greater international recognition. Unusually, the cover of this photographic book did not contain an image; instead, the images conjured from the text Hall had written were successfully embraced as representing the image content of the book. Part of the cover reads: 'Black is considered to be a political and cultural, not a genetic or biological, category. It is a contested idea, whose ultimate destination remains unsettled. And "identity" is understood as always, in part, an invention; about "becoming" as well as "being"; and subject to the continuous play of history, culture and power. What makes it possible to compare the work of these photographers across their significant differences is their common historical experience of living in a racialized world.'[6]

Phaidon agreed that no one image could represent the book as a cover image; Stuart's text was image enough. This also was a radical departure for Phaidon's marketing department. The book has sold well and effectively as a narrative on visual culture, representing an incisive intervention across the study of photographic history. The book prized open a gap in our understanding of the work that images produce. It highlighted an explosive visual force that was at play from within a wide range of black experiences. *Different* laid a solid foundation for much of what we were to build across our relationship at Autograph ABP.

Notes

1. Stuart Hall, 'Black Narcissus', *Autograph ABP* newsletter (1991), 3.
2. Stuart Hall, 'Reconstruction Work', *Ten 8* 2, no. 3 (1992): 107.
3. Stuart Hall, 'Critical Decade: Black British Photography in the 80s', *Ten 8* 2, no. 3 (1992): 107.
4. David A. Bailey and Stuart Hall, 'The Vertigo of Displacement', *Ten 8* 2, no. 3 (1992): 20.
5. Stuart Hall, 'Vanley Burke and the "Desire for Blackness"', in *Vanley Burke: A Retrospective*, ed. Vanley Burke and Mark Sealy (London: Lawrence & Wishart, 1993), 12–15, 15.
6. See the cover of Mark Sealy and Stuart Hall, *Different: Contemporary Photography and Black Identity* (Wien: Phaidon Press, 2001).

Centre for Contemporary

Cultural Studies

University of Birmingham

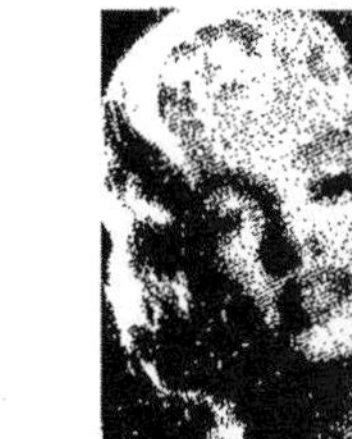

6⁴

Report

7.1969

12.1971

Centre For Contemporary Cultural Studies
Annual Report: 1966 - 1967

4th

University of Birmingham

January 1968

Part V
The International Expansion and Extension of Cultural Studies

The International Expansion and Extension of Cultural Studies

Part V begins with chapter 19, Dick Hebdige's semi-autobiographical account of his own 'relocations' from the CCCS in Birmingham to Goldsmiths and then on to California—in a career that is a rather like an emblematic 'one-man story' of the development—and internationalisation—of British cultural studies itself. Many significant threads of the narrative the conference was designed to articulate are represented here. In offering this account, Hebdige highlights the contrast between his own positive appropriations of North American culture, which has been his home for twenty years now, and the negative responses of Richard Hoggart and his family when they visited the United States in the 1950s. Although Hoggart could, in principle, see the attractions of the 'loose limbed assurance' of that affluent North American suburban culture (especially when contrasted with the much narrower cultural confines of 1950s Europe), he nonetheless found it too uncomfortably 'foreign' and felt the need to promptly get back to his own 'native' soil.

In a critique of simplistic forms of anti-Americanism, Hebdige has previously written about the necessary ambivalence of British working-class tastes in relation to American popular culture and its complex (and sometimes subversive) relations to traditional forms of class culture in the United Kingdom. In all of this, he might be said to stand in intellectual opposition to Hoggart's position on these issues. Nonetheless, there is a strong historical tie between them—it was Hoggart who interviewed Hebdige as an undergraduate applicant to the English department at Birmingham and offered him a place to study there, and it was Hoggart again who helped to bring Hebdige to work at Goldsmiths when he was Warden in the 1980s. The tightly knit mode of these connections is not incidental; as noted later, the renaming in Stuart Hall's honour of the building in which the conference was held had all the more resonance in the context of the college's previous move to rename its main building in honour of Hoggart.

To that extent, the autobiographical dimension of Hebdige's account is central to its purpose, as he then goes on to explore the profound difference between the more nationally focussed model of cultural studies developed by Hoggart's generation and its quite different inflection in the context of the intellectual and diasporic displacements instituted in the forms of cultural studies developed by Stuart Hall. Hebdige is careful to point out the profound differences between the paradigms of 'homeland and belonging' developed by Hoggart (as indicated earlier) and Hall—themselves no doubt related to their very different personal experiences of place, migration, home and empire. However, he also stresses how much we all owe to *both* Hoggart and Hall. Later, Hebdige offers a vivid in account of his own participation in the creation of a 'utopian' subcultural multiracial space in Birmingham in the 1970s. He then moves from the optimism of that historical moment in the British politics of race to the dystopian shock of being in a very white part of Los Angeles on the day in 1992 that the police were cleared by the jury in the Rodney King case. However, his emphasis is not simply on the substantive differences between the two experiences but on what, in his view, a cultural studies perspective in the tradition of both Hoggart and Hall should insist on: the recognition of our inevitable implication in what is happening around us and our continuing intellectual, ethical and political 'responsibility to and in the moment.'

In an account in chapter 20 of the contrasting ways in which Stuart Hall's work has been read specifically in Brazil, Liv Sovik, while speaking less autobiographically than Dick Hebdige, nonetheless grounds her account of the process of the appropriation of Hall's work not simply in the context of Latin American cultural studies, but in the particular phases of the recent Brazilian cultural and political history that have shaped her own life. To some extent, her account can be read as a sort of 'sociology of knowledge' that attempts to explain why it was that in specific periods, different aspects of Hall's work were taken up in Brazil. As she notes, at different stages, Hall was read there as a Marxist, as media analyst and, only later, as a theorist of identity, diaspora and globalisation.

We must recall here Hall's own insistence on the *uses* of theory and the necessarily provisional, and context-specific nature of its accomplishments. In that context, it is perhaps not too much to imagine that Hall himself would be delighted to see this account of how it was that, in the various phases a Brazilian history, following the disintegration of the military dictatorship of the 1970s, people in Brazil found his own revisionist Marxism and, in particular, his account of the dynamics of authoritarian populism in the United Kingdom to be a useful theoretical resource they were able to then 'translate' into the Brazilian context. Likewise, ever since having been introduced to the work of semioticians such as Eliseo Verón by Latin American visitors to CCCS in the 1970s, Hall also took great pleasure in the resonance between his own work and that of the Latin American media theorists to whom Sovik refers here (Jesús Martín-Barbero and Néstor García Canclini in particular). Her explanations of the quite particular take-up of Hall's theorisation of diaspora in Brazil is of special interest, based as it is on the notion of Brazil having an analogous relationship to Europe as that of the Caribbean. If we are to understand the modalities of cultural translation and displacement, it is evidently at the same time crucial that we recognise the precise logic of such particularities, which do connect different concrete instances. In this case, that particularity concerns the terms of the analogy between the highly developed categorisations and hierarchies of skin colour to be found in both the Brazilian and Caribbean contexts. As she notes, in conclusion, these diasporic societies with their traditions of 'malleability, irony and self-reflection' may perhaps offer us all more hopeful models of social relations for the future than can be found in any more permanently 'settled' cultural context.

Kuan-Hsing Chen's analysis in chapter 21 of the significance of Stuart Hall's role in inspiring cultural studies work throughout East Asia over the last twenty years focuses not simply on the intellectual content of the ideas, but also on their modes of institutionalisation in a range of cultural studies projects. As Chen notes, these include venues such as the *Inter-Asia* journal, which Chen himself co-edits (established in 1995); the Cultural Studies Association in Taiwan (1998); and the Cultural Typhoon network in Japan (founded in 2003). In the first place, Chen is careful to recognise that, rather than cultural studies being an entirely 'new' import to the region, it is better understood as having provided a stimulus for the 'rediscovery' of pre-existing (but long-marginalised) indigenous traditions of cultural history and cultural analysis. The moment of its legitimation, centring on the British Council–sponsored 'launch' of Hall's *Critical Dialogues in Cultural Studies* book in Tokyo in 1996, is then not to be understood not as some ex nihilo form of cultural importation, but in terms of its integration with a range of different, pre-existing intellectual and indeed political formations throughout East Asia.

Here, Chen's account (like Sovik's in relation to Brazil) focuses on the perceived relevance in the region of Hall's earlier analysis of authoritarian populism in the United Kingdom. In East Asia in the 1990s, the years of post-war authoritarianism, anti-Communism and statism were already being undermined by a variety of political and social movements. As he notes, the relevance of cultural studies in East Asia can only be understood properly in this broader context—in which connections were being made not only with the emerging intellectual positions, but with the various dimensions of the democratisation process that were emerging in Taiwan and Korea, in mainland China in the wake of the Tiananmen Square events, in Indonesia and in India. If, as is commonly recognised, Hall himself was not simply an academic, but rather a public intellectual, then despite his own modesty in the matter, Chen (as the initiator and long the mainstay of the *Inter Asia* journal and its subsequent offshoots) and his colleagues have very effectively modelled their interventions on Hall's exemplary political, and intellectual, practice.

The account Chen offers is an extremely persuasive one of a mode of practice that has involved not simply emulating or popularising Hall's work—or that of British cultural studies in general—but rather of taking on board his insistence on the necessity for any specific analysis of a given conjuncture to be effectively revamped, rethought and 'translated' if it is to be 'exported' and transposed so as to be genuinely useful in intellectual and political work elsewhere. This work of 'cultural translation'—and of critique, reformulation and 'renewal from the margins'—is evidently central to the project of cultural studies in an era of globalisation.

Iain Chambers's contribution to this section in chapter 22 poses the question of what is deemed to be marginal by whom. He focuses on the necessary lessons that can be learnt from the various poor 'souths' of the world. He focuses on the south of Europe, most notably highlighted by the mediated spectacle of migrants and refugees attempting to sail the Mediterranean on flimsy craft to reach that 'better life' they see in potential, if only they can breach the walls of Europe's securitocracy. Chambers is concerned with exposing the conceptual limits of European humanism and the rationalist/nationalist requirements of Euro-American modernity. He highlights the way in which European humanism's fate is now articulated around the question of who can be admitted to the 'promised land' of Europe. In raising the south 'as a political and historical question', rather than simply a matter of geography, Chambers questions the taken-for-granted conceptual landscape within which the population of rich North Western Europe lives—and thus exposes its particularity. He recognises not only that its assumptions and privileges cannot be universalised, but more radically that the *continued* exclusion of the poor south is, in fact, the price that would have to be paid for the continuation of Europe's hegemony over the material and political resources it has currently sequestered.

It is in this context that he invokes the notion of the migrating soundscapes of the Mediterranean—including the sounds of the Arab, Berber and Islamic worlds—as a way of escaping the 'historical and political cage' of a singular understanding of the present, in favour of a creolised landscape. There, we might better hear subaltern histories singing the 'bluesology', as he puts it, of different modernities, which productively 'contaminate' established cultural forms by giving voice to other genealogies and counter histories. This voicing does more than just add a supplementary set of 'exotic' examples to a conventional perspective: It exposes the universalistic presumptions of that hegemonic culture for what they are—mere particularities, held in place by power. It is also designed to offer a map of other places from which we might start, in order to better conceptualise the (necessarily) transnational conjuncture in which Europe's problems (like everyone else's, these days) must be seen—simply, as Tzetvan Todorov[1] once put it, as those of 'another among others'—rather than as an unquestioned point of origin (or 'nature') from which all forms of difference (or monstrosity) are to be measured.

Note

1. Tzvetan Todorov, *The Conquest of America: The Question of Other* (Norman: University of Oklahoma Press, 1999).

Home and Away: Cultural Studies as Displacement

19

Dick Hebdige

There's a passage in Richard Hoggart's autobiographical trilogy, *A Measured Life: The Times and Places of an Orphaned Intellectual* where he's recounting his first impressions of America from 1956, when he'd spent a year as a visiting professor with his young family at the University of Rochester in upper New York state and he's contrasting what he calls the 'pinchbeck assumptions of [1950's] Europe' with the 'larger, more loose limbed assurance' of his white, middle-class American hosts rocked in the cradle of the affluent suburban idyll, secure in their king-size beds and well-equipped kitchens, behind their brilliantly lit, un-curtained windows, which he describes as 'bright human assertions of belonging against the alien largeness of the land'.[1] He sums up the contrast in one line: 'The lengthening femur of the American West compared with the little bow-legs of rickety, lined men trotting up snickets in Lancashire to borrow a hand-cart so as to shift a fourth-hand mangle.'[2]

The incongruity, the disparities in scale played out on the page and in the mouth in the clash between the long, rolling vowels of the New and the hemmed-in fricatives and glottal stops of the working-class Old World. Having lived for twenty-two years now in the United States—and not just in the United States, but in California, and especially having worked the last thirteen years at University of California, Santa Barbara—I think it's safe to say I can see what he's getting at. I stayed, of course—and he, of course, most emphatically didn't, in America that is. 'All the members of the family had enjoyed themselves [in America] very much indeed,' he writes, 'but knew they would go back. The youngest said, with childish conviction, "I'm English and should be in England",' and that in a way was psychologically true for all of us.'[3] He ends the chapter by drawing the familiar analogy between the pull of home and the stubborn rootedness of an un-pottable native plant: 'I am too immersed in, too much of, one culture, not a particularly fine plant but one which withers in almost any soil but his own.'[4]

Iain Chambers, of course, in *Border Dialogues*, and Paul Gilroy, in *The Black Atlantic*, have explored the dialectical tension, as Gilroy puts it, between cultural roots and diasporic routes: 'r-o-u-t-e-s'—*rowts* as we say it in America; *rowt*: it rhymes with *nowt*. They explored that tension between roots and routes to great effect, but here's Stuart on the subject in an interview from 1997:

> There is no single origin—and the movement outwards, from narrower to wider, is never reversed. It's connected with the notion of hybridity, so it's connected with the critique of essentialism. But the notion of diaspora suggests that the outcome of the critique of an essentialist reading of cultural transmission is not that anything goes, is not that you lose all sense of identity, it is the consequential inscription of the particular positionalities that have been taken up. The history depends on the routes. It's the replacement of roots with routes. There are no routes which are unified. The further back you go, something else is always present, historically, and the movement is always towards dissemination.[5]

As a friend of mine said recently on reading that passage to herself out loud, you can see what Stuart saw in Henry James. I can hear Miles Davis in it, too—the sense of someone going at it at full

DJ/music promoter, Mike Horseman (1949-2015) at the turntables: The Shoop at the Golden Eagle, Hill Street, Birmingham, circa 1977 (photo: Bernard G. Mills)

tilt, fully present in the moment, given over in the act of thinking about what comes next, abandoned in an ecstasy of concentration yet simultaneously detached, relentlessly pursuing the ineffable: always on the move. Anyone who ever heard Stuart Hall speak in public, even those who didn't go along with what he said, knew they were in the presence of something out of sight, something out of this world. How many people have you met who've told you they heard Stuart speak once and have never forgotten it—even when they couldn't summarize exactly what it was he said? Try summarizing Henry James. Try summarizing Miles Davis.

Now, I'm not going to try in the five minutes I have remaining to bridge the gulf that separates these two paradigms of homeland and belonging—Stuart Hall's and Richard Hoggart's; let's just say they're different. However, I know how much I and many thousands like me and many thousands more no doubt *nothing* like me owe them both. In a more particular, more pointed sense, I feel especially privileged and indebted because, thanks in different ways consecutively to Richard and to Stuart, I *went* to Birmingham and found myself indelibly marked and made over in the process by that journey. To use Stuart's terminology, 'the positionalities taken up' there in the early 1970s form for me, in the profoundest possible way, a consequential intimate inscription.

Alongside and beyond the frenetic centre spaces—the reading groups, the workshops and the seminar room—I'd mention as separate but vitally connected the Shoop sound system I happened to help run from the early to mid-1970s above a pub on Hill Street in Birmingham's city centre. The Shoop was a heaving hybrid space that, as the 1970s wore on, served for me as the prototype and crucible of UK urban subculture's briefly actualized utopia. It was a space carved out and occupied by the people who used it, people who on a weekly basis assembled there en masse in defiance of the infamous sus laws and the spatialized apartheid imposed elsewhere throughout the city centre by Birmingham's police force.[6]

And then, after a long interlude spent working the provincial UK art school teaching circuit, I was offered a home when Richard was presiding as the rector in the eighties here at Goldsmiths, somewhat east of where I'd been raised, as they say in the States— as if human beings were a kind of fodder crop, like corn or hay. I got to teach here in the Communications department for several years before finally jumping ship in 1992 to take a job as dean of Critical Studies at California Institute of the Arts (Cal Arts), a

The Shoop, circa 1977 (photo: Bernard G. Mills)

Under pressure from the local CID, the Irish landlord insisted we play 'no more than 10 percent black music'. Turning a deaf ear, Horseman dutifully nodded and went on playing what he always played: The Shoop, circa 1977 (photo: Bernard G. Mills)

small, radically experimental arts school in northern LA County—'The Other CIA,' as the official Cal Arts T-shirt slogan put it in the nineties—set up, paradoxically, on Disney's dime in 1972 at the height of the Californian counterculture.

I was meant to sign the contract somewhere on Wilshire Boulevard in downtown LA on April 29, 1992, which happened to be the day the Rodney King verdict came down, and I was biding my time hanging out at the Getty Research Centre, then located, appropriately enough, over a bank in Santa Monica, at a desk next to one that bell hooks—like me, on a short-term research fellowship—had recently vacated waiting for the call: the Cal Arts call, but also, like everyone else across Southern California that day, waiting for the verdict from the all-white jury in suburban Simi Valley in Ventura County not far south of Santa Barbara on the four policemen charged with the use of excessive force in the arrest of Rodney King when the not guilty verdict came down, and the city combusted in unfiltered fury at the outrage of the acquittal in the face of copious and damning citizen video sousveillance. And a young, female librarian, pale with the burden of the moment and her mission, came hurrying through the stacks, urging us all to make our way to the exit, to go home and batten down the hatches, while she apologized profusely for the inconvenience—this unseemly interruption of our important scholarly endeavours (checking art auction catalogues, etc.). I remember looking up and saying: 'Please don't apologize. It's not your fault. You weren't on that jury'—a comment that solicited first a puzzled, then, I thought—or did I just imagine it?—a vaguely disapproving expression, an expression, more precisely, of distaste.

Stuart is the person who taught me how I might begin to weigh that look—how to look back through someone else's eyes as in a mirror and not to step aside, to see how we're all of us implicated not just in what is happening now, but in what might happen next, our responsibility to and in the moment. And my responsibility right now is to stop, because I've run out of time; my eight minutes are up, and I'm painfully aware I haven't addressed the topic of this panel: Cultural Studies in a Global Context. I'll just end by saying how honoured and how sad I am to be here today with everyone else to honour Stuart's legacy and to have an opportunity also to remember Richard Hoggart, to see them both brought together here at Goldsmiths at last—if not under one roof, exactly, then at least on the same campus under two.

Notes

1. Richard Hoggart, *A Measured Life: The Times and Places of an Orphaned Intellectual* (New Brunswick: Transaction Publishers, 1994), 166.
2. Ibid. The sentence comes at the end of a paragraph that serves as a retrospective postscript to the critique of Americanization and post-war consumer culture mounted in *The Uses of Literacy*, which was published in the United Kingdom during Hoggart's stint as a visiting scholar in the English Department at Rochester: Even thirty years ago, the houses would be full of things, things everywhere—multiple televisions, hi-fi gear, cameras, videos [sic]; and the gardens cluttered with aluminium picnic equipment bought by mail-order from Cincinnati. Yet that is not in most people acquisitiveness; they don't really believe in possessions; they give away very easily; about possessions they are transcendentalists. If you are a visitor from Europe they will load you with goods, their own goods; a 'shower' (the old pioneer word for gifts to help you settle in is exactly right) of goods. The nonchalance of the well-filled belly perhaps, not the pinchbeck assumptions of Europe but a more loose-limbed assurance for most, not just for the traditionally well-to-do. The lengthening femur etc.
3. Ibid., 170.
4. Ibid., 171.
5. Stuart Hall interviewed by Peter Osborne and Lynne Segal, 'Interview—Stuart Hall, Culture and Power', *Radical Philosophy*, no. 86 (November/December 1997): 34.
6. For more elaborated, illustrated accounts of the Shoop sound system, see Dick Hebdige, 'The Worldliness of Cultural Studies', *Cultural Studies* 29, no. 1 (2015): 32–42; and Dick Hebdige, 'Afterword', in *Subcultures, Popular Music and Social Change*, ed. The Subcultures Network (Newcastle upon Tyne: Cambridge Scholars Publishing, 2014), 267–294.

20 Stuart Hall, Brazil and the Cultural Logics of Diaspora

Liv Sovik

For the academic press that published *Da diáspora*,[1] it was a bestseller from the start. When it came out in 2003, the first two thousand copies of the collection sold in a matter of four months. Where did the interest in *Da diáspora* come from? Hall's name had circulated for more than twenty years. *On Ideology*, the CCCS volume of which the introduction began, 'This journal is conceived as a contribution to discussion about the nature and theory of "ideology", mainly within the Marxist tradition', was published in Brazil in 1980,[2] just as the military regime was beginning to make the transition to civilian rule in earnest. It contains Hall's 'The Hinterland of Science: Ideology and the "Sociology of Knowledge"', in which he discusses the history of the term *ideology*, arguing that it is a relatively underdeveloped concept in Marxist theory.

Hall was first translated when the Brazilian military dictatorship was beginning to come to an end. The process of redemocratization, or *abertura*, was announced by the head of the military government, President Geisel, in 1974, but uncertain until the early 1980s (there were numerous right-wing bomb attacks from 1980 to 1981) and only complete in 1988. This process allowed a diversity of opinion to emerge. During the 1970s and early 1980s, despite police informants in the classroom, self-censorship and official censorship of the press until 1978 and of books until some years later,[3] intellectual life continued to be lively and to receive influences from abroad. The underlying political question centred on how to understand the coup and the defeat of resistance to it. What had gone wrong? What had to be rethought?

230

A sign of the degree to which these questions were asked in the light of contemporary theory is that Michel Foucault visited Brazil to lecture at the Catholic University of Rio de Janeiro from May 21–25, 1973, a time of brutal political repression. His lectures, collectively entitled *A verdade e as formas jurídicas* (*Truth and Juridical Forms*), were published the following year, although they only came out in French in Foucault's *Dits et écrits* in 1994. In the lectures, Foucault directly addressed the left intellectual's dilemma with regard to Marxism's apparent objectivity. Its certainties had guided much of the opposition to the regime but were inadequate to explain its failures.

> The question is this: there is a tendency that, a bit ironically, we could call academic Marxism, which consists of looking for the ways in which the economic conditions of existence may be reflected and expressed in man's consciousness. It seems to me that this form of analysis, traditional in university Marxism in France and in Europe, has a serious defect: it supposes that the human subject, the subject of knowledge, even the forms of knowledge are, in a way, already and finally given, and that economic, social and political conditions of existence do nothing more than deposit or impress themselves on this finally given subject.[4]

Foucault's aim was to be done with academic Marxism's 'philosophically traditional' subject.[5]

Thus, when the first of Hall's work arrived in Brazil, it was received by at least two sides of a debate: academic intellectuals who took the poststructuralist path and those who remained Marxist, many of them eventually becoming interested in Gramsci. Hall was then read in retrospect, by the poststructuralist and postmodernist sides, as having been useful in trying to save the Marxism of radical opposition to the regime from facing its inevitable defeat not only by the regime but the forces and distractions of consumer culture. Hall's 'wrestling' with Marxism is often read as affiliation even today, even as his work is read as high theory—though sometimes as high theory that is somehow not quite high enough. When, for example, he considers *ideology* to be a term that is still useful to describe culture 'harnessed to particular positions of power' or reclaims Althusser, Hall has been thought to rather simple-mindedly disregard post-Marxist theoretical advances, perhaps Foucaultian poststructuralism itself, and certainly Jean Baudrillard's acute apprehension of the sliding surfaces of contemporary social life.[6]

The prehistory of Hall's reception in Brazil as diasporic intellectual had a second phase. Venício Lima, a professor of communication at the University of Brasília who was among the first to speak of cultural studies in Brazil, understands that Hall's first major impact came through the publication in Portugal in 1993 of the third chapter of *Policing the Crisis*, on 'the social production of the news'.[7] In the early 1990s, too, informal typescript translations into Spanish of such media studies classics as 'Encoding/Decoding' entered Brazil from Argentina. Hall's work on identity came to light a little later. 'Cultural Identity and Diaspora' was published in the journal of the government heritage institute Instituto do Patrimônio Histórico e Artístico Nacional (IPHAN) in 1996.[8] 'The Centrality of Culture',[9] 'Who Needs Identity?'[10] and the long essay 'The Question of Cultural Identity', from the massive Open University textbook *Modernity and Its Futures* (1996), all came out between 1996 and 1997. They were translated by Tomaz Tadeu da Silva, often in collaboration with the feminist scholar and queer theorist Guacira Lopes Louro, both professors of education in Rio Grande do Sul, southern Brazil. Hall's real bestseller is 'The Question of Cultural Identity', translated as a small book titled '*A Identidade Cultural na Posmodernidade*'[11] and estimated by its current publisher, Lamparina, to have sold more than forty thousand copies.

In the 1990s, in the field of communication, cultural studies came to be associated with reception research, for which 'Encoding/Decoding' is a founding text, and with studies of youth culture, for which *Resistance through Rituals* is a model. This way of reading Hall via reception theory was consolidated by the association of British cultural studies with Latin American cultural studies and the work of Jesús Martín-Barbero on mediation, Néstor García Canclini on hybrid cultures and consumption, and Guillermo Orozco on critical reception theory, television and media literacy. The focus here is on popular agency and the problems of method and subjectivity involved in studies of what people and 'the people' think.

Race and racism only emerged clearly to the Brazilian audience as an object and priority in Stuart Hall's work from 2000 onwards. In that year, he came to a comparative literature conference in

Salvador, an important centre of black Brazilian culture, and delivered a keynote speech entitled 'Diasporas, or the Logics of Cultural Translation'. (In literary studies in Brazil, Hall's work and cultural studies have been grafted onto a long tradition of cultural criticism in which the distance between the lettered and unlettered has been discussed since well before the advent of mass culture in the 1960s.) In 2003, Dawoud Bey's diptych of portraits of Hall appeared on the cover of the *Da diáspora* collection, revealing his blackness, surprising to many. When, for a newspaper interview published in January 2005, Heloisa Buarque de Hollanda and I asked him why he thought interest in his work was so high in Brazil, he attributed it to his having thought about the diaspora. Maybe, he said, it 'has to do with the fact that the Caribbean has a relationship to European cultures very similar to Brazil's. That is the theme that underpins practically all of my work. In the end, I am always writing about that. It is what I am talking about when I write about hybridity, creolization, diaspora. I think that in Brazil people feel very touched by this issue.'[12]

If Hall's work resonates in Brazil because of his work on the diaspora, there are those too who contest or relativise that focus, whether by bringing Hall back into the fold of media studies;[13] rejecting the figure of the diasporic intellectual in favour of the exile, imagined as more proper to Latin America and effective in facing post-9/11 US imperialism;[14] or painting Hall as a rather naïve linguistic theorist for whom black identity is realized through self-affirmation.[15] Even so, his work has made a major contribution to the public and academic discussion of race in Brazil, helping to move it on from the parameters established by the Unesco studies of the 1950s. This research, provoked by the experience of Nazi anti-Semitism, examined the particularities of Brazilian racial classificatory systems in search of models of cordial race relations. Although these studies did not confirm the cordiality or absence of racism, they were not able to dislodge from common sense the idea that Brazil had had a 'softer' slavery, a less violent racism than the United States, or that the unit of analysis was the nation or country. The diaspora as a paradigm for thinking about cultural processes on both local and global scales and about the cultural production of the black Atlantic was interlinked and mutually constituted: This is one of Hall's major contributions to Brazilian intellectual debate in fields including literary studies, anthropology and sociology, all of which have long critical traditions of examining Brazilian culture.

This contribution came precisely at a time when black diasporic cultural forms such as hip-hop were headline news. Enormously popular among the urban poor and MTV's middle-class audience, the hip-hop wave that came to the attention of the mainstream media at the end of the 1990s did not depend on mainstream media to survive. Hip-hop artists sold millions of CDs at concerts attended by tens of thousands of people at a time, advertised on local radio, while some refused to perform for middle-class audiences (the members of which they referred to as *playboys*) at conventional concert hall venues. The underlying issue was that hip-hop presented the voice of black urban youth in an understandable, moral form that helped the middle class understand differently the objects of its moral panic: drug trafficking, urban violence across class lines and black youth.

On the other hand, the same year *Da diáspora* was published, 2003, the first racial university entrance quotas were established, at Rio de Janeiro's state university, as an attempt to close the educational gap between white and non-white sectors of the population. The policy was then applied, rather unevenly, to the federal university system, becoming general policy in 2012, when such quotas were judged constitutional by the supreme court. The controversy over this policy and, to a lesser extent, forms of affirmative action at private universities, marked public debate for a decade. The quotas, the moral panic, the new profile of university student were all, to use Hall's terminology, *theoretical moments* and *interruptions* by new actors, in a context with an added complicator: the growing feeling, in many places and disciplines, that epistemological models of traditional science based on ideas of discovery and revelation no longer held sway—as Foucault had said in his lectures in 1973. This was the setting in which Hall's work on diaspora was embraced as helpful in understanding Brazilian society and politics in the mid- to late 2000s.

Summarising his views of diaspora in 2000, Hall said that diaspora produces a hybridity that is 'an agonistic process . . . marked by an ultimate undecidability'. It is 'haunted by a profound sense of loss', 'a process through which cultures are required to revise their own systems of reference, norms and values by departing from their habitual, in-bred rules of transformation,' framed by 'radically a-symmetrical relations of power' and an awareness of 'the over-determining moments of conquest and colonization and slavery'. He concluded his lecture in an upbeat way, saying that 'the path of diaspora is the pathway of a modern people and a modern culture', but on review, the difficulties stand out: 'This "narrative" has no guaranteed happy ending,'[16] he wrote.

The period since Dilma Rousseff's re-election has been a time of regression, in Brazil, with right-wing demonstrations in favour of impeaching the recently elected president, middle-class resentment of supposed advantages granted to beneficiaries of social income policies, dismantling of policies favouring broader access to higher education and of democratic cultural policy, and reduction of the rights of labour. Although there is not a threat of military coup, wondering how and why the Workers' Party governments went wrong is a necessary exercise, and, under the circumstances, it calls to mind that the same question about what went wrong was asked during the military regime. If Hall was read as a Marxist high theorist the first time around and a reception and media studies theorist in the meantime, what can we gain from the logic of his thinking about diasporic societies? How can Hall's legacy of thought on the diaspora, so evidently useful to so many people in the recent period of policies aiming at reducing inequality in Brazil, be used to think about the politics of a country in its current state? There are no answers to these questions at the moment, but perhaps a rereading of his work in light of recent events would yield greater emphasis of the violence of the processes by which diasporas come into being, of the conquest and colonization and slavery.

Notes

Parts of this article were published in the "Tribute to Stuart Hall" issue of *MATRIZes*, University of São Paulo 10, no. 3 (2016): 15–29. Reproduced by permission.

1. Stuart Hall, *Da diáspora: Identidades e mediações culturais*, ed. Liv Sovik, trans. Adelaine La Guardia Resende et al. (Belo Horizonte/Brasília: Editora UFMG/Representação da UNESCO no Brasil, 2003).
2. Stuart Hall et al., *Da ideologia* (Rio de Janeiro: Zahar, 1980).
3. Flora Süssekind, *Literatura e vida literária: Polêmicas, diários e retratos* (Rio de Janeiro: Zahar, 1985), 22–24.
4. Michel Foucault, *A verdade e as formas jurídicas,* trans. Eduardo Jardim and Roberto Machado (Rio de Janeiro: NAU Editora, 2003), 7–8.
5. Ibid., 10.
6. Ciro Marcondes Filho, 'Stuart Hall, *Cultural Studies* e a nostalgia da dominação hegemônica', *Communicare* 8, no. 1 (2008): 25–42, 32.
7. Venício Lima, *Cultura do silêncio e democracia no Brasil: Ensaios em defesa da liberdade de expressão (1980–2015)* (Brasília: Editora Universidade de Brasília, 2015), 104.
8. Stuart Hall, 'Identidade cultural e diáspora', *Revista de Patrimônio Histórico e Artístico Nacional* 24 (1996): 68–75.
9. Stuart Hall, 'A centralidade da cultura', *Educação e Realidade* 22, no. 2 (1997): 15–46.
10. Stuart Hall, 'Quem precisa da identidade?' In *Identidade e Diferença: A perspectiva dos Estudos Culturais*, ed. Tomaz Tadeu da Silva (Petrópolis: Vozes, 2000): 103–133.
11. Stuart Hall, *A identidade cultural na posmodernidade*, 8th ed., trans. Tomaz Tadeu da Silva and Guacira Lopes Louro (Rio de Janeiro: DP&A, 2003).
12. Heloisa Buarque de Hollanda and Liv Sovik, 'O papa negro dos estudos culturais: Entrevista de Stuart Hall', *Jornal do Brasil* (cultural supplement), January 3, 2004, 3.
13. Lima, *Cultura do silêncio e democracia no Brasil*, 102–103.
14. Vera Follain de Figueiredo, 'Exílios e diásporas', in *O papel do intelectual hoje*, ed. Izabel Margato and Renato Cordeiro Gomes (Belo Horizonte: Editora UFMG, 2004), 133–148, 141.
15. Marcondes Filho, 'Stuart Hall, *Cultural Studies* e a nostalgia da dominação hegemônica', 33.
16. Stuart Hall, 'Diasporas, or the Logics of Cultural Translation', *MATRIZes* (University of São Paulo) 10, no. 3 (2016): 47–58, http://www.revistas.usp.br/matrizes/article/view/124647/121874.

Stuart Hall and the Inter-Asia Cultural Studies Project

Kuan-Hsing Chen

I saw Stuart Hall in Asia only once; that was in Tokyo, in March 1996. I somehow have the impression that he visited mainland China earlier in the 1990s, but there does not seem to be any record. The 1996 Tokyo trip was documented in the *Dialogues with* (or *among*) *Cultural Studies* book in Japanese, published around 1999.[1] Stuart was invited to bring a group of the Birmingham alumni (if I recall correctly, David Morley, Charlotte Brunsdon, Colin Sparks and others were there) to join in dialogues with Japanese intellectuals and scholars. Stuart's counterpart was Hanasaki Kohei, a highly respected activist and intellectual and cultural critic, who was amazed to find his own work had something to do with cultural studies. I went to Tokyo at Stuart's invitation to launch the newly released volume, *Stuart Hall: Critical Dialogues in Cultural Studies*, edited by David Morley and I.[2] It was through Stuart that I was introduced to, and later became a close friend and ally of, Yoshimi Shunya. Shunya was then a young faculty member, put in charge of organizing the conference, and is by now a central figure leading the cultural studies movement in Japan; he has recently finished his duty as the vice president of Tokyo University.

In many inter-Asia cultural studies gatherings over the past fifteen to twenty years, I heard Shunya often refer back to the 1996 encounter with Stuart. The Tokyo dialogue was not exactly a means to endorse the formation of cultural studies in Japan because, according to Shunya's account, there had existed a long intellectual tradition of cultural history and sociology of culture since the 1930s, which formed the basis for Japanese cultural studies in the 1990s. To my understanding, the similar stories to articulate local discursive formation of cultural studies in the 1990s were also told in Korean, Chinese or Taiwanese, Indonesian and Indian instances, all with different trajectories and specificities. For instance, Taiwan's cultural studies formation overlapped with the popular cultural criticism movement of the late 1980s and early 1990s, which was an integral part of the larger democratization movement; that wave of cultural criticism mediating through popular presses and magazines was in fact a continuation of the modern literati culture formed in the late nineteenth and early twentieth centuries. It was through the encounter between existing intellectual formations and cultural studies that cultural studies in Taiwan began to emerge in academic institutions, with a self-conscious attempt to link with wider social and political movements. I think this still holds true for many of the partners involved in the Inter-Asia Cultural Studies (IACS) project.

For Shunya, the moment of the 1996 encounter had a long-lasting impact, motivating and empowering those young audiences packed in the university's stadium to listen to Stuart's keynote in Tokyo. Perhaps it was a similar experience that many of us had in the 1985 International Communication Association (ICA) conference held in Hawaii, when Stuart's speech reverberated through the entire lecture hall. My own proposition is that had it not been for Stuart's work, practices and persona as a whole, that semi-institutional turn or many other projects under the name of cultural studies would not have taken place. Japan's Cultural Typhoon network (2003 to present) and Taiwan's Cultural Studies Association (1998 to present) have been established as non-governmental organizations, located more in the social world to be in dialogues with the currents of political transformation. This identification with cultural studies then generates wider liaisons and connections, within and across borders. IACS and its related evolving programs are concrete expressions of a specific kind of cultural studies inspired by Stuart.

There was an earlier moment of the neo-Marxist, New Left side of Stuart that entered East Asia in the late 1980s, when South Korea and Taiwan (and to some extent Japan) went through a structural shift from the downfall of post-war authoritarianism, anti-Communism and statist developmentalism to an ambiguous new era, now labelled as *neoliberal*. In Taiwan, the moment was marked by the lifting of martial law, opening of political spaces, and booming of the social and political movements. It was in this conjuncture, still in the years of the Cold War, that Stuart's work on authoritarian populism and formulation of popular democratic struggle was used to analyse the local political configurations and to break the nationalist hegemony of the integrationist versus separatist binary and to energize the nascent autonomous social movements of the left. (It is as though one wing of left thought had to traverse West Indies and the United Kingdom to cross-fertilize thinking and actions in post-authoritarian Taiwan, where all things left had been almost decimated.)

There is not enough space here to unpack the complexities of the debate. Suffice it to say that, empowered by Stuart's analysis of Thatcherism, a local popular democracy position or grouping was slowly emerging in the process of confronting concrete political events, such as the June 4, 1989, Tiananmen event, to open up a space for the new social movements that have continued to operate for the past twenty-five years or so. Because of this earlier moment of Marxist connections, when cultural studies began to enter the academic field in East Asia in the late 1990s it was always and already understood as part of a larger political project. (Today, in mainland China, Stuart's work is taken more seriously by the younger faculty in the research institutes of Marxism and Leninism, such as in Nanjing University.) As you could imagine, with a long history of red purge, involving mass killings in the capitalist bloc of Asia, cultural studies' close ties with Marxism is a big problem for the academic establishment. In this sense, institutionalization of cultural studies always means occupying a minor space within the academy so as to work somewhere else.

In the year 2000, the *Inter-Asia Cultural Studies* journal started publication. One of the events to launch the journal was held in Birmingham, during the Crossroads conference, and Stuart was invited as a keynote speaker. He came to the gathering to endorse the project, and in his short speech he mentioned how pleased he was to be able to read critical works available now in English directly out of Asia. What Stuart did not realize was that over the past fifteen years the journal has been forced to deliver materials published in English (note that the editorial office in Taiwan is a non-English-speaking, Mandarin language environment) four times a year and was thus able to create an archive of knowledge; without the journal, such an archive would not have existed.

The IACS project has continued to grow from a loose network of concerned individuals to a larger society established in 2005, with a biannual conference for younger generations to meet in the region. Since 2006, a biannual gathering, the East Asian Critical Journals and Magazines Conference, was launched, and IACS has been an active agent. With the IACS Society, we have built another layer, a consortium of IACS institutions, serving since 2010 to establish a biannual summer school for graduate students to build friendships earlier in their lives. In 2010, we initiated social thought dialogues between India and China. In 2012, an independent Inter-Asia School was founded to create the Asia Circle of Thought, recognizing and facilitating the circulation of work of important Asian thinkers via multilingual translation and publication projects. In 2015, we organized the Bandung/Third-World Sixty Years series across Asia, in which the Hangzhou Forum brought together thinkers and intellectuals from Asia, Africa, Latin America and the Caribbean to revitalize the incomplete intellectual project of the Third World links. In short, multilayered intellectual networks of solidarity have emerged in the post–Cold War era to connect and reconnect intellectual circles in Asia and beyond. Almost all these ongoing projects and programs have been either conducted in the name of cultural studies or facilitated by the IACS network.

More recently, to keep Stuart's ideas alive and to track how his work has become source of thought in different parts of Asia, we organized a double panel in the 2015 IACS Conference at Airlangga University, Surabaya, Indonesia. The panel included scholars of different generations from China, India, Indonesia, Japan, Korea, Taiwan and Thailand. From the presentations and compilations of translations of Stuart's work in different languages, we began to understand which aspects of the work were relevant to specific locations.[3] After the Surabaya gathering, we took a field trip to Bandung and the nearby rural villages in Garut, studying the land-occupying movement led by the Peasant Union (SPP), and we had the extraordinary chance to interact with members of the Confederation of the Indonesian People's Movements (KPRI), a larger umbrella organization to integrate diverse groups including peasants, workers, women, aboriginals, fishermen, environmental groups and more. We were told by the theorist leader of the movement that Stuart's work on Gramsci, in particular on race and class, and his theory of articulation were instrumental for thinking and building the popular democratic movement.

As Stuart remarked at one point, IACS has 'positively and irrevocably transformed the cultural studies project itself'. Perhaps Stuart was right, but he himself may not quite know the extent to which that transformation still carries his spirit. As members of the IACS project, we want to acknowledge Stuart's inspiration and support. I personally confess (likewise for my friend Shunya Yoshimi, and perhaps many of you sitting here may share part of this sentiment): Without seriously thinking about it, the moments of encounters with Stuart have changed the trajectories of our intellectual life (i.e., the name of cultural studies, the commitment for political engagement and working for larger causes), and a lasting attachment with Stuart has directly or indirectly initiated and shaped many critical works. This acknowledgement and confession may well be too late, yet I imagine Stuart sitting here among us to listen with his usual encouraging smile.

Notes

1. The presentations in the conference were translated in T. Hanada, S. Yoshimi and C. Sparks, eds., *Dialogues with* (or *among*) *Cultural Studies* (Tokyo: Shinyo Publisher, 1999). See also the conversations between Stuart Hall and Naoki Sakai, "A Tokyo Dialogue on Marxism, Identity Formation and Cultural Studies," in *Trajectories: Inter-Asia Cultural Studies*, ed. Kuan-Hsing Chen (London: Routledge, 1998), 360–378.

2. Kuan-Hsing Chen and David Morley, eds., *Stuart Hall: Critical Dialogues in Cultural Studies* (New York: Routledge, 1996).

3. The presentations are being revised and will hopefully be published in the IACS journal in the future. For compilations of Stuart Hall's work in Japanese translation by Hiroki Ogasawara, in Korean by Yougho Im, in simplified Chinese by Zhang Liang and in conventional Chinese by Kuan-Hsing Chen, see the Inter-Asia journal website: http://www.tandfonline.com/toc/riac20/current.

22 Mediterranean Archives, Sounds and Cultural Studies

Iain Chambers

Although much of his life was embedded in Englishness and British metropolitan life, Stuart's intellectual formation and biographical trajectory brought an edge to all of that, which native Britons have always found difficult to replicate. Just as Frantz Fanon, another boy with a 'sound colonial education', crossed and confuted French colonial culture and metropolitan thought, Stuart reshuffled the cultural pack. He went on to deal non-authorised versions of modernity, and bet on a possible series of belongings that drew British culture into unsuspected combinations involving diaspora, creolisation and the uncertainties attendant on claiming identity—whether national, racial, social or sexual.

In this spirit, pursuing cultural studies under Mediterranean skies as a pedagogical and political project, I wish to argue that the rationalist and nationalist requirements of Euro-American modernity—to the will of which all seemingly has to be rendered transparent (these days, increasingly reduced to the implacable metaphysical glow of the 'market' on a computer screen)—necessarily come to be undone and located on an altogether more extensive and less provincial map.

The Limits of Democracy

This critical journey could commence from the extreme south of Europe—so far south as to be below the northernmost tip of Africa. The island of Lampedusa, located on the African continental shelf some 200 km to the south of Tunis and Algiers, is politically part of Europe. Here, the so-called Third World brushes up dramatically against the First World in scenes of desperate migrants and refugees being rescued from sinking vessels and human traffickers before being isolated, identified and despatched to camps. Lined up on the quayside prior to being shipped to Sicily, each is given a plastic bag containing a two-litre bottle of water, a panino and a telephone card to phone home; for the men, there is also a packet of cigarettes. Here, the multiple souths of the planet crack and infiltrate the modernity that has consigned them to silent histories. Here, the arbitrary violence of legality, rights and citizenship are most brutally exposed. For if the watery cemetery of the present-day Mediterranean is witness to the necro-politics of global capital, then it equally registers the very limits of European humanism. A legal-juridical regime that pretends universal valency, while, as Frantz Fanon famously noted in *The Wretched of the Earth*, it continues to massacre mankind on every street corner, in every angle of the world, or else simply leaves it to sink beneath the waves, consigning the anonymous to the abyss between the law and justice, emerges in all of its arbitrary violence.

Here, the migrant's body, rendered an object of economical, legal, political and racial authority, exposes in all its naked brutality the occidental imperative to reduce the world to its needs. It simultaneously reopens the global colonial archive that initially established this planetary traffic in capital, bodies, merchandise and legalised annihilation. The walls—between the United States and Mexico, between Israel and the Occupied Territories, between South Africa and the rest of the continent, between India and Bangladesh, between Australia and the Timor Sea—go up. They are, of course, both material and immaterial, composed of fluid and fluctuating borders to control a traffic in bodies that is simultaneously a traffic in potential capital, resources and accumulation.[1] What is apparently kept out is an inherent component of the walled world of securitocracy and its design on the planet.

This is the political economy of location and the dark underbelly of the global formation of the modern world. Here, the multiple souths of Europe, of the Mediterranean, of the globe are rendered both marginal and paradoxically central to the reproduction of that economy. If the whole world were considered equally modern, then the competitive logic that divides and drives modernity would collapse. The cancellation of the inequalities, property and differences that charge the planetary circuits of capitalist accumulation would render the concept superfluous. As

James Baldwin captured it: 'It is not even remotely possible for the excluded to become included, for this inclusion means, precisely, the end of the *status quo*—or would result, as so many of the wise and honored would put it, in a mongrelisation of the races.'[2] The subversion of this historicist and racial accounting of time and 'progress' undoes historical time as it is presently understood—for the 'south' as a political and historical question is, above all, about the power exercised on those held in its definitions.

After all, the democracy and citizenship that we claim in the West fully depends—in both its economic structures and cultural tissues—on the subordination and exclusion of the bodies and histories of those who inhabited the colonial world and who continue their lives in the postcolonial polity. Not only has our 'freedom' been structurally dependent on the extension of non-freedoms (slavery, indenture, genocide) elsewhere, but the liberal formation of modern, European democracy on both sides of the Atlantic is riddled with perversities of power and property that make its citizens the bearers of planetary injustice. The *rule of law*—that is, the universal claims of a property-owning class and its political economy to legislate for the world—not only reveals the arbitrary and unilateral powers of a European-derived sovereign will on the planet; at the same time, and this is what most interests me, it exposes that same logic to both translation and betrayal. Ideas about citizenship, democracy and the public sphere are everywhere taken up and embodied by subjects practising the multiple languages of modernity. In the immediacies of the simultaneously local and transnational spaces of the contemporary city, lives, cultures and prospects are both inhabited and appropriated. All this is part of what David Featherstone has called the 'geographies of subaltern connection.'[3]

To return to Lampedusa and consider the historical archive of this space—the Mediterranean—is to trouble the prevalent historical placeholder of the modern nation state. It is to query what has come to be considered the *natural* form of historical formations; but history, as Hannah Arendt consistently argued, clearly is not only narrated, lived and perceived through the nation.[4] This is to question both a political order of knowledge and its direct inscription in the disciplinary protocols of modern sociology, political science, area studies, anthropology and historiography, not to mention the assumed authority of national literatures and languages. Working in a Mediterranean web of transnational histories and their presence and effects on multiple scales suggests even more: The conceptual landscape peculiar to one of its shores—in particular, its northern, hegemonic European one—is now exposed to very different understandings and unsuspected variations.

Migrating Sounds

We are drawn into a shifting geography of memory (and forgetting) where meaningful details connect with forgotten futures: a dynamic interweaving of past, present and future collated in the intensities of the present sustained, for example, in a sound. Listening to the musical sounds of the Mediterranean, we can hear different archives and chart diverse geographies from those proposed in the accredited versions of its formation secured in the historical and political cage of the nation state. When the ninth-century Muslim dandy Abu l-Hasan 'Ali Ibn Nafi', better known as Ziryab, brought from Baghdad to Cordova his compositions and musical innovations for the oud, he was not simply traversing Dar al-Islam. His musical passage left a profound cultural trace. Today, this music has been reworked and re-proposed by Naseer Shamma, who is also from Baghdad.[5] As a contemporary event, this recording and performance of music from Islamic Spain opens a hole in time. More suggestively, it proposes, to echo Gilles Deleuze and his noted work on the baroque, a fold in the regime of linear temporality that renders physical and temporal distance proximate, immediate and contemporary.[6] The intimation of another Mediterranean, sustained in sound, provokes a critical interruption in its present configuration. Not only does the homogenous alterity associated with Muslim culture in contemporary definitions break down, but that alterity also comes undone, to be replaced by an altogether more complex historical and cultural composition in which the Arab, Berber and Islamic world turns out to be internal to Europe's formation.

To work in this manner of receiving and reworking the archive—not as a mausoleum, an accumulation of dusty documents or a museum technology narrating the nation, but as a living and ongoing site of critical elaboration and a redistribution of responsibilities for the future, as Derrida would have put it—is not only to recover from the rubble of the past materials to conceive of a diverse today and tomorrow. It also permits, through interrupting a singular understanding of the present, new circuits of connections and understandings to emerge. Not only does the past never fully pass, it also spills out of the narrow definitions prepared for its presence in the present. Once again, the privileged placeholder of the nation as the site of historical explanation and identification proves unsatisfactory. A Mediterranean musicality suggests altogether more extensive and unfinished business.

Here, the sounds of an archive, of an altogether deeper history and longer series of rhythms previously reduced to silence, disturb and interrupt the codification of historical time as the privileged site of a universal rationality: the simultaneous point of departure and arrival of occidental reason. The sounds of Ziryab's maqams spill out of the oud into sub-Saharan Africa and subsequently across the Atlantic, via the black diaspora induced by the racist slave trade. They will later be deposited in the blue notes of Stuart's adored Miles Davis. In this instance of ninth-century Arab music dubbing the Mediterranean, reassembling and putting it together with a different cut and mix, there opens an interval in time that ushers in other temporalities for sounding out the present: music as method. Thinking with sounds as processes and practices, as living archives, we encounter unsuspected genealogies, other modalities to rhyme, rhythm and reason the world that ruffle and disturb the singularity of the approved narrative.

Altogether more recently, in the port city of Naples, occupied by the Allied Forces in 1943, and subsequently the headquarters of NATO and the US Seventh Fleet, street life and club life have been crossed in a significant musical mix. Local Neapolitan song, itself a profoundly urban and commercial tradition, proposed a harmonic ambivalence—the *glissando*, the throttled vocals on the edge of breakdown—easily susceptible to the inclinations of the blues and its subsequent offspring. Despite its autochthonous declarations, sedimented in local Neapolitan song is a deeper archive that takes us back and outwards into an altogether more extensive Mediterranean musicality. Here, the microtonalities of Arab singing and instrumentation turn out to be not too distant from the tangled harmonies found in the voices of local singers.

In September 1981, in Piazza Plebiscito, in front of a public of two hundred thousand, Pino Daniele plays *I Know My Way*.[7] The line-up is that of a classical rock band: electric guitar and bass, drums and percussion, keyboards and a saxophone. *I Know My Way* is sung in a mixture of English, Neapolitan and Italian over a funk riff interspersed with electric guitar arpeggios and solos that could have arrived directly from Buddy Guy in Chicago—yet the sound is ultimately a local idiom. Tradition here is crossed and transformed through the translation of sounds from other subaltern histories, provoking a renewal in the seeming continuity of the same. Blue veins in the metropolitan body, traced on the skin of the city, challenge the cliché in a syncretisation of sounds and sentiments, producing a further unplanned cultural and critical space. These are also the traces subscribed to by the Neapolitan dub group Almamegretta, proclaiming their Afro-Phoenician ancestry over dub rhythms that have arrived from the Caribbean via London. Over a heavy bass riddim, Hannibal once again conquers Italy—'Africa, Africa, Africa'—and a negated "Black Athena" reverberates in the "Suud" of Italy and Europe, where once we were all wops and without papers[8]

Here, music mines modernity in another key. Visceral intensities are doubled and disseminated, echoed in dub, to relay the insistence of histories from below, from 'way, way below'.[9] Born elsewhere—in the racisms of the urban jungles of North America, in the slave-drenched histories of the Caribbean—such cultural sensibilities and musical suggestions also unfolded in the city under the volcano. Between Paul Gilroy's black Atlantic and Mediterranean blues, it becomes possible to trace an ecology of rhythms, beats and tonalities that generate sonorous cartographies in which, as Steve Goodman would put it, 'sound comes to the rescue of thought'.[10] Listening to this blue archive—a bluesology that plays and replays modernity, exploring the gaps between its official notes—unsuspected sounds and sentiments cross, contaminate and creolise the landscape: in the Caribbean, in the Mediterranean—and in the modern world. Such musical maps produce forms of interference that give voice to hidden histories, negated genealogies, rendering them audible and perceptible. The importance of the sound lies not only in its narrative force, but also in its capacity to sustain critical perspectives. Such sounds direct us toward what survives and lives on as a cultural and historical set of resources able to resist, disturb, interrogate and interrupt the presumed unity of the present.[11] As such, they promote counter-histories of the Mediterranean, of modernity, disseminating intervals and interruptions in the well-tempered score that the hegemonic accounting narrates to itself under the teleological dictatorship of Euro-American 'progress', thereby systematically rendering the rest of the planet underdeveloped and structurally not yet 'modern'.

Cultural Studies as an Incurable Wound

As it travels into other geographies, sustained in translation and confronting the indecipherable that registers the complexities of historical differences, the critical configuration of cultural studies in transit also returns to reinvest its so-called origins and sources with further interrogations. So cultural studies under Mediterranean skies proposes a formation that is necessarily uncoupled from a social and historical objectivity, the universality of which always and only reconfirms me. This has meant thinking and living with processes that cross, confuse and confute the perspective that insists that all should be represented and rendered transparent to Western eyes. To inhabit *this* threshold, where conformity and the consolidated break down, is to work with fragments and acknowledge Walter Benjamin's understanding of history as an accumulation of ruins that continue to pile up as the past refuses to pass.

Such lessons from the souths of the world—simply hinted at here—exceed the framing of European rationalism and nationalism and cut into the existing corpus of knowledge and power. They leave an *incurable wound*. They also constitute a critical rendezvous with the cut that cultural studies has left in the disciplinary pretensions and premises of the human and social sciences. For me, neither Europe nor its disciplinary practices, powers and knowledge can ever be the same again. To practice cultural, and what I today might call Mediterranean, studies is precisely to operate this cut. It cannot be healed; it continues to bleed. It returns us to Stuart's far wider and altogether more troubled and unstable world without guarantees: a world that continues to draw us on.

Notes

1. Sandro Mezzadra and Brett Nielson, *Border as Method; or, The Multiplication of Labor* (Durham, NC: Duke University Press, 2013).

2. James Baldwin, *No Name in the Street* (New York: Vintage, 1972), 87–88.

3. David Featherstone, *Resistance, Space and Political Identities: The Making of Counter-global Networks* (Oxford: Wiley-Blackwell, 2008).

4. Hannah Arendt, *The Origins of Totalitarianism* (New York: Schocken Books 2004).

5. Naseer Shamma, *Maquamat Ziryáb—Desde el Eúfrates al Guadalquiver* (Pneuma 2003).

6. Gilles Deleuze, *The Fold* (London: Continuum, 2006).

7. For a version from 1983, see https://www.youtube.com watch?v=fFTOeIS4 1DI&feature=youtu.be.

8. The song titles refer to diverse recordings by Almamegretta. For example, *Figli di Annibale*: https://www.youtube.com/watch?v=jp4wLi5Ptog; *Black Athena*: https://www.youtube.com/watch?v=PMXVp2b2jqk; and Almamegretta's singer Raiz with *Wop*: https://www.youtube.com/watch?v=btJ-07ak2q0.

9. Robin D. G. Kelley, *Race Rebels: Culture, Politics, and the Black Working Class* (New York: The Free Press, 1994), 1.

10. Steve Goodman, *Sonic Warfare: Sound Affect and the Ecology of Fear* (Cambridge, MA: MIT Press, 2010), 82.

11. I explored reading the Mediterranean and modernity with music as method in Iain Chambers, *Mediterraneo Blues: Musiche, malinconia postcolonial, pensieri marittimi* (Turin: Bollati Boringhieri, 2012).

POLICING in Hackney

1945-1984

A Report
Commissioned by
The Roach Family Support Committee

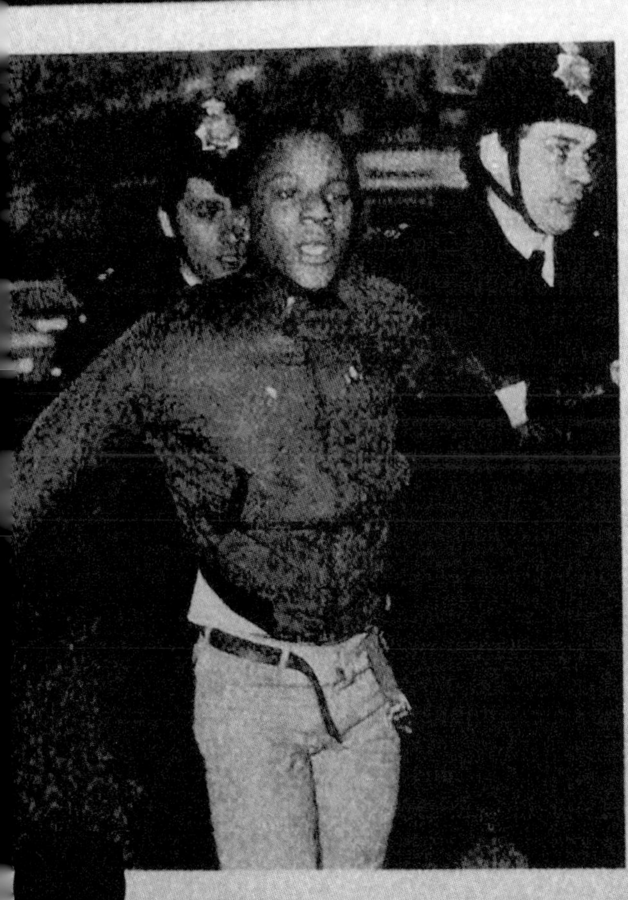

Produced by
an Independent Committee of Inquiry

Foreword by Professor Stuart Hall

Part VI
The Intellectual Legacies of Policing the Crisis

The Intellectual Legacies of Policing the Crisis

As with many of those who first met and were influenced by Hall by way of his writing—rather than on television—Angela Davis admits that, initially, she had no idea he was black. Her first encounter in the 1960s with Hall's writing was in the *New Left Review*, as Angela Davis describes in her keynote, 'Policing the Crisis Today' (chapter 24). She 'met' Hall through his work, notably *Policing the Crisis: Mugging, the State, and Law and Order* in the 1980s and in person at key conferences in the early 1990s, where his contribution 'What Is This "Black" in Black Popular Culture?' (defined in terms of finding who we ourselves are) was critical for Davis. She describes one of Hall's famous conference interventions— this one almost physical, between Stephen Steinberg and Cornel West—and Hall's special capacity 'to bridge intellectual gaps, to traverse theoretical and political positions' and thus resolve conflicts in a constructive manner.

Davis identifies the continuing relevance of *Policing the Crisis* in two respects. One is as a pivotal text for both radical criminology and critical prison studies, which currently addresses the over-representation of blacks and Hispanics in the largely privatized 'prison industrial complex'. The other, twenty-five years after its original publication, is how the collectively authored book helps to frame her response to racist state violence, as manifested in the then-recent uprisings in Ferguson, Missouri, following the death of Michael Brown and the all too numerous similar cases that have fuelled support for Black Lives Matter in the United States and internationally. To conclude, Davis calls for a present-day conjunctural analysis, in which race, crime and the often-neglected 'intimate violence' within personal relationships is subject to the kind of investigation that Hall and his collaborators pioneered.

23 *Policing the Crisis Today*

Angela Y. Davis

I am profoundly grateful for the opportunity to participate in this conference dedicated to the life, work and legacies of Stuart Hall. I thank Julian Henriques, the curator of the Stuart Hall Week here at Goldsmiths, and I express my deepest gratitude to Catherine Hall.

I must admit that I was somewhat surprised to receive the invitation to provide the keynote for this memorial conference. After all, I have lived and worked at a certain distance from the exciting swirls of research, teaching and activism anchored by Stuart's writing, his mentoring and his work more generally as a public intellectual. If I think about his influence in terms of concentric circles, I was indeed involved in several circles—but far more removed than many of the participants in this conference. I am therefore extremely happy for the opportunity to hear those who have built more directly on Stuart Hall's theoretical and activist legacies—some of whom I have already met and some of whom I have not—and am all too aware of my own inadequacies in the position of being charged with delivering a keynote at this international conference.

This conference engages us in conversations, acquaints and reacquaints us with projects, and begins the process of considering Stuart's legacies, which have already vastly transformed individuals, theories, fields and movements. It is precisely this capaciousness that so many of us experienced as the generosity of Stuart's ideas and interventions. He helped to make Marxism more open, even if lacking the guarantees we could not avoid desiring. He helped to shift our epistemological focus from discipline-based theories and methods to problems—the possible but always contingent resolution of which would require us to consult many disciplines—and, indeed, to think beyond the framework of disciplines, and to also recognize the production of knowledge in venues other than academic ones—in other words, also through political practice. And all of this he accomplished with the most wonderful, most unforgettable smile.

After I last saw Stuart, shortly before he passed away, I felt compelled to reflect on the many ways his influence had marked my own life. I first encountered the name Stuart Hall as a young person eagerly reading *New Left Review*. I must admit that I had no idea then that he was black—but in those days, we had not yet learned how to embrace, disavow or express disinterest in such identities. It was during this time that I found my way to the thought and teachings of Herbert Marcuse, who would eventually become my primary mentor both as an undergraduate and graduate student. By the time I might have had the opportunity to meet Stuart Hall through Marcuse, who had been an avid reader of *New Left Review*, Stuart had already left the journal's editorship some years before. When I travelled to London in 1967 to attend the Dialectics of Liberation Conference, where Marcuse made a pivotal intervention, I did meet Robin Blackburn, who then represented the *New Left Review*, along with Stokely Carmichael and a number of black British intellectuals and activists. In the same way that Stuart often reflected on the alternative lives he might have led had he decided to return to Jamaica as did many of his cohort, I have often speculated on how an earlier encounter with Stuart Hall in person might have shifted my own trajectory.

Although I would not meet him in person for many years, I rediscovered his writings through various paths and in various venues. I first encountered *Policing the Crisis: Mugging, the State and Law and Order* through the journal *Crime and Social Justice*—which survived the dismantling of the radical School of Criminology at University of California, Berkeley, and which continues to be published today under the title *Social Justice*. When I joined the faculty in History of Consciousness at the University of California, Santa Cruz, I began to understand what a powerful influence the work of the CCCS under Stuart Hall's leadership had exerted on new interdisciplinary knowledge formations inside and outside the academy.

I met Stuart at two conferences that took place in the early 1990s: the 1991 Black Popular Culture Conference at the Dia Foundation in New York and the 1994 Race Matters Conference inspired by the publication of Cornel West's book of the same title.[1] The two conferences and subsequent anthologies framed many of the major questions that would guide explorations of race, identity and culture over the next decades. In retrospect, Stuart's valuable interventions, in serving as bookends for the two collections, raised issues that would remain at the centre of these explorations. Stuart's essay 'What Is This "Black" in Black Popular Culture?' is the opening contribution in *Black Popular Culture*,[2] directly following Gina Dent's introduction, which dwells in part on Stuart's analysis of the mythic nature of popular culture. Popular culture is not, in Stuart's words, 'where we find who we really are . . . It is where we discover and play with identifications of ourselves, where we are imagined, where we are represented, not only to audiences out there who do not get the message, but to ourselves for the first time.'[3]

In the Race Matters anthology, *The House That Race Built*,[4] edited by Wahneema Lubiano, Stuart's contribution, 'Subjects in History: Making Diasporic Identities', is positioned at the end of the book, accentuating the way it radically troubles the notion of identity that tends to define the process of political organizing. The question is not, as he put it, 'How do we effectively mobilize those identities which are already formed? so that we could put them on the train and get them onto the stage at the right moment', but rather, 'How can we organize . . . human subjects into positions where they can recognize one another long enough to act together, and thus to take up a position that one of these days they might live out and act through as an identity? Identity is at the end, not the beginning, of the paradigm.'[5] During this present conjuncture, even as we are poised to open a new era of political struggle, both the question of popular culture and the question of identity remain central.

Lubiano has described a revealing moment during the latter conference, which celebrated the publication of Cornel West's book *Race Matters*. She describes an extemporaneous debate between Stephen Steinberg and West that resulted from Steinberg's critique of *Race Matters*—especially his observations about black nihilism, a debate that had surfaced previously at the Black Popular Culture Conference:

> Cornel jumps to his feet to respond to Stephen. A couple of guys in the back shout at Cornel that Stephen is right; some people in the audience heckle Cornel while others defend him. Cornel pantomimes mock indignation . . . There's more shouting, and things are getting quite heated. At that point, Stuart walks to one of the microphones and says 'I feel that I ought to place my body between Cornel and his interlocutors in order to save him' and the entire audience starts laughing. Then they quiet and listen to Stuart give a measured, nuanced, and useful defence of Cornel's work while at the same time affirming most of Stephen's critique. It was a fascinating moment.[6]

Stuart was so unusual in his capacity to bridge intellectual gaps, to traverse theoretical and political positions and to change his own position when it seemed the right thing to do. No one could mistake his intellectual generosity—not only offering us the gift of his always discerning and insightful observations, but also always willing to learn from others. He not only talked to his peers, but learned from younger people as well.

When I was asked how I wished to frame my remarks for this session, I immediately thought about these questions of popular culture, political identities and processes of moving across theoretical and political positions. Simultaneously, I asked myself how we might learn directly from *Policing the Crisis* as we grapple with the widely reported 2014 uprising in Ferguson, Missouri. When I was last in this part of the world three months ago, I was struck by the scale and intensity of European responses to the story of Michael Brown's death and the subsequent protests in Ferguson, Missouri. For example, in Savona, Italy, a town of sixty thousand people, virtually everyone I encountered posed urgent questions about the death of Michael Brown, who had been had been killed in August by the police in a small town one-third the size of Savona, in the Midwestern United States What about this current historical conjuncture enabled massive responses—and not only in the United States and Europe—to what was simply one out of an infinite number of examples of a form of racist state violence that reaches back to the era of slavery? Four days ago, the failure to indict Darren Wilson, the police officer who killed Michael Brown, further intensified the protests. What were referred to as spontaneous demonstrations erupted throughout the United States, including in Oakland, California, where I live. In an unprecedented action, demonstrators, who paraded through the city, monitored by police on the ground and in helicopters above, succeeded in shutting down a major freeway for a significant period of time. Calls for economic boycotts circulated throughout the St. Louis area. The slogan and gesture, 'Hands up, don't shoot', recapitulating the reported stance of young Mike Brown before he was shot down, was rapidly adopted. 'Black Lives Matter', a phrase coined by Patrisse Cullors, Alicia Garza and Opal Tometi in the aftermath of the failure to indict George Zimmerman in the 2012 Trayvon Martin case,[7] became a wildly popular twitter hashtag, a political slogan circulating around the world and a movement, as well as an organization. Numerous demonstrations are taking place in Europe and in other parts of the world as well. How, then, do we make sense of these developments? Can *Policing the Crisis*, published more than thirty-five years ago, help us navigate the complexities of this moment?

Policing the Crisis opens with the case of three youth of different racial backgrounds, who were given excessively long sentences after a trial on robbery and assault. As we know, the text opens with an attempt to understand an instance of mugging and concludes with an analysis of the social, cultural, ideological and economic crisis that became the terrain for the development of Thatcherism. As the authors point out in the preface to the second edition, 'This book ends by making connections and offering explanations that would not have been anticipated at the beginning.'[8] What is significant for the present moment is how this study demonstrates the crafting of collective consent to increased state repression, which appears to be spontaneous, through various cultural and ideological channels.

A deeply collaborative and interdisciplinary work, *Policing the Crisis* examines neoliberalism as it began to take shape during the Thatcher and Reagan eras. In the new preface, published in 2013, the authors reflect on the legacy of the CCCS: 'In a post-1968 participatory spirit, CCCS was committed to collective modes of intellectual work, research and writing, in which staff and graduate students worked together. The ethos, project and practice of the Centre were therefore crucial for the form that the project took. Indeed, this collective authorship is one way in which PTC is widely viewed as an exemplary text.'[9] It is true that *Policing the Crisis* became a pivotal text in radical criminology—but I want to emphasize how central it also has been to the development of the emergent field of critical prison studies and, within and beyond the academy, to the development of contemporary prison abolitionism as a basis for theory and practice in the era of neoliberalism. A growing number of scholars who work in history, legal studies, geography, feminist studies, literature and cultural studies associate their work with the field of critical and interdisciplinary prison studies. As it has thus far evolved, this emergent field would be inconceivable without the example of *Policing the Crisis* and the intellectual and political legacies it represents.

One of the collaborative research clusters explicitly organized around the theoretical and methodological approaches of *Policing the Crisis* was Critical Resistance: Beyond the Prison Industrial Complex in spring 2000, which followed on the heels of a major conference that brought together scholars, activists, artists, advocates, as well as former and current prisoners. This residential research group associated with the University of California Humanities Research Centre grew out of an effort to encourage scholars to directly address the growing prison crisis, the rising numbers of people in US jails and prisons, the disproportionate numbers of black and Latino people behind bars and the increasing involvement of major capitalist corporations in the punishment industry. At the time, we were attempting an analysis that considered the efforts at ideological closure that were rendering it increasingly difficult to engage in serious public conversations about the persistence of racism in the post–civil rights era. We argued that the soaring prison population with its manifest racial disparities was perhaps the most salient example of the structural racism undergirding contemporary social institutions—an example of the way racism was hiding in plain sight.

Those of us who organized the 1998 conference that preceded the research group had strategically chosen to highlight what we called—drawing from Mike Davis's formulation—the *prison industrial complex*. We gave ourselves the charge—inspired by Stuart Hall—of 'disarticulating' crime and punishment so that punishment could be critically examined outside its usual causal relation with crime, with the aim of investigating ways of comprehending the new economic, political and ideological stakes in a rising prison population that were linked to the decline of the welfare state and directly related to global capitalism and its various structural adjustments throughout the world—both north and south.

We knew that our analysis had to be feminist—not simply in the sense of attending to gender, but also in the sense of attending to the circuits that lead from the intimate to the institutional, from the public to the private and from the personal to the political. Thus, the move toward abolition—prison abolition—is also a way of raising the question of the work the state does within and through our emotional life—the landscapes forged by our feelings that often appear to be autonomously produced. As this process was formulated in *Policing the Crisis*: 'Each of the phases in the development of our social formation has thus transmitted a number of seminal ideas about crime *to* our generation; and these 'sleeping forms' are made active again whenever common-sense thinking about crime uncoils itself. The ideas and social images of crime which have thus been embodied in legal and political practices historically provide the present horizons of thought inside our consciousness; we continue to "think" crime *in them*—they continue to think crime *through us*.'[10] Now that some of these ideas appear to be in the early stages of unravelling—at least with respect to policing practices in US black communities—we could clearly benefit from a more expansive, transdisciplinary investigation of contemporary policing, prisons, racism, the state, popular culture and political resistance.

I make these comments as an initial, tentative response to Stuart's comments during a riveting interview conducted by Sut Jhally in 2012. The comments point out that through their collaborative scholarship, the authors 'almost casually, almost by chance . . . hit on the moment of transition between two major conjunctures'. Remarking that it is not possible to say that nothing has changed since then, Stuart emphasizes the degree to which the dimension of the market has become much more important to processes of policing and social control. These changes, he says, 'oblige us to do a Policing the Crisis now', to perform a 'conjunctural analysis of your own and put race and crime at the centre and see what happens'.[11]

State violence increasingly relies on the use of the 'war on terror' as a broad designation for the project of twenty-first century Western democracy and as the primary contemporary justification of anti-Muslim racism. The so-called war on terror has further legitimized the Israeli occupation of Palestine and has solidified the repression of immigrants as it has led to the militarization of local sheriffs' and police departments, including university police. That the US Department of Defense Excess Property Program has systematically transferred military equipment to local police was dramatically demonstrated when protestors responding to the killing of Michael Brown in Ferguson, Missouri, were confronted by local police officers dressed in camouflage uniforms, armed with military weapons, backed up by armoured military vehicles, and tossing into the crowd the same military-grade tear gas used by the Israeli army on Palestinian resisters. How would a contemporary conjectural analysis examine the various ways in which Islamophobia and the war on terror have transformed state practices of racism?

In the Global North, the history of people of African, Latin American, Asian and indigenous descent has always revealed the deployment of racialized state violence. The persistence of anti-black racism has become even more conspicuous in the United States during the administration of a black president, whose very election was extensively represented as heralding the advent of a new, 'post-racial' era. The sheer volume of police violence directed against black youth is beginning to be acknowledged as boldly contradicting the lingering assumption that police killings in black communities, as repetitive as they may be, are, after all, aberrations. Trayvon Martin in Sanford, Florida, and Michael Brown in Ferguson, Missouri, are only the most widely known of the countless numbers of black people killed by police or vigilantes during the Obama administration. As we begin to learn about the outrageous numbers of black male targets of state violence, it is important to note that we rarely hear about the women—Rekia Boyd in Chicago, for example—who may succumb less frequently to police violence, but who nevertheless deserve to be acknowledged. Moreover, a full engagement with state violence requires a serious investigation of the homophobic and transphobic dimensions of racism. As oppositional sensibilities to racist state violence emerge, so too have we begun to recognize the degree to which professional sports concerns have concealed a pandemic of intimate violence. How might a contemporary conjunctural analysis address the connection between state violence and intimate violence, including on university campuses?

In the recent period, we can trace state involvement in racist violence back to Stephen Lawrence and Amadou Diallo, through Oscar Grant, Jordan Davis, Eric Garner and Trayvon Martin. In the same judicial district as the case of George Zimmerman, who admitted to shooting Trayvon Martin, there is also the case of Marissa Alexander, who fired a warning shot to prevent her abusive husband from attacking her. The same prosecutor who failed to obtain a conviction of Zimmerman recently threatened Alexander with three, twenty-year sentences to be served consecutively in order to force a plea deal. A final question: What if an examination of the contemporary moment that, in the tradition of *Policing the Crisis*, placed race and crime at the centre were launched by the case of Marissa Alexander? How might an analysis be developed that would vigorously work this conjuncture?

Notes

1. Cornel West, *Race Matters* (New York: Vintage Books, 1994).
2. Gina Dent, ed., *Black Popular Culture* (Seattle: Bay Press, 1992).
3. Stuart Hall, 'What Is This "Black" in Black Popular Culture?', in *Black Popular Culture*, ed. Gina Dent (Seattle: Bay Press, 1992), 21–33, 32.
4. Wahneema Lubiano, ed., *The House That Race Built: Black Americans, U.S. Terrain* (New York: Pantheon, 1997).
5. Stuart Hall, 'Subjects in History: Making Diasporic Identities', in *The House That Race Built: Black Americans, U.S. Terrain*, ed. Wahneema Lubiano (New York: Pantheon, 1997), 289–300, 291.
6. '"Stuart Hall" (Wahneema Lubiano Comments, Stuart Hall Event, 17 March 2014)', *Cultural Studies* 29, no. 1 (2015), 12–16.
7. See Alicia Garza, 'A Herstory of the #BlackLivesMatter Movement by Alicia Garza', *The Feminist Wire*, October 7, 2014, http://www.thefeministwire.com/2014/10/blacklivesmatter-2/.
8. Stuart Hall et al., *Policing the Crisis: Mugging, the State and Law and Order* (London: Palgrave Macmillan, 2013), xi.
9. Ibid., 10.
10. Ibid., 171; italics in original.
11. Sut Jhally, 'Stuart Hall: The Last Interview', *Cultural Studies* 30, no. 2 (2015): 332–345, doi: 10.1080/09502386.2015.1089918.

Part VII
Biographies and Institutional Histories

Biographies and Institutional Histories

As explained in the introduction, the pieces included here have their origin in a conference that took place at Goldsmiths, University of London in November 2014. Indeed, in the wake of Stuart Hall's death, the building in which the conference took place was renamed in his honour—and the naming ceremony took place on the conference day itself, November 28, 2014.

In terms of Hall's specific connections to Goldsmiths, there was an important prehistory to the renaming of the building in which the conference took place. One part of this prehistory concerned the college's close relations not only to Hall himself but also to his predecessor at the CCCS in Birmingham, Richard Hoggart. Hoggart was Warden of Goldsmiths in an earlier period, and a few years prior to Hall's death, another of the college's buildings had been renamed in his honour. This has produced a highly appropriate architectural symmetry: Now, across the college green from the Richard Hoggart Building, lies the Professor Stuart Hall Building—named in honour of the person who succeeded Hoggart at the original CCCS and led it through its most successful period of development. To that extent, the history of British cultural studies is now architecturally inscribed in the Goldsmiths campus. The connection goes very deep—for Hall had come very close to joining Goldsmiths on two occasions. When Hoggart came to Goldsmiths as Warden in the late 1970s, he tried hard to persuade Hall to follow him here—an invitation that Hall felt he had to refuse because of his continuing responsibility for the CCCS.

By the early 1990s, having subsequently moved from Birmingham to spend a decade at the Open University, Hall had come to feel that he was ready for what he described as 'one last Big Challenge' before the end of his career. Thus, positive discussions were held with a view to Hall's transferring to Goldsmiths. Unfortunately, due to funding cuts, this move proved impossible; to everyone's disappointment, the initiative faded away. However, on his retirement from the Open University in 1997, Hall was made an honorary degree holder at Goldsmiths, and his relation to the college was formalised. Of all the many honours he received, that one was of particular significance for him. Hall was subsequently made a research fellow of the Media and Communications department and worked closely with the department, appearing regularly as a speaker at events variously sponsored by the departments of Media and Communications, Visual Cultures, Sociology and the Cultural Studies Centre.

Hall's links to Goldsmiths were myriad; this was, after all, the place where a variety of his own/CCCS's ex-students, friends and collaborators found the most convivial home for their own intellectual work at different times—including Sally Alexander, Les Back, Paul Gilroy, Dick Hebdige, Julian Henriques, Isaac Julien, Andy Lowe, David Morley, Angela McRobbie and Bill Schwarz, among others. However, the linkages were not merely personal—beginning, as he did, as a Henry James scholar and ending up not simply as professor of sociology (at Open University) but as the inspiration for a whole new generation of artistic work in film, video and photography concerned with matters of race, ethnicity and culture, Hall's own intellectual formation exactly matches—and indeed, helped to shape—the distinctive identity Goldsmiths enjoys today as a college specialising in the Humanities, Arts and Social Sciences. He personally was—and continues to be—the inspiration for a great deal of our work. Many of us owe him a great intellectual debt—which all the contributions to this book reflect in their own ways, even if this debt is by definition, one that can never be repaid.

Conversations, Projects and Legacies represents an attempt not so much to repay that intellectual debt, but to begin a new series of conversations, debates and lines of enquiry that will take the legacy of Stuart Hall's particular type of cultural studies through into new areas for the future. Many of those who attended the conference found it a profoundly emotional event as much as an intellectual one. Indeed, it is impossible not to be affected by

Stuart's work—even for those who did not have the good fortune of meeting or working with him in person. The conference was the culmination of an entire week of activities at Goldsmiths, opening with the showing of John Akomfrah's three-screen installation, *The Unfinished Conversation* (2013). The conversations between those who took part in the talks, screenings, discussions and exhibitions of the week had that special convivial energy Stuart was so well-known for inspiring.

This collection is designed to be as comprehensive as possible, but of course it could never be exhaustive. Inevitably, the geographical location of the conference and the links explained earlier between Goldsmiths and CCCS has led to a positive focus on those interlinked institutional histories—and on the early CCCS days that (as documented in Mahasiddhi's photoessay in chapter 24) have been such an important aspect of our intellectual and political formation. This is indeed how the *legacy* in our title runs: through Hall's former students to our students today—a legacy of which we are very proud. In this connection, it is important also to recognise that Hall was always deeply invested in institutional politics—in building collectives and institutions that could pursue intellectual and political projects over the longer term. For him, the goal was never just to produce intellectual *content* (to use today's terminology) but rather to continually build collectivities, project groups and institutional structures through which that 'content production' could be enabled—whether at CCCS, with INIVA and Autograph ABP (Association of Black Photographers) at Rivington Place, at The Open University, or here at Goldsmiths.

Right: Mahasiddhi (Roy Peters) as a Soviet-era astronaut

BACK IN
THE CCCS

24 *Back in the* CCCS: A Photoessay

Mahasiddhi (Roy Peters), with notes by Bob Lumley

In 1963, Richard Hoggart founded the Centre for Contemporary Cultural Studies at the University of Birmingham. He appointed Stuart Hall, who took over running the Centre from 1968 until 1979. Both these preeminent and innovative thinkers died in 2014, but their legacy lives on. This series of portraits is a very personal account of some of the alumni who passed through the Centre, including me; I was there as Roy Peters, between 1975 and 1979. The idea was born out of a conversation in 2010 with Roger Shannon, who has lent an encouraging and formative hand throughout. Michael Green, a lecturer at CCCS when I arrived, was also a keen advocate, but sadly he died before the first photograph had been taken. I wanted to celebrate the Centre and acknowledge my own roots, beginning with friends I made during my time there and eventually broadening to include acquaintances and influences. It is very much a work in progress and far from complete.
—Mahasiddhi

Like Mahasiddhi (aka Roy Peters), the photographer shown on the first page of this photoessay wearing a space helmet, I was at CCCS in the 1970s. I knew almost every face in the exhibition of the portraits that accompanied the fiftieth anniversary conference in Birmingham. Even if we'd not met up for some time, it was like a parallel reunion that assembled some thirty people. I greeted them in my head: 'You haven't changed a bit'; 'I almost didn't recognise you'; 'I remember that smile.' But, photographs don't talk back. For most readers, the photographs are photographs, and perhaps only a few faces, such as Stuart Hall's, are familiar. So, some additional words of explanation and contextualisation might be helpful.

The idea for 'Back in the CCCS' (as in The Beatles' number 'Back in the USSR') was conceived in a conversation with Roger Shannon in 2010, and from the very start it was a project of Mahasiddhi's making. It was not the result of a commission, nor was it designed to document CCCS membership. It didn't try to be systematic or comprehensive in terms of those included, and here, in this book, it is a much-reduced selection. In many ways, the project has been like a working paper in cultural studies—a work in progress rather than a finished, final product. The analogy is particularly appropriate because the photographer is giving back in images things he first explored at the Centre where he studied approaches such as semiotics and texts such as Stuart Hall's 'The Determinations of the Newsphotograph'. This exhibition can be seen as part of a personal journey, a return, a bringing together.

There is also an ethical dimension to the project that helps explain the special quality of the portraits. When he started out as young man, the photographer would make his subjects assume poses that made for striking results: 'Let's put your head in that goldfish-bowl and see how it looks' (in Mahasiddhi's words). With this project, the approach has been more about negotiation and about collaboration with the person photographed. The portrait photograph is, as Richard Avedon says, always a performance, 'a picture of someone who knows he is being photographed'. And again: 'We all perform. It's what we do for each other all the time, deliberately or unintentionally. It's a way of telling about ourselves in the hope of being recognised as what we'd like to be.' What we have here in 'Back in the CCCS' are not snapshots for private consumption. Yet there is a personal feeling to them that comes from the relationship of trust and even complicity between photographer and photographed. You can see/hear in some images the conversation that is momentarily punctuated, the shared laughter.

Historically, portraits of this kind have shown women and men in specific surroundings and with carefully chosen objects that attest to status, profession, membership of a corporation, belief. Dress and pose are likewise coded. In this gallery of photographs, these cultural signs are not so self-evident. In the original exhibition, one portrait gave prominence to the West Brom Football Club emblem, and another showed the artist in his studio, but mostly they have placed the subject in a domestic interior, or a garden provided the setting with a greater or lesser degree of detail. The office or study with books and computer screen scarcely feature as they do in canonical academic portraits. We are mostly at home. The portraits taken in public spaces and locations are markedly urban: the Birmingham snooker hall; Euston Road, London, at night; the back of a brick building with street signage.

Not all the portraits are obviously situated. In some, the background is deliberately out of focus or opaque. There were technical problems to solve. In the age of digital photography, images can be virtually invented, as shown by the portrait of the photographer as Yuri Gagarin. Here, an anorak has changed colour, and a crash helmet has metamorphosed for use in outer space—an ingenious creation using Photoshop, made by Stuart Hall (not the director of CCCS but a fellow photographer). However, Mahasiddhi did not allow himself to use these options. While still using a digital camera, he deliberately gave himself anachronistic technical constraints. The lighting is dramatic in some photographs, but mostly the photographer has chosen to use 'natural' light: 'Technically, it is something I might have done forty years ago'—medium-format camera, use of the tripod, slow shutter speeds, two lenses, minimal cropping. At the same time, the taste for performance and drama is there, and photographer and photographed each take part. In the exhibition, bathroom mise-en-scène was used, respectively in the portraits of Richard Dyer and Paul Willis, in ways that gesture towards classic movie moments: *Psycho* and the shower cubicle, and Jean-Paul Belmondo reading in the bath in Godard's *Pierrot le fou*. The snooker hall brings to mind both *film noir* and the Sheffield Crucible. The aesthetic is precise: precision of image, technical perfection. You can *not like* the photograph, but cannot question its technical skill. Clearly, the photographer is a master of colour[1] and composition; he visualises the geometry of lines in which figures stand and places subjects in relationship to a painting or a garden shrub with unforced deliberation.

A sense of time passing and the passage of time has been closely associated with photography since its invention. The deaths of first Stuart Hall and then Richard Hoggart in 2014, and the earlier loss of Michael Green, Ian Connell and Martin Culverwell made this association deeply felt in the 2014 exhibition. But then, everyone portrayed could not (and cannot) avoid the sense of 'then' and 'now', and the anticipation of the day when a photograph will remain, but not us. Viewers and readers too are brought into this train of thought by association. As Susan Sontag wrote: 'All photographs are *memento mori*. To take a photograph is to participate in another person's (or thing's) mortality, vulner-ability, mutability. Precisely by slicing out this moment and freez-ing it, all photographs testify to time's relentless melt.'

This observation brings us back to the power of the still photo-graph. It is worth pondering that Stuart Hall returned to his early interest in photography with his and Mark Sealy's book *Different: Contemporary Photographers and Black Identity*. In John Akom-frah's film *The Stuart Hall Project*, there is, appropriately, a haunt-ing sequence in which enlarged photographs appear in a wood among the trees blowing in the wind. The CCCS pioneered studies in the still image and in the moving image (film and television). It produced future practitioners and researchers. The photographic work of Mahasiddhi over the years is also testimony to this CCCS legacy. May the working paper, the work in progress, go on.

Note

1. The exhibition at Birmingham University in June 2014 was of colour photographs. The colour images from this exhibition can be accessed at https://backintheccss.wordpress.com/.

Stuart Hall
at his home in Moseley,
Birmingham, circa 1978

My first memory of Stuart on the inaugural MA course is of him coming in with what seem like a hundred books under his arms, as if he's going to quote from them all. But they stay piled on the desk as he began to roll into his trademark 'mapping the field' expansiveness. As more and more people came to realise, Stuart had the rare gift and intelligence of expressing the dialectical movement of ideas and politics in his very character and presence. This was the way he worked with people, talked to (diverse) audiences, disputed and laughed his way through issues and built up his (often provisional, inclusive) solutions. He never gave less than his full attention and time to students, episodic interlocutors, political activists, and the legions of questioning colleagues who just liked being around him. He was never on the lookout for someone more important to talk to.

Gregor McLennan
CCCS student 1975–1980

Gregor McLennan
Professor of Sociology,
University of Bristol

My intellectual life was shaped by my sense that the exciting but often difficult work of the Centre was aiming to find a different way of bringing politics and intellection together. Whether thinking about continental philosophy (an enduring passion), popular music and youth culture (my project at CCCS), the state of kids, the rise of the right or the failure of the left, the trajectory of my academic life's work (and more) began at CCCS.

Lawrence Grossberg
CCCS student 1975–1980

Lawrence Grossberg
Distinguished Professor of Communication and Cultural Studies, University of North Carolina, Chapel Hill

It was an important influence in my successive career, mainly due to the interdisciplinary perspectives that cultural studies provided. I live in Naples, teach Italian to immigrants and continue research in a PhD programme in cultural and postcolonial studies, along with a European-wide research project on migration and the modern museum.

Lidia Curti

It was *the* crucial turning point in my intellectual and emotional life. There, I learnt to undo inherited sense, Englishness and myself, and reassemble it all elsewhere in another (critical) space. It marked and traversed the limits of academia—both then and now—and propelled us all before the wider and more vibrant horizons of intellectual work attuned to a politics of change.

Iain Chambers

Lidia Curti
Retired, now teacher of Italian
to immigrants in Naples, Italy

Iain Chambers
Professor of Sociology,
University of Naples 'L'Orientale'

I encountered an ongoing commitment to collective interdisciplinary work: breaking the boundaries that separate disciplines, questioning the values of established intellectual traditions and thinking about the sociopolitical implications of my work.

Frank Mort

Frank Mort
Professor of Cultural Histories,
University of Manchester

My time at Birmingham University CCCS allowed me to develop an idea of the kind of scholar and intellectual I wanted to be. I am immensely grateful for being given that opportunity. The influence of Stuart Hall has been a defining feature of my research and my teaching over four decades. I very much hope something of Stuart's spirit will continue to animate academic life for a long time to come. My own objects of study over this time have retained something of the CCCS style and content. Perhaps the key achievement of the Centre in the 1970s is that its work found such a substantial intellectual readership.

Angela McRobbie

Angela McRobbie
Professor of Communications,
Goldsmiths, University of London

It rescued me from a not very happy line of development (learning to be a manager!) and gave me ways of thinking and working with others that still underpin most of what I do.

John Clarke

John Clarke
Emeritus Professor,
Faculty of Arts and Social Sciences, The Open University

The Centre taught me many things, including the pleasures (and of course, the inevitable difficulties) of collective intellectual work, in dialogue with others, and not as an isolated pursuit. But most of all, it taught me the importance of interdisciplinarity. When I got in touch with him, Stuart Hall suggested I should come along to the next Media Group meeting and 'see how it went'. So I did and I stayed for the best part of a decade.

David Morley

David Morley
Professor of Communications,
Goldsmiths, University of London

Part pressure cooker, part shoestring neo-Marxist think tank and DIY publishing hub, the Centre in the early 1970s was more like a squat—an extended occupation—than a regularized academic research unit. It was a crowded, open, driven space, un-owned for long by any one agenda, and, for better or worse, that became my model of what critical work should be: an urgent interrogative address by any means necessary and available to whatever's lining up on the horizon. The Centre stretched me way beyond my range. It taught me to stay focused and to feel at home, even—and especially—when at a loss. I feel beyond lucky to have been there—on the edge/at the Centre—at that time.

Dick Hebdige

Dick Hebdige
Professor of Art Studio and Film and Media Studies,
University of California, Santa Barbara

I loved working in subgroups, and the thrill of some of these shared projects has subsequently fed into both my teaching and research. Intellectually, the wide interests that took me to CCCS, and were there expanded, have meant that my work is always ambitious in relation to existing disciplinary boundaries.

Charlotte Brunsdon

Charlotte Brunsdon
Professor of Film and Television Studies,
University of Warwick

My time at CCCS was for me a completely formative, wonderful time, which I look back on with great pleasure. I can't help contrasting the collective ethos of the Centre with the much more corporate, instrumental approach to intellectual life that now increasingly dominates universities.

Bill Schwarz

Bill Schwarz
Professor in the School of English and Drama,
Queen Mary, University of London

Much of what I produced subsequently continued to be produced collectively (and was the better for it). At CCCS, I learnt to
take the everyday world seriously, which I continue to see as a
starting point both for research and for thinking through issues.

Tony Jefferson

Tony Jefferson
Emeritus Professor, Keale University

Being at the Centre meant being in the middle of a wonderful experiment in collective learning and research. For me, it was the start of a new way of thinking about things—and the start of many friendships.

Bob Lumley

Bob Lumley
Professor of Italian Cultural History,
University College London

Afterword

Catherine Hall

This book is a record of a very special day—Friday, November 28, 2014—a day that was very much in the spirit of Stuart. We gathered to remember and to celebrate him. I listened to everything with close attention and was moved by the demonstration of what Stuart's life and thought had meant to so many people. His friends, colleagues and co-workers expressed their political passions, capacity for intellectual rigour and wondrous imaginations. Their words were sparkling, their presentations inspiring. We laughed, cried and cheered. It was a day of joy and sorrow, remembering and celebrating together, holding on to what Stuart had meant and would continue to mean for us. We had the kind of talk that Stuart would have loved. Goldsmiths had made a remarkable week of it—with special teaching, exhibitions, John Akomfrah's installation *The Unfinished Conversation*, the commemorative plaque and specially commissioned artwork at the entrance to the splendid new Professor Stuart Hall building and the event to mark its installation. They did him proud.

Stuart is buried in Highgate Cemetery; it's not hard to find him. Just turn right at Marx and take the first left, as one friend pointed out to another. The historian Macaulay liked to work on the dead because they could not answer back. 'With the dead there is no rivalry', he wrote. 'In the dead there is no change. Plato is never sullen. Cervantes is never petulant. Demosthenes never comes unseasonably. Dante never stays too long'. But I find that the dead live on in our hearts and minds and can speak to us.

Contributors

John Akomfrah
Founder, Smoking Dogs Films

Avtar Brah
Professor Emerita of Sociology, Birkbeck College, University of London, UK

Charlotte Brunsdon
Professor of Film and Television Studies, University of Warwick, UK

Iain Chambers
Professor of Sociology, University of Naples 'L'Orientale', Italy

Kuan-Hsing Chen
Professor in the Graduate Institute for Social Research and Cultural Studies, National Chiao Tung University, Taiwan

John Clarke
Professor Emeritus, Faculty of Arts and Social Sciences, The Open University, UK

James Curran
Professor of Communications, Goldsmiths, University of London, UK

Angela Y. Davis
Distinguished Professor Emerita, History of Consciousness and Feminist Studies, University of California Santa Cruz, USA

David Edgar
Playwright; former Professor of Playwriting Studies, University of Birmingham, UK

Lawrence Grossberg
Distinguished Professor of Communication and Cultural Studies,
University of North Carolina, Chapel Hill, USA

Catherine Hall
Professor Emerita, Modern British Social and Cultural History,
University College London, UK

Dick Hebdige
Professor of Art Studio and Film and Media Studies, University of
California, Santa Barbara, USA

Julian Henriques
Professor of Media and Communications, Goldsmiths,
University of London, UK

Tony Jefferson
Professor Emeritus, Keele University, UK

Bob Lumley
Professor of Italian Cultural History, University College London, UK

Mahasiddhi (Roy Peters)
Independent photographer, Birmingham, UK

Doreen Massey
Professor Emerita of Geography, The Open University, UK

Angela McRobbie
Professor of Communications, Goldsmiths, University of London, UK

Caspar Melville
Lecturer in Global Creative and Cultural Industries, SOAS,
University of London, UK

David Morley
Professor of Communications, Goldsmiths, University of London, UK

Frank Mort
Professor of Cultural Histories, University of Manchester, UK

Michael Rustin
Professor of Sociology, University of East London, UK

Bill Schwarz
Professor in the School of English and Drama, Queen Mary,
University of London, UK

Mark Sealy
Director, Autograph ABP (Association of Black Photographers), UK

Liv Sovik
Professor of Communications, Universidade Federal do Rio de
Janeiro, Brazil

Lola Young
Campaigner and Independent Crossbench Member of the House
of Lords, UK

Index

Page numbers followed by *f* refer to figures.